Dropout Prevention

The Guilford Practical Intervention in the Schools Series

Kenneth W. Merrell, Founding Editor
T. Chris Riley-Tillman, Series Editor

www.guilford.com/practical

This series presents the most reader-friendly resources available in key areas of evidence-based practice in school settings. Practitioners will find trustworthy guides on effective behavioral, mental health, and academic interventions, and assessment and measurement approaches. Covering all aspects of planning, implementing, and evaluating high-quality services for students, books in the series are carefully crafted for everyday utility. Features include ready-to-use reproducibles, lay-flat binding to facilitate photocopying, appealing visual elements, and an oversized format. Recent titles have Web pages where purchasers can download and print the reproducible materials.

Recent Volumes

Coaching Students with Executive Skills Deficits
Peg Dawson and Richard Guare

Enhancing Instructional Problem Solving:
An Efficient System for Assisting Struggling Learners
John C. Begeny, Ann C. Schulte, and Kent Johnson

Clinical Interviews for Children and Adolescents, Second Edition: Assessment to Intervention
Stephanie H. McConaughy

RTI Team Building: Effective Collaboration and Data-Based Decision Making
Kelly Broxterman and Angela J. Whalen

RTI Applications, Volume 2: Assessment, Analysis, and Decision Making
T. Chris Riley-Tillman, Matthew K. Burns, and Kimberly Gibbons

Daily Behavior Report Cards: An Evidence-Based System of Assessment and Intervention
Robert J. Volpe and Gregory A. Fabiano

Assessing Intelligence in Children and Adolescents: A Practical Guide
John H. Kranzler and Randy G. Floyd

The RTI Approach to Evaluating Learning Disabilities
Joseph F. Kovaleski, Amanda M. VanDerHayden, and Edward S. Shapiro

Resilient Classrooms, Second Edition: Creating Healthy Environments for Learning
Beth Doll, Katherine Brehm, and Steven Zucker

The ABCs of Curriculum-Based Evaluation: A Practical Guide to Effective Decision Making
John L. Hosp, Michelle K. Hosp, Kenneth W. Howell, and Randy Allison

Curriculum-Based Assessment for Instructional Design:
Using Data to Individualize Instruction
Matthew K. Burns and David C. Parker

Dropout Prevention
C. Lee Goss and Kristina J. Andren

Stress Management for Teachers: A Proactive Guide
Keith C. Herman and Wendy M. Reinke

Dropout Prevention

C. LEE GOSS
KRISTINA J. ANDREN

THE GUILFORD PRESS
New York   London

© 2014 The Guilford Press
A Division of Guilford Publications, Inc.
370 Seventh Avenue, Suite 1200, New York, NY 10001
www.guilford.com

Printed in the United States of America

This book is printed on acid-free paper.

Last digit is print number: 9   8   7   6   5   4   3   2

Library of Congress Cataloging-in-Publication Data

Goss, C. Lee.
     Dropout prevention / C. Lee Goss, Kristina J. Andren.
        pages cm. — (The guilford practical interventions in the schools series)
     Includes bibliographical references and index.
     ISBN 978-1-4625-1620-9 (paperback)
     1. High school dropouts—United States.   2. Dropout behavior, Prediction of.   3. Youth with
social disabilities—Education—United States.   4. School improvement programs—United States.
5. Educational change—United States.   I. Andren, Kristina J.   II. Title.
     LC 146.6.G67   2014
     371.2′913—dc23
                                                                            2014013581

To Jonathan, my soul mate,
and our three daughters, Brittany, Heather, and Lauren—
you fill my life with joy and inspiration
—C. L. G.

To Owen, who will climb every mountain,
and Elsa, who will move them
—K. J. A.

About the Authors

C. Lee Goss, PsyD, NCSP, is a lecturer in the Educational and School Psychology Programs at the University of Southern Maine. She has provided school psychology services, professional development, and consultation for schools and districts in multi-tiered, system wide prevention and early intervention methods. In private practice, Dr. Goss takes a collaborative and comprehensive multidisciplinary approach to supporting children and adolescents at risk for academic, social, and mental health problems that often result in underachievement and school failure. Her research interests include prevention, early intervention, and problem-solving methods to inform effective interventions and dropout prevention.

Kristina J. Andren, PsyD, NCSP, has practiced as a school psychologist in Maine schools since 2005. She served as Assistant Professor of Educational and School Psychology at the University of Southern Maine, and continues to be affiliated with the University as a supervising licensed psychologist for PsyD school psychology interns and practicum students and as a member of the School Psychology Advisory Board. Dr. Andren's research interests include assessment and intervention within a multi-tiered systems of support (MTSS) framework. Her current work focuses on the application of MTSS methods—such as response to intervention—to reading initiatives, schoolwide practices, and dropout prevention.

Preface

A national conversation about the high incidence of students dropping out of school has begun. What has been termed a dropout "crisis" or "epidemic" is not a high school problem or an urban problem, nor one that can be solved with new funding, policies, or teachers alone. We as a nation have an obligation to invest in our children and their future successes. Effective dropout prevention methods enhance outcomes for individual students, families, schools, and their communities, directly influencing future educational and economic aspirations. The need for user-friendly resources on evidence-based dropout prevention and intervention practices is clear. This book provides information on protective factors and risk factors associated with dropping out of school, current evidence-based dropout prevention and intervention methods, and applicable resources.

Another goal of this book is to articulate the relevance of previous educational research and evidence-based practices that support implementation of multi-tiered systems of support (MTSS) throughout the grades as essential components of effective dropout prevention and intervention methods. The expansion of the current MTSS model to include parent, family, and community partnerships in a comprehensive approach to dropout prevention is emphasized. In Part I, Chapters 1–3 lay the foundation for systemwide prekindergarten through 12th-grade dropout prevention efforts. In Part II, Chapters 4–6 focus on early identification of students at risk, on problem-solving practices for students in need of additional support, and on evidence-based interventions for students in the elementary grades. In Part III, Chapters 7–10 provide information and guidance on early warning systems, problem solving, and the best opportunities to intervene at the secondary levels. Most chapters contain illustrative case examples, which are fictional and do not represent known individuals. Each chapter concludes with a summary of "big ideas." Finally, the Appendix offers sample checklists and other practical resources for schools that are taking steps toward these challenging yet essential goals for all students.

During the writing of this book, the tragic school shooting in Newtown, Connecticut, occurred. It happened close to home in a small New England village, with the unimaginable sudden loss of 20 young children and 7 adults, including the mother of the shooter, teachers, the school principal, and a school psychologist. This tragic event vividly illustrated that the significant problems faced by our nation in education, mental health, and violence prevention are not restricted to low-performing schools and impoverished neighborhoods, but transcend all educational and socioeconomic populations.

As seen in too many previous cases of gun violence in our schools and communities, the signs of disengagement from school and university settings, combined with mental health problems, were evident long before the violent acts occurred. We know that prevention extends beyond the school grounds. True prevention involves collaboration between family systems and the entire educational and larger communities to build relationships, foster a caring school climate, facilitate meaningful involvement, and cultivate a sense of belonging throughout the school and community. A body of research has clearly supported a public health approach for school-based prevention and early intervention methods. A public health model invests in prevention efforts and identifies early warning signs of troubling behavior to offer coordinated, individualized, consistent, and culturally sensitive support for a student's academic, behavior, and health needs. This type of integrated framework offers the best research-to-practice solutions available to begin to solve these very complex societal issues that frequently overlap with education.

The ultimate goal of this book is to advocate for best practices to foster school success for all students. In that process, the research shows that we can identify students at risk in the early stages of a problem, when we can be most effective in preventing the high incidence of school dropout that plagues our youth and our nation. Because students who drop out of school are at significantly higher risk for medical and mental illnesses, these efforts also hold great promise for implementing more effective mental health interventions for those in need.

As many before us, including our mentors, have said, "it takes a village." The critical components of an effective dropout prevention program include collaboration with parents and families, community partnerships, student engagement, and multiple levels of evidence-based academic and behavior instruction targeted to individual student needs. Because the research shows that dropping out is a process, not an event, this book is offered as a resource to assist educators, specialists, and clinicians in implementing effective dropout prevention methods from prekindergarten through high school graduation.

Acknowledgments

We extend heartfelt appreciation and gratitude to our mentors, Drs. Rachel Brown and Mark W. Steege, who provided extraordinary leadership, instruction, and advice throughout our master's and doctoral training in school psychology, and then beyond, as professional colleagues at the University of Southern Maine. Rachel and Mark, we have benefited from your willingness to model and share your expertise in best practices in school psychology. As national leaders and trainers, you proactively teach and reinforce the skills needed by future school psychologists to embrace an international paradigm shift occurring in school psychology and education service delivery. We share your passion about the potential to improve academic and behavior outcomes for all students so that they may experience school success.

We also extend our appreciation to Dr. Jennifer Robert, who contributed tremendously to this book, and to Natalie Graham, T. Chris Riley-Tillman, and Mary Beth Wood for their editorial expertise and guidance. Perhaps most important, we would like to thank our spouses, Jonathan and Stefan, and our families for their continuous support, enthusiasm, senses of humor, and professional encouragement.

Contents

PART I. SYSTEMWIDE DROPOUT PREVENTION

1. The Dropout Crisis
3

High School Completion Benefits Everyone   4
International Educational Status   5
Why Do Students Drop Out?   6
Dropping Out Is a Process, Not an Event   6
Individual Variables   7
Home and Family Variables   7
School Variables   8
Community Variables   8
Protective Factors   8
Turning the Tide   9
Educational Legislation   9
School Reform   10
Multi-Tiered Systems of Support   11
Summary   13

2. School, Family, and Community Partnerships
14

School Reform for Dropout Prevention   14
A Sense of Belonging   14
The Role of Consensus and Team Building   16
Family Collaboration   18
School Readiness   19
Family Engagement in Schools   19
Community Partnerships   24
Summary   27

3. Academic and Behavior Links to Inform Dropout Prevention Methods
28

Academic and Behavior Links   28
Research to Practice   30
Student Engagement   31
Focus on Reading   32

Dropout Prevention and MTSS   33
Summary   36

PART II. DROPOUT PREVENTION AT THE ELEMENTARY LEVEL

4. A Process, Not an Event: Early Identification of Dropout Risk   39

Risk Indicators   39
   School Engagement   40
   School Readiness   41
   Academic Performance   42
   Attendance   44
   Behavior   45
   Retention   45
Early Identification   46
   Summative and Formative Assessment   47
Universal Screening Recommendations   49
   Academic Screeners   50
   Behavioral Screeners   51
A Team Approach   51
Summary   52

5. Tier 2 and Tier 3 Problem Solving at the Elementary Level: 53
Are We Closing the Gap?

The Problem-Solving Model   53
   Identify and Define the Problem   55
   Explore Alternative Interventions   56
   Apply Selected Intervention   56
   Look at Effects   56
Data Management Systems   57
   Academic Assessments: Curriculum-Based Measurement   58
   Behavioral Assessments   58
Data-Based Decision Making   61
   Rates of Progress   61
   Benchmark Scores   63
Summary   64

6. Early Intervention: Elementary Evidence-Based Resources   65
with Jennifer L. Robert

The Importance of *Early* Intervention   66
Why Evidence Matters   67
Tier 1   68
   Core Instruction   70
   Tier 1 Reading Instruction   71
   Tier I Math Instruction   73
   Positive Behavioral Interventions and Supports   73
   Family Involvement   76
Tiers 2 and 3 Targeted Interventions   77
   Attendance   78
   Academic Interventions   78
   Executive Functioning Skills   80
   Behavioral Interventions   84
   Progress Monitoring   87
Summary   88

PART III. DROPOUT PREVENTION IN MIDDLE SCHOOL AND HIGH SCHOOL

7. Time Is of the Essence: Early Warning Systems for Middle School and High School 93

At-Risk Indicators 93
Attendance 95
Academic Performance 96
Behavior 97
Early Warning Systems 98
Early Warning Systems within MTSS 99
Developing EWS 101
Summary 102

8. Tier 2 and Tier 3 Problem Solving at the Secondary Level 105

Problem Solving 105
Identify the Problem 106
Define the Problem 108
Explore Alternative Interventions 109
Apply Selected Intervention 111
Look at Effects 112
Summary 114

9. Middle School and High School Evidence-Based Resources
with Jennifer L. Robert 115

Tier 1 115
Universal Screening 116
Effective Teaching Practices 117
Reading Instruction 117
Math Instruction 119
Mentorship and Coaching 119
Tier 2 and Tier 3 Targeted Interventions 119
Academic Interventions 121
Behavioral Interventions 122
Targeted Transition Interventions 125
Executive Functioning 125
Community Collaboration 126
Clinical and Mental Health Support 128
Intervention Integrity 128
Professional Development 129
Summary 130

10. The Role of Technical Education, Alternative High Schools, and Postsecondary Options in Dropout Prevention 131

Career and Technology Education 131
Work-Based Learning 133
Career Academies 133
Benefits of CTE 133
Alternative Schooling 134
Postsecondary Options 137
Characteristics of Successful Programs 138
Student Engagement 138

Relationship Building   *139*
Flexibility   *139*
Summary   140

11. Conclusion: Time for a Change   **141**

The Promise of Converging Research   141
Facilitating a Paradigm Shift in Education   143
Future Directions   144

APPENDIX. REPRODUCIBLE MATERIALS

Appendix A. Checklist for Monitoring and Improving Family Engagement   **147**

Appendix B. Academic Intervention Record Form   **149**

Appendix C. Building an Early Warning System   **151**

Appendix D. Evidence-Based Interventions   **152**

Appendix E. Online Resources for Dropout Prevention and Intervention Methods **156**

References   **159**

Index   **173**

Purchasers can download and print Appendices A, B, C, and D
from *www.guilford.com/goss-forms*.

PART I

SYSTEMWIDE DROPOUT PREVENTION

CHAPTER 1

The Dropout Crisis

Today, there are many successes in America's schools. Even in the toughest communities, facing the most significant challenges, we see examples of educators and families preparing our nation's youngsters for success in school and life. But, in far too many communities across America, we continue to face educational challenges that jeopardize the futures of our young people, and in turn our country. Right now, 25 percent of all of our youngsters and 40 percent of our minority youngsters are not finishing high school with their peers. This lack of high-quality education has dramatic consequences for individuals, society, the economy, and even our national security.... Failure is not an option. Opportunity must be the way.
—GENERAL COLIN POWELL AND ALMA J. POWELL (in Balfanz, Bridgeland, Bruce, & Fox, 2012)

Current graduation rates reflect a dropout crisis for the United States with considerable social and economic implications. Educational and economic research evidence shows substantial individual, school, state, national, and global adverse outcomes related to high dropout rates. Consequently, dropout prevention, a topic of important national interest, has been identified as an essential priority in education and current school reform efforts. A review of 2009 high school completion and dropout rates in the

> **Approximately 37% of African American students, 35% of Native American students, and 34% of Hispanic students do not graduate from high school.**

United States indicates that 75.5% of U.S. high school freshmen graduate on time (National Center for Education Statistics, 2011). Although this rate has improved by almost 4 percentage points since 2000, it has been hovering in the low- to mid-70s range for the previous 30 years (National Center for Education Statistics, 2011). Provisional data from 2010 indicate further improvements, with nationwide graduation rates climbing to 78.2% (Stillwell & Sable, 2013). Even with recent increases, this translates to nearly 7,000 students who drop out daily, culminating in over 1 million American youth who drop out of school every year (Alliance for Excellent Education, 2011). The data reveal a more troubling picture for racial minority students: only 63.5% of African American, 65.9% of Hispanic, and 64.8% of Native American students graduate from high school (Balfanz et al., 2012). For a description of how these numbers are calculated, see Box 1.1.

3

BOX 1.1. Making Sense of the Statistics

Estimates of graduation and dropout rates vary according to which definition of high school completion and methodology for calculation are used. Historically, states have been inconsistent in methods used to estimate their graduation rates, resulting in unreliable data from state to state. In 2008, the U.S. Department of Education established common requirements for calculating and reporting graduation rates, which are based on the 4-year adjusted cohort graduation rate. Consistent with the definition in the No Child Left Behind Act of 2001, this represents the percentage of students who graduate with a regular diploma within 4 years after starting ninth grade. Cohort-based graduation rates provide a more accurate picture of timely school completion, as well as a more accurate comparison of graduation rates across schools, districts, and states. Without sufficient longitudinal data, until these requirements are fully implemented, current rates are approximated by using the Averaged Freshman Graduation Rate (AFGR) or the Cumulative Promotion Index (CPI). Although these estimates may yield slightly different dropout rates and economic implications, they consistently point to a dropout crisis in this nation (Balfanz et al., 2012; Chapman, Laird, Ifill, & Kewal Ramani, 2011).

In a report titled *The Silent Epidemic*, developed for the Bill and Melinda Gates Foundation, Bridgeland, Dilulio, and Morison (2006) illuminate the unintentional process of dropping out of school from the students' perspective, as well as the serious personal consequences and limitations associated with dropping out of high school. In a quest to understand why students dropped out of school, national focus groups, personal interviews, and a survey were conducted. The researchers learned that although some students dropped out because of academic challenges—and research shows that core course failures are predictive of dropout (Balfanz & Herzog, 2005; Balfanz, Herzog, & Mac Iver, 2007)—most high school dropouts who participated in the study reported average grades and career aspirations that required education beyond high school. Survey respondents reported feelings of alienation at school. They believed no one noticed or cared whether they failed to show up for class. More than half of the respondents reported that their classes were uninteresting and irrelevant. Overall, personal circumstances and an inadequate response by the schools were identified by the researchers as the primary reasons these capable students dropped out, regardless of culture, socioeconomic factors, and geographical variables. As this report articulates, to galvanize a nation and develop solutions to this national educational epidemic, we must begin by clearly identifying and understanding the barriers to on-time high school completion.

HIGH SCHOOL COMPLETION BENEFITS EVERYONE

The national dropout crisis has extensive individual, societal, and economic consequences. Dropping out of school is correlated with a host of negative outcomes, including higher rates of unemployment, lower earnings, poorer mental and physical health, higher rates of criminal behavior, and divorce. Additionally, parents who didn't complete high school are more likely to have children who drop out of high school themselves, perpetuating the tragic cycle (Bridgeland et al., 2006). Individuals who don't graduate from high school are more likely to use public assistance, to rely on government health care, and to be incarcerated, resulting in higher government expenditures (Belfield & Levin, 2007). Simultaneously, lower individual earnings translate to substantially lower tax revenue for local, state, and federal governments.

High school graduates have longer life expectancies, are more likely to have children who graduate from high school, and are more likely to vote and volunteer in their communities (Alliance for Excellent Education, 2011; Belfield & Levin, 2007). Compared with students who don't complete high school, the average annual income for an individual with a high school diploma is approximately $8,000 to $9,000 higher (Alliance for Excellence in Education, 2011; Bridgeland et al., 2006). Recent earning statistics show that college graduates earn more than double the annual income rates that high school dropouts can expect to earn, which translates to about $1 million more over a lifetime (Bridgeland et al., 2006). Additionally, in economic downturns, or recessions, high school graduates are more likely to locate and maintain employment. Since December 2007 the unemployment rate for all education levels has skyrocketed, but high school dropouts faced the most difficulty finding jobs, with an unemployment rate of 14.3%, compared with 9.6% for high school graduates, 8.2% for individuals with some college credits or associate's degrees, and 4.3% for individuals with bachelor's degrees or higher (U.S. Bureau of Labor Statistics, 2011). Most jobs in the United States now require some college education beyond high school. To meet future demands of employers and continue to be competitive in a global economy, our nation needs a more skilled and educated workforce.

> Each new high school graduate would generate an estimated $200,000 or more in government savings and higher tax revenues.

INTERNATIONAL EDUCATIONAL STATUS

Internationally, recent research shows that the United States ranks 17th in literacy, 26th in mathematics, and 21st in science achievement. Whereas other countries have increased their educational outcomes, the United States has seen no significant improvement since the Programme for International Student Assessment (PISA) testing began in 2000 (Organization for Economic Cooperation and Development, 2013). Recent estimates project that the future domestic workforce demands will require higher levels of education among U.S. workers. However, without significant improvements in the high school and postsecondary completion rates, the nation is on track to fall short by up to 3 million postsecondary degrees by 2018 (Carnevale, Smith, & Strohl, 2010). These sobering statistics highlight the magnitude of the dropout crisis in America. To sustain America's economic and political stature for future generations there is an immediate need for effective dropout prevention methods in public education. Although the dropout crisis is real, research shows that the barriers to achieving a high school diploma and postsecondary educational opportunities are not insurmountable. Encouragingly, research has identified early warning signs to identify students at risk for dropping out as well as potential solutions to reverse this alarming trend.

WHY DO STUDENTS DROP OUT?

Bridgeland et al. (2006) report that almost every elementary and middle school student voices ambitions that include high school graduation and at least some college. The researchers investigated the reasons students gave for dropping out of high school by surveying and interviewing a sample of ethnically, racially, and geographically diverse 16- to 24-year-olds who did not complete high school. A summary of research findings showed that a lack of supervision, low parental involvement, perceptions of minimal teacher interest, irrelevant courses, and academic challenges were important variables that contributed to disengagement, absenteeism, and a lack of motivation prior to students' dropping out of school. More than half of the participants reported that they often missed class in the year before dropping out. Almost half of the students cited boring and irrelevant classes as a major reason for leaving school. The majority of respondents indicated that they were not motivated or inspired to work hard, completing less than an hour of homework daily, if at all. Too much freedom, low parental involvement, and socializing with people who were not interested in school were other common experiences. In hindsight, the majority of participants expressed great remorse about dropping out of school and a strong interest in returning to school with students their own age. The majority of respondents (81%) reported that graduating from high school was important to success in life. If they could relive the experience, 74% of the participants said they would have stayed in school.

> **Identifying the reasons that students report for dropping out can help schools, families, and communities identify potential solutions to the dropout crisis.**

DROPPING OUT IS A PROCESS, NOT AN EVENT

Finn (1989) reported that dropping out of school is a process of disengagement that often begins early in the prekindergarten to elementary school years. A student's decision to drop out of school often encompasses not just one but a multitude of factors that involve individual, family, school, and community variables (see Figure 1.1). These factors are frequently identified as push-out and pull-out effects (Kortering & Braziel, 1999). Push-out effects are defined as situations or experiences within the school environment that heighten students' feelings of alienation and failure, such as problems getting along with teachers, suspension and expulsion, low grades, an impersonal or intolerant school environment, bullying and harassment, social isolation, lack of involvement in co-curricular activities, and academic and/or behavior problems that reinforce feelings of school failure. Pull-out effects are defined as external factors that weaken and distract a student from the importance of school completion, such as adolescent pregnancy, poor economic circumstances and financial responsibilities, opportunities for employment, and caretaking responsibilities. Post hoc research examining the reasons *why* students drop out of school indicates the existence of push-out and pull-out effects in many schools (Jordan, McPartland, & Lara, 1999). Interest-

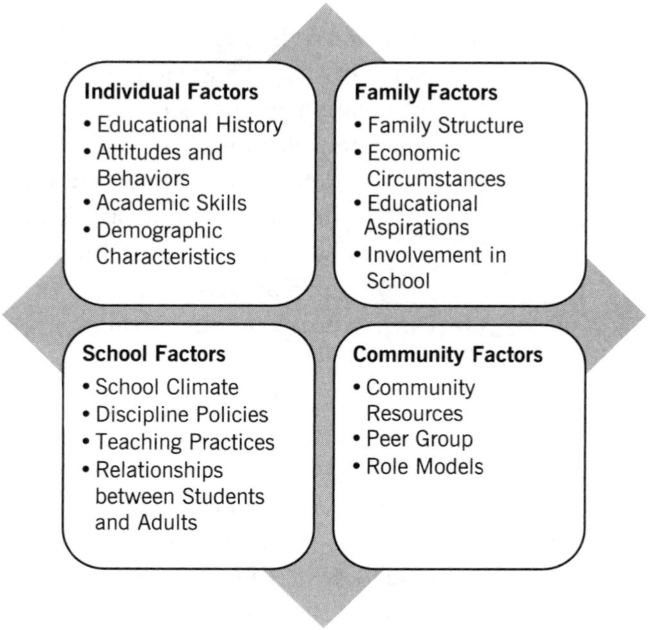

FIGURE 1.1. Factors contributing to dropout.

ingly, students who leave school most often cite push-out factors as reasons for dropping out (Dynarski et al., 2008).

Individual Variables

A student's educational history, including early school readiness, past academic achievement, retention, and school changes due to high mobility, have an impact on future school success. Mediating variables appear to be school attitudes and behavior, such as educational expectations and goals, attendance, and active participation in classroom and co-curricular activities. Research has identified demographic trends in dropout rates: female students, Asian and Caucasian students, and students with high English language proficiency tend to have higher graduation rates than male students, African American, Hispanic, and Native American students, and English language learners (Rumberger & Lim, 2008).

Home and Family Variables

Identified home factors that contribute to dropout risk include lack of materials and environmental conditions to support homework, and a lack of involvement, supervision, and educational expectations and aspirations on behalf of parents and caregivers (Dynarski et al., 2008). Rumberger and Lin (2008) found that family structure, resources, and events matter; students living with both parents have higher graduation rates than students who live in other family arrangements. Changes in the family, particularly stressful events such as moving, death, chronic illness, and divorce, increase the risk of dropping out. Students with a sibling who dropped out of school are also at a greater risk for dropping out.

Additionally, misalignment of expectations across school settings and between home and school contributes to academic and behavior problems and potentially impedes early detection and intervention efforts. These mixed messages about academic achievement and behavioral expectations have been shown to increase student risk for school performance problems and dropping out (Dynarski et al., 2008).

> When we strive to increase graduation rates, we are not simply counting diplomas. We strive to help students complete school with the skills and confidence to be successful after school.

School Variables

Rumberger and Lim (2008) determined that student and family characteristics account for most of the variance in dropout rates; however, about 20% can be attributed to school characteristics. Research shows that for schools in affluent communities, which tend to have higher graduation rates, the effects appear to be indirect and related to other school variables. Students are more likely to drop out in school environments with high rates of misbehavior and classroom disruptions. Conversely, higher graduation rates are correlated with academic environments characterized by active student engagement in classroom activities and assignment and homework completion. School size does not appear to have a consistent effect on dropout or graduation rates; however, there is strong evidence that small classes (ratio of 15:1) in early elementary school are correlated with better high school graduation rates. At the high school level, evidence suggests that compulsory attendance beyond age 16 leads to lower dropout rates, whereas exit exams appear to have a low but negative correlation with on-time high school completion.

Community Variables

Along with families and schools, communities play a crucial role in child and adolescent development. Children who live in impoverished communities face greater socioeconomic risk factors for dropping out; however, the correlation with dropping out is not direct, and many children who attend school in high-poverty neighborhoods complete school. Furthermore, students who live in affluent communities are at an increased advantage for access to community resources and positive role models and mentors.

Protective Factors

A review of the research shows that a number of studies examined dropout prevention factors (Finn, 1989; Hammond, Linton, Smink, & Drew, 2007; Rumberger, 1987, 2004) and the literature on the related phenomenon of student engagement (Fredricks, Blumenfeld, & Paris, 2004; National Research Council, 2003). For each push-out and pull-out effect

TABLE 1.1. Protective Factors

Pull-in factors	Push-in factors
• Positive school climate • Caring relationships with adults • Participation in co-curricular activities • Sense of belonging at school • Match between student and learning environment	• Family involvement in school • Academic and motivational support for learning • High educational aspirations • Supervision and monitoring

described earlier, there must be a counter "push-in" and "pull-in" effect that increases student engagement and the likelihood of staying in school. A selection of these protective factors is shown in Table 1.1. The literature underscores that further analysis of the push-out effects that students identify as the primary reasons they become disengaged from school prior to dropping out offers important opportunities for schools to design effective school-based prevention and protective factors.

TURNING THE TIDE

Educational Legislation

The nation has been invested in school reform and school improvement initiatives dating back to the 1960s. The No Child Left Behind Act (NCLB) of 2001 is the most recent version of the Elementary and Secondary Education Act (ESEA), and contains Title I, Improving the Academic Achievement of the Disadvantaged. In 1965, ESEA was the first major legislation passed by Congress to provide funding to public schools (see Box 1.2). The reauthorization of NCLB in 2001 advanced the original legislation and public school funding to emphasize the implementation of evidence-based practices for participating students. NCLB defines evidence of effectiveness as "programs that have been found through scientifically based research to significantly improve the academic achievement of participating children or have strong evidence that they will achieve this result," along with implementation and progress monitoring procedures to ensure that the programs are effective at the student level (NCLB, 2002).

We have the largest body of scientific research to guide us in implementing evidence-based reading instruction practices, which are highly correlated with future academic achievement and school success. Numerous government initiatives have targeted reading skills and school readiness as a national priority. The Head Start program promotes school preparation for low-income children by providing early educational, health, and social services. Reading First is a program through the U.S. Department of Education aimed at teaching all children to read by the end of third grade, by incorporating research-based teaching practices and assessment methods in the early elementary classroom. Early Reading First is a federal initiative that focuses on the preschool years. Early Reading First grants are

---

BOX 1.2. A World-Class Education

In March 2010, the Obama administration released its blueprint for revising the Elementary and Secondary Education Act.

> Every child in America deserves a world-class education. Today, more than ever, a world-class education is a prerequisite for success. America was once the best educated nation in the world. A generation ago, we led all nations in college completion, but today, 10 countries have passed us. It is not that their students are smarter than ours. It is that these countries are being smarter about how to educate their students. And the countries that out-educate us today will out-compete us tomorrow.
>
> —President Barack Obama (U.S. Department of Education, 2010)

---

designed to improve early education centers to foster the development of early cognitive, language, and reading skills that are so important for school readiness and success.

Other examples of current federal grants to accomplish these educational legislative initiatives include the Race to the Top and School Improvement Grant (SIG) programs. Race to the Top provides states with over $4 billion for school reform initiatives to improve student achievement outcomes that educators and policy makers expect to directly and indirectly improve dropout rates. The SIG program, sponsored by the Department of Education, awards states $3.5 billion in federal grants to target the lowest performing schools, with reports of states utilizing 40% of these funds to target high school improvement plans. Additionally, the U.S. Department of Education presently provides $50 million to states and districts to create, implement, and sustain dropout prevention and recovery programs through the High School Graduation Initiative.

School Reform

The primary goal of school reform movements is to increase academic achievement and school completion rates. Research shows that we accomplish these goals best when we make a more relevant and engaging experience for all students by aligning teaching and instruction to a student's current skill and need levels within general education. Providing universal evidence-based prevention and early intervention methods benefits everyone, including special education students, who would benefit from additional instruction opportunities, and gifted and talented students, who would benefit from enrichment and advanced placement or college-level courses in high school. To implement such changes at the individual student level, we must recognize that dropout prevention requires systems-level reform, including leadership, data-based resource allocation, policies that support schoolwide implementation of evidence-based practices, and tools to identify and document success.

Recent research has highlighted the important role of teachers and teacher support (Lam et al., 2012) in promoting student engagement and positive student attitudes toward school. Teachers need professional development and support to implement proven classroom management, academic, and behavior methods to effectively address the needs of most students. Implementation of school reform efforts should be guided by research evidence and relevant student data. A holistic approach with a comprehensive prekindergarten to grade 12 strategic district plan is needed to address the varying student needs at the elementary and secondary levels. Elementary school marks the optimum opportunity for prevention and early intervention methods. By middle and high school, time is of the essence. Unresolved student problems increase the magnitude of risk at each grade level, along with the efforts needed for effective intervention.

MULTI-TIERED SYSTEMS OF SUPPORT

Although middle and high school are critical periods for early detection and effective intervention for students at risk for dropping out of school, there is considerable evidence that students begin disengaging long before they arrive at the secondary levels. Retrospective studies show that students at risk for dropping out can be identified with reasonable accuracy in the elementary years (Barrington & Hendricks, 1989). Because dropping out of school is a multifaceted process that often begins early in school, it is essential that we adopt a systemwide approach to dropout prevention that extends from prekindergarten to high school graduation.

As in public health initiatives, a population perspective is needed to positively influence our national dropout crisis. Methods to identify children and adolescents at risk for dropping out as early as possible, when intervention is most effective, as well as growth indicators sensitive to small increments of progress, are essential to reversing the dropout trend and getting children back on track for school success. A growing body of research supports the implementation of multi-tiered systems of prevention and intervention for academics and behavior to foster student engagement, positive social interactions, and academic achievement for all students (Brown-Chidsey & Steege, 2010). As in the public health model, multi-tiered systems of support (MTSS) are made up of three tiers, or levels of prevention. Primary prevention (Tier 1) is aimed at reducing the number of children who develop academic or behavior problems and consists of the core academic and behavior instruction that is delivered schoolwide. Students who do not respond to evidence-based Tier 1 instruction will be identified through universal screening or early warning systems as needing more strategic intervention support at Tier 2. Secondary prevention (Tier 2) uses targeted supports to remediate problems before they escalate and may include small-group academic instruction, homework, study, and organizational skills support, or behavior plans and contracts. Tier 2 interventions are designed to reduce academic and behavior problems and facilitate progress toward Tier 1 status. For those students who do not respond to increased Tier 2 support, tertiary prevention (Tier 3) involves the most intensive services for students most in need. Typically, students at Tier 3 require one-to-one or very-small-group interventions and frequent (daily to weekly) progress monitoring. At this level, a comprehensive psychological evaluation or functional behavioral assessment (FBA) is often initiated to determine appropriate school, medical, clinical, family, and/or community supports.

In education, MTSS methods originated at the elementary levels with research on response to intervention (RTI) and positive behavioral interventions and supports (PBIS) that showed that evidence-based instruction and strategically applied multi-tiered interventions were effective for preventing and reducing risk factors for students with academic and behavior difficulties. MTSS methods can also be useful in identifying students ready for enrichment and additional academic challenges. Essentially, the ultimate goal of MTSS is to provide quality instruction at a student's current skill level, when student engagement and learning are best achieved.

At the elementary level, MTSS focuses on prevention, which research shows can be accomplished with evidence-based core academic (reading and math) and behavioral instruction for all students at Tier 1. Universal screening of all students determines who would benefit from additional instruction in the early stages of a problem, when intervention is likely to be most effective. Current research evidence supports the expectation that 80% of students will respond to Tier 1 methods when they are implemented with integrity. Schools that have less than 80% response at the Tier 1, or core, instructional level should examine their curricula to answer four important questions:

- Does the research evidence support the core curricula for the school population?
- Are literacy, math, and behavior instruction implemented with integrity?
- Is the master schedule organized to provide students with the recommended instruction time?
- Are selected literacy, math, and behavior instruction well matched for the student population?

There is growing recognition and research support that MTSS can be applied at the secondary levels with some fundamental differences in infrastructure in order to facilitate early detection and rapid response. At the secondary level, the opportunity for prevention and early identification has passed. At this point, MTSS focuses on remediation with optimal results, as time is of the essence.

The Institute of Education Sciences published a dropout prevention practice guide, which identified six main practices that were found to be effective in decreasing high school dropout (Dynarski et al., 2008). These six practices are listed in Table 1.2. The parallels to

---

TABLE 1.2. Recommendations for Dropout Prevention

1. Utilize data systems to identify students at risk.
2. Assign adult advocates to students at risk.
3. Provide academic support and enrichment.
4. Implement interventions for improving behavior and social skills.
5. Personalize the learning environment.
6. Provide rigorous and relevant instruction.

Note. From Dynarski et al. (2008).

existing MTSS frameworks are clearly identified in the dropout prevention practice guide and are extended to include methods of enhancing student engagement and school, family, and community partnerships. Put together, these provide an excellent framework for schools to use in developing comprehensive dropout prevention action plans.

SUMMARY

Dropout rates in this country have sparked national debate, national and educational research, political action, school reform efforts, and media campaigns. In a rapidly changing and highly competitive global economy, with simultaneous reductions in educational, medical, and mental health resources, the current school failure and dropout rates are contributing to a national focus on this immediate crisis. Current research shows that students who drop out disengage from educational settings long before they get to high school and rarely, if ever, close the gap on previously identified socioeconomic or public health measures compared with high school graduates. Along with an overall lower life expectancy, students who don't complete high school face limited employment and earning opportunities.

Just as there are multiple factors identified in the research literature and by students themselves that contribute to the dropout crisis, there are multiple places where solutions can be applied. Early identification of disengagement and other warning signs, as well as efforts to build protective factors, are important for promoting school completion and will be explored in more depth throughout this book.

BIG IDEAS

- The dropout crisis has serious individual, economic, social, and national security implications.
- Dropping out of school is a process, not an event, and it can begin before a student even enters elementary school.
- The decision to drop out of school is influenced by many individual, family, school, and community factors.
- Research evidence identifies early warning signs and prevention and intervention methods that are effective for reducing risk for dropout.

CHAPTER 2

School, Family, and Community Partnerships

Statewide efforts to improve student outcomes and reduce dropout rates often focus on establishing standards for student achievement and holding schools accountable for meeting these expectations. In order for schools to meet standards for student performance, they must have the capacity and coordination to implement systemic reform (Supovitz, 2008). Researchers for the California Dropout Research Project (Supovitz, 2008) described the problem of building capacity as nested within different layers of the system: school, district, community resources, state and federal government. Each of these layers contributes an important role to school reform, with leadership needed at all levels. Dropout prevention research also emphasizes the valuable contributions of family and community collaboration to foster student achievement (Dynarski et al., 2008). This chapter provides recommendations and guidance to facilitate family participation and communication to enhance student success and graduation rates. The interplay of these factors is illustrated in the case example in Box 2.1.

SCHOOL REFORM FOR DROPOUT PREVENTION

We must foster school environments where teachers have the time to collaborate, the opportunities to lead, and the respect that all professionals deserve. We must recognize the importance of communities and families in supporting their children's education, because a parent is a child's first teacher. We must support families, communities, and schools working in partnership to deliver services and supports that address the full range of student needs.
—President Barack Obama (U.S. Department of Education, 2010)

A Sense of Belonging

School climate transcends all educational programs and strategies. It is a concept that is difficult to define, measure, and develop; however, numerous studies have pointed to the

---

BOX 2.1. Case Example: Daniel

Daniel was a ninth-grade student attending a large urban high school. He lived with his mother and two younger sisters, and the family had moved frequently throughout his childhood. He enrolled in a new high school in October following another move. Daniel's mother, who worked at night, had limited involvement in school activities and was rarely at home to supervise the children after school. Daniel relied on public transportation to get to school, and the trip took over an hour, making it difficult for him to arrive on time. When he was present, Daniel often sat by himself and sketched in his notebook. He had not made new friends at school and was not involved with any school-based extracurricular sports, clubs, or activities. Near the end of first quarter, Daniel was failing math and English.

Through academic screening assessments and teacher and parent interviews, the school problem-solving team and school psychologist learned that Daniel's academic skills were about a year behind grade level. Daniel voiced concern about his academic performance and difficulty keeping up with assignments and expressed aspirations to attend college. After the problem-solving team reviewed relevant data and considered alternative strategies and supports, Daniel began receiving Tier 2 academic support, including Read 180, targeted math instruction and practice, and study skills assistance, during daily intervention and enrichment blocks. Additionally, to increase Daniel's interest and involvement in school activities and opportunities to interact with peers who shared similar interests, he began participating in school and community events. Given his interest in drawing, these included art classes and set design projects with a community theater group. Along with public transportation support, the team also made efforts to improve home–school communication and collaboration by scheduling and coordinating weekly phone and/or e-mail updates on attendance, assignments, course performance, and extracurricular activities. The weekly updates increased a sense of parent involvement and support.

Practical Application to Dropout Prevention

Daniel was first brought to the attention of the problem-solving team when he was identified as having attendance and academic problems. Covered in more detail in Chapter 4, these factors are highly predictive of dropout risk. This process brought to light other signs of disengagement that were addressed through home, school, and community supports.

---

school climate, particularly one characterized by caring relationships, fairness, respect, and high academic expectations, as a major factor in enhancing student engagement, academic achievement, and school completion. If dropping out of school involves a process of disengagement, then fostering student engagement must be a priority in helping students stay in and complete school. Students who feel a sense of community and belonging at school are less likely to drop out (Dynarski et al., 2008; Christenson, Sinclair, Lehr, & Hurley, 2000; Christenson & Thurlow, 2004; Janosz, Archambault, Morizot, & Pagani, 2008). If students build meaningful relationships and feel a sense of connectedness and relevance at school, the school becomes a place they want to be. Developing a personalized learning environment and maximizing students' sense of connectedness is no small task and requires commitment and cooperation among several groups. School leadership, as well as school, family, and community collaboration, are essential.

Small, personalized school environments are associated with higher student achievement, attendance, and graduation rates (Dynarski et al., 2008). Even in large, traditional schools, this can be achieved by creating smaller "school-within-a-school" learning communities or establishing teams of teachers. This type of environment allows more personalized attention from teachers, including knowledge of individual challenges and motivation, close monitoring of academic progress and behavior, and support in specific areas of difficulty. Whether it comes from teachers, counselors, other school staff, or volunteers, students benefit from a "second shift" of familiar and caring adults (Koughan & Robertson, 2012) to help them stay on track.

> "Through relationships that convey high expectations, students learn to believe in themselves and in their futures, developing the critical resilience traits of self-esteem, self-efficacy, autonomy, and optimism" (Benard, 1995).

Small learning communities can be established according to grade level (e.g., a ninth-grade academy) or by theme (students select a particular professional or curricular area of focus, such as science, business, or the arts). An added benefit of smaller learning communities is the ability to form interdisciplinary teaching teams, which facilitate more innovative instruction, curriculum choice, and individualized teacher attention. Even schools that are not ready for systemic reform associated with the school-within-a-school model can make positive changes in this direction by establishing teaching teams, creating smaller classes, and providing extended time in the classroom through block scheduling and advisory periods (Dynarski et al., 2008).

The Role of Consensus and Team Building

There is wide national agreement that the traditional factory model educational delivery system is no longer relevant for modern students in a global technological age. To redesign traditional systems to support small, personalized learning environments that foster a sense of belonging, we must first invest in consensus building to develop the capacity and infrastructure for effective implementation.

The MTSS Framework

The MTSS framework provides an excellent foundation for the alignment and integration of evidence-based dropout prevention components. The National Association of State Directors of Special Education (NASDE) offers tremendous guidance in implementing MTSS, with RTI blueprints at the district (Elliot & Morrison, 2008) and school (Kurns & Tilly, 2008) levels. As the NASDE blueprints outline, the implementation of MTSS typically proceeds through three stages, identified as (1) consensus building, (2) infrastructure building, and (3) implementation.

Three Stages of School Reform
1. Consensus building
2. Infrastructure building
3. Implementation

CONSENSUS

In the context of dropout prevention, consensus building is best achieved from a district-wide perspective (PreK–12), as the research clearly identifies that risk of dropping out is a process that occurs over time (Dynarski et al., 2008). Consensus building begins by communicating dropout prevention concepts and research, within an MTSS framework, to all educators and stakeholders. This is the time when the evidence and purpose of dropout prevention is taught, discussed, and embraced. An important caveat and lesson learned from MTSS implementation is the recognition that consensus does not require 100% of staff to buy in. Although it is a laudable goal, 100% enthusiastic staff support for system change is probably not realistic. Although some educators embrace change and the inherent challenges involved in systems change, resistance to change is a common human reaction. Thus leadership is essential to ensure that schools move forward in the journey of implementing best practices by providing ongoing professional development in conjunction with clear goals and expectations for school and district outcomes.

INFRASTRUCTURE

To begin building infrastructure, district and individual school sites examine their current practices as compared with the critical components of effective dropout prevention methods identified in the research. A systematic inventory of current curricula, practices, assessments, and all school resources is an important first step. Next, to identify current areas of success and prioritize areas of need, it is important to gather districtwide and schoolwide data on student engagement, attendance, achievement, problem behaviors, and high school completion rates. This analysis provides baseline data to inform districtwide and schoolwide priorities. Then an action plan is developed to systematically address any potential gaps between current practices and benchmark goals. The action plan is reviewed regularly to assess progress toward the district and school goals and to celebrate achievements. New goals and priorities are determined on the basis of student engagement, attendance, behavior, academic, and on-time graduation outcomes.

IMPLEMENTATION

The third stage involves ensuring that the systems and structures, in conjunction with professional and community resources, are identified and developed to execute dropout prevention methods in a continuous multi-tiered system. To carry out these recommendations effectively, teachers will benefit from participation in professional learning communities and ongoing professional development in the areas of curriculum and instruction. Therefore, support and resources from school leaders, including principals and superintendents, are essential. Development of a master schedule that incorporates the precious resource of time for parent communication, community partnerships, professional collaboration, and analysis of district, school, and individual student data is a primary implementation component.

Without question all three phases of implementing an MTSS framework for dropout prevention require leadership, ongoing professional development, and efficient resource allocation. Districts with a well-established MTSS foundation are clearly at an advantage, with leadership, consensus, infrastructure, and evidence-based prevention and early intervention practices already in place. School districts in the beginning or early stages of MTSS implementation can benefit from the lessons learned from MTSS practices already implemented in many schools nationwide. A substantial body of research already exists on the positive outcomes of identifying and resolving problems in the early stages, before a child becomes more at risk for dropping out of school. Examples of user-friendly, evidence-based text resources available to guide MTSS implementation and application efforts include, but are not limited to, Brown-Chidsey and Andren (2012); Brown-Chidsey, Bronaugh, and McGraw (2009); Brown-Chidsey and Steege (2010); Burns, Riley-Tillman, and VanDerHeyden (2012); Chafouleas, Riley-Tillman, and Sugai (2007); Glover and Vaughn (2010); Jimerson, Burns, and VanDerHeyden (2007); and Shapiro (2011).

FAMILY COLLABORATION

Across cultures worldwide, a common area of agreement is care and concern for our children. Typically, families of all cultural backgrounds, education, and income levels encourage their children, express interest and concern about their school experiences, and urge them to do well in school. Historically, many of these families seek a better educational and employment future for their own children. Most parents and family members understand that school success leads to better employment opportunities and requires academic, behavioral, and social skills and thus strive to support children in their school experiences. International research and evidence from successful family and parental partnerships show that *all* families can, and do, have positive effects on their children's learning (Henderson & Mapp, 2002). Consequently, another key ingredient of dropout prevention for all students is meaningful family involvement. In this chapter, the term *parent* refers to any family members who fulfill a parenting role, including stepparents, grandparents, other relatives, and foster parents.

Historically, the modern American family has changed in many ways since the evolution of American public education. Research shows that parental and family expectations and active participation in a child's education are highly predictive of school engagement and on-time high school graduation. A growing body of evidence shows a strong correlation between parental involvement and student achievement. New evidence suggests that a school's effort to engage parents can have a positive impact on the home environment and, in turn, on student performance. School-based efforts to improve family engagement lead to more attention to learning activities at home, parent–child interactions concerning learning, and better learning outcomes at school (Redding, Langdon, Meyer, & Sheley, 2004). Parent engagement in schools is linked with improved student behavior, motivation, attendance, social skills, and academic achievement. In addition, parent engagement serves as a protective factor against drug and alcohol use (Centers for Disease Control and Prevention,

2012; Michigan Department of Education, 2004). As with the implementation of school-based interventions, the earlier parents get involved, the more beneficial their involvement will be. Furthermore, the positive effects of their involvement last through high school (Michigan Department of Education, 2004). Thus a fundamental first step in developing meaningful dropout prevention plans is establishing positive relationships with parents and families. This topic is discussed more thoroughly in *Collaborating with Parents for Early School Success: The Achieving–Behaving–Caring Program* (McConaughy, Kay, Welkowita, Hewitt, & Fitzgerald, 2010).

School Readiness

The impact that families have on their children's learning and school achievement begins long before they set foot in school. Isaacs (2012) reported that children from low-income families typically start kindergarten with language and prereading skills well below national norms, and almost half of low-income children are not ready for school when they enter their first classroom. Importantly, the research also highlighted the positive impact that quality early educational opportunities can have on later school success. Effective prekindergarten programs that support parent involvement and family collaboration offer important opportunities for detecting academic or behavior problems as they emerge and for establishing protective factors shown to be highly predictive of school success.

Attendance and engagement in preschool programs such as EduCare and Head Start have been shown to be highly effective in improving early childhood rates of school readiness. In the early stages of childhood development, effective home–school partnerships improve attendance in prekindergarten programs and positive school engagement. Additionally, programs and interventions that engage families in supporting their children's learning at home are linked to higher student achievement (Henderson & Mapp, 2002).

Family involvement in the preschool years presents opportunities for parents and teachers to work together to support children's development of essential language, literacy, mathematics, and social skills. Simultaneously, this positive relationship facilitates development of positive learning environments at home. With increased attendance and engagement, students have more exposure and opportunities to practice early literacy and numeracy skills, social skills, and age-appropriate classroom behaviors. Given the correlation between attendance, school engagement, academic achievement, and behavior regulation skills, these additional preschool learning opportunities are crucial elements of dropout prevention in the early stages of child development.

Family Engagement in Schools

To develop effective school-based parent and family partnerships and sustain positive relationships, schools must adopt the attitude that *all* families are invested in their children's education and are appreciative of assistance and guidance in their efforts to support their chil-

> **Schools will discover new resources when they see families and communities as valuable assets.**

dren's learning. Successful family partnership programs focus on relationship building as an initial goal and embrace four key characteristics identified by Henderson and Mapp (2002) and defined in Figure 2.1: a joining process, welcoming, honoring, and connecting.

Common barriers to family engagement in schools include families' lack of understanding or knowledge of schools and how to help their children succeed in school, geographic isolation or lack of transportation, time and scheduling issues, personal history of negative school experiences, the perception that older children do not need or want their parents to be involved in school, and the reluctance of teachers and administrators to invite families to participate in school activities and decision making (Michigan Department of Education, 2004). To overcome these obstacles and promote a collaborative approach to achieving student success, there are numerous steps that schools and communities can take. Development and implementation of both in-school and out-of-school initiatives are necessary as many parents and family members are not frequent visitors to school facilities. The National Parent–Teacher Association (PTA) has identified six standards of parent and family involvement efforts that are linked to increased engagement and school success (Michigan Depart-

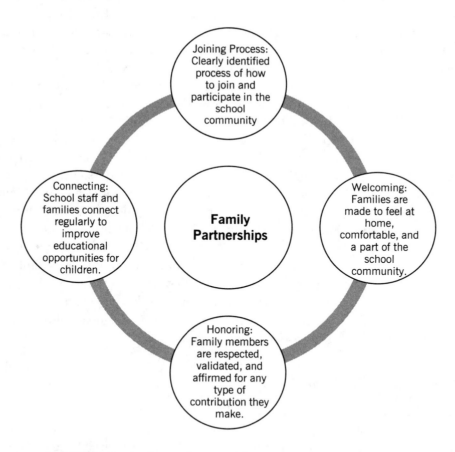

FIGURE 2.1. Qualities of successful parent partnership programs.

TABLE 2.1. Six Standards for Parent and Family Involvement

1. Regular, two-way communication.
2. Promotion and support for parenting role.
3. Partnership in student learning.
4. Volunteering.
5. School decision making and advocacy.
6. Community collaboration.

Note. Based on Michigan Department of Education (2004).

ment of Education, 2004). These are listed in Table 2.1 and described in more detail in the following sections.

First, efforts to engage families start with communication. Regular, two-way communication between school and home helps develop trust, potential for problem solving, and parents' commitment and ability to help their children achieve at school. Teachers and administrators play a critical role in reaching out to parents, and these efforts lay the foundation for openness and involvement. To establish effective communication with families, schools should use a variety of communication tools and numerous opportunities to interact, including technology for general information and updates, as well as informal activities that foster contact and relationship building among school staff and families. Examples include coffee hours, potluck dinners, parent education and training opportunities, cultural festivals, book clubs, and performing arts, music, and sports events.

Through regular communication, parents must be kept informed about student progress and behavior, including positive news and work samples. Behavior research has shown that in numerous settings, the optimum ratio of positive messages to counterbalance negative messages is 5:1 (Flora, 2000). Traditionally, particularly at the secondary levels, phone calls home are to relay negative messages. Taking the time to routinely reach out to parents with positive messages has the potential to significantly improve parent and school communication and foster parent engagement, receptivity to school concerns, and partnerships throughout school. In turn, parents must be given the opportunity to comment on their children's performance, share information about strengths and goals, and voice parental concerns. Information on school activities, courses, policies, procedures, expectations, and student services should also be provided clearly and consistently. Taking into consideration possible barriers, such as schedules, transportation, language, and child care, schools can develop strategies to accommodate families' unique needs and meet these standards. Following is a list of recommendations for facilitating involvement with families who are not proficient in English:

- Arrange for translators if needed.
- Understand your own cultural context.
- Share cultural traditions and norms.

- Create small, friendly settings.
- Invite families and communities to tell their education stories.
- Ask families about their expectations for their children.

The second standard for improving family engagement is to provide support for the parenting role and responsibilities. This involves promoting positive parent–child relationships, showing respect for families and their traditions, and connecting families with needed resources. For example, the transition year for schools offers a prime opportunity to connect with parents and offer education, resources, and support relevant to preparation for the transition year changes. Schools that offer prekindergarten have a unique opportunity to offer early childhood parenting support in literacy and prosocial behaviors—areas research has shown are highly predictive of school success. Similar to themes that are developed for curricula, cultural diversity within schools offers an opportunity to celebrate and educate the school community about different cultures and parenting perspectives.

Educators play an important role in informing families about school expectations for student learning and can guide families in parent–child activities through events such as literacy and math nights.

Third, parents play an important role in their child's learning, and empowering them with the knowledge and tools to help at home can have a significant impact on students' academic achievement. Parent conferences, workshops, school assembly events that incorporate a series of small skill lessons (e.g., literacy, math calculation, organization, study skills, resources), or written material are all means of helping parents to understand classroom expectations, to learn how to monitor and assist with homework, to discuss school learning and activities with their children, and to promote good study skills. The main objective is to involve parents as partners in teaching and learning, educational decision making, goal setting, and to convey through these interactions that education is valued.

These messages are communicated at home and in the school, as shown by the fourth standard: volunteering. Parents don't need to have a special talent or expertise to contribute in the classroom. They don't even need to be present during the school day; parents with scheduling or transportation constraints can still be invited to participate before or after school or from home. Welcoming families into the school and providing regular, meaningful opportunities for them to volunteer builds confidence in the schools, provides needed support to teachers, and communicates commitment and caring to students. Acknowledging parents for their participation and contribution fosters a sense of belonging and partnership. This requires organization, training, and a truly inviting school climate.

Beyond the scope of involvement with their own children or local schools, parents are encouraged to participate in systems-level decision making and advocacy (Standard 5) and community collaboration (Standard 6). This type of family involvement is associated with greater student achievement and public support. By joining groups such as PTAs, advisory committees, and governance bodies, parents can represent the concerns of families and influence policy, curricular, and other decisions. The school's role in this is to solicit parental participation, to provide accessible forums for discussing and resolving concerns, and to give parents representation on school committees. In collaboration with the greater community, schools can serve as a link between families and community resources by sharing information, establishing partnerships, and involving students, parents, and community members in mutually beneficial community service and school volunteer programs. An example of a parent involvement program is described in Box 2.2.

Schools that have been successful in increasing parent engagement have several common characteristics. These include establishing a trusting and respectful relationship with families, emphasizing learning objectives, and connecting with families outside of school. Importantly, efforts to engage families must be inclusive and wide-ranging, making many connections with parents over time. Parent engagement can be fostered in numerous informal ways, such as everyday communication of attitudes and expectations and opportunities for connection and relationship building. Alternatively, a school may increase family engagement by implementing a targeted intervention, for example, that involves parents in school decision making, provides parent education in home reading and study skills, or engages in outreach in the form of home visits and family nights (Redding et al., 2004). Figure 2.2 provides numerous examples of both informal and targeted strategies for promoting family engagement in schools, and a checklist in Appendix A serves as an assessment tool for schools striving to improve family engagement.

BOX 2.2. First-Day Program

Purpose

To break down the barriers with parents and the community by making the first day of school a celebration with special activities that include everyone. The First-Day Program is an attempt to involve parents who are not typically involved with their children's schools.

Examples of First-Day Program Activities

- Workshops that are held in different languages (if required) that help explain:
  o Strategies for helping students study at home.
  o How to maintain parent–school communications.
  o The school's rules.
  o The outcome of absenteeism.
- School parades and celebrations are held with parents, teachers, and students.
- Teachers and students pack picnic lunches and eat together on the athletic fields or playgrounds of the school.
- Teachers provide information to parents about their reading programs and how they can support their child's reading at home.
- Community resources are provided, such as library cards for students who participate in the First-Day Program.
- Local businesses come together and allow parents paid time off to attend the school event.

Embrace Partnerships and Share Power.
- Discuss and plan how families want to be engaged.
- Consult all families about policies.
- Involve families in action research.
- Provide access to principal and school staff.
- Facilitate connections to community groups.
- Invite families to staff training.
- Support families' involvement in decision making.

Build Social and Political Connections.
- Promote families' connections with each other, school staff, and community groups.
- Invite school officials to the school to respond to families' concerns.
- Give families information about how the system works.

Acknowledge the Knowledge Base of Families.
- Identify community assets.
- Identify parent interests and areas of expertise.
- Invite parents to volunteer in the school on special topics.

Short-Term and Long-Term Joining Activities.
- Greet visitors at the door in a family-friendly way.
- Set up an open-door policy that meets the needs of families and staff.
- Make "good-news" phone calls home at least once a month about a child's progress.
- Hold events in places other than at school, such as churches, community centers, etc.
- Provide child care, translation, and food at meetings.
- Provide tips for parents on reading and math in newsletters, book bags, and report cards.
- Make sure all materials are translated into the language spoken at home.
- Conduct home visits designed to welcome families to school again.
- Hold workshops and seminars for parents to help with understanding technology, preparing for college, teen years, and homework.
- Engage in "first day of school" events.
- Conduct more frequent parent–teacher–student conferences.

FIGURE 2.2. Strategies for enhancing family involvement.

COMMUNITY PARTNERSHIPS

The dropout problem does not belong to the school district alone, nor can it be solved by schools alone. Rather, dropout prevention is the responsibility of the whole community. Lower graduation rates have an impact on the economic development of a community and are linked with lower tax revenue, greater reliance on government health care and social services, less civic activity, and higher crime rates. As a collective problem, building community collaboration ensures that efforts will be shared among involved parties, such as the superintendent, students, parents, local businesses, the media, universities, public safety officials, faith-based organizations, cultural groups, and community and youth organizations.

Academic interventions are often the focus of dropout prevention methods. Additionally, mentorship, coaching, and tutorial support are linked with increased student participation and academic achievement. There is research support for numerous programs that provide students with adult mentors and tutors (Dynarski et al., 2008). For example, well-designed after-school and weekend tutoring programs can help improve academic skills and student engagement when the type and intensity of interventions are matched to students' needs. Summer enrichment programs allow students to catch up on high school credits and help prepare students for transitions to the next year. Because schools face limited resources in terms of time and staff, administrators are encouraged to establish community partnerships and to reach out to local organizations, universities, and businesses to volunteer time and provide work space. Establishing relationships with service organizations such as the YMCA, Rotary International, and the local Chamber of Commerce are good places to begin outreach to local business organizations to develop mentorship and volunteer training opportunities. Schools benefit tremendously from partnerships with their state universities and community colleges, as well. Collaboration with universities offers an opportunity for coordination of supervised professional preservice training, practica, and internship opportunities, as well as access to college-level courses for students in need of enrichment beyond high school course offerings. The explosion of courses available globally via the Internet is rapidly becoming a new frontier of educational opportunities that is beyond the scope of this book, but global online instruction clearly represents another opportunity to provide strategic alternative educational supports for students. All collaborative efforts should be guided by protocols, training, and supervision, with clearly defined educational criteria, as well as program and individual outcome goals. Examples of some creative community collaborations are provided in Table 2.2.

> **Parents and community members should:**
> - **Be involved.**
> - **Feel invited to make a contribution.**
> - **Feel a welcome by the school and their children.**

School engagement is often characterized as complex transactions between personal and family characteristics and the school environment. A review of intervention research suggests that, along with affective and psychological factors (a student's perceptions of adult, peer, and family support for learning and school completion), a student's cognitive perceptions of the relevance of schoolwork and expectations for success influences educational outcomes (Finn, 1989; Sinclair, Christenson, & Thurlow, 2005). This suggests that school-based efforts to provide relevant and personally meaningful learning experiences are likely to increase student engagement. Additionally, research has shown that school engagement has a direct influence on academic achievement in adolescence, above and beyond a number of inherent familial risk factors (Johnson, McGue, & Iacono, 2006). Community members, in partnership with schools, can play an important role in engaging students in applicable and motivating work-related experiences to foster student engagement and provide additional mentorship opportunities. Opportunities for students to begin thinking about and planning for postsecondary education or employment options include interactive career days, college campus tours, and information sessions with postsecondary admissions or financial aid offices. In addition, it is recommended that schools partner with local businesses and organizations to provide internships, service learning projects, paid employment, and simulated job interviews.

TABLE 2.2. Examples of Community Collaborations

21st Century Community Learning Centers

This program supports the creation of community learning centers that provide academic enrichment opportunities during nonschool hours, particularly for students who attend high-poverty and low-performing schools. Students participate in after-school homework help and social development activities such as sports and the arts.

Foster Grandparents Program

The Foster Grandparents Program (FGP) provides role models, mentors, and friends to children in schools. The FGP is a community service model in which volunteers, generally ages 55 and over, work with youth who are at risk or have special needs. These volunteers provide tutoring, mentoring, and support for teachers and students in preschool through college.

An Achievable Dream

An Achievable Dream is a K–12 academy located in Newport News, Virginia. This program is an example of a collaborative partnership between the public school system and the business community, providing students with intensive instruction in basic skills, extended-school-day and summer programming, enrichment programs, technology, personal development programs, and parent involvement opportunities.

Project U Turn

Project U Turn is part of a nonprofit youth network in Philadelphia that provides services to students across all grades and helps keep high school students engaged and on track through graduation. Student Success Centers help youth design secondary readiness plans and provide academic, social, postsecondary, and career support.

Community leaders, including civic leaders and school board officials, are charged with the responsibility for advancing the community and have the opportunity to allocate resources and organize efforts needed to make meaningful changes for our children. Their role in dropout prevention should be comprehensive, including addressing transportation issues, ensuring that the school is a safe environment, and building community collaboration. There is a movement toward creating school-based health centers, which provide physical and mental health services within the school walls. Through these centers, communities can ensure that students and families receive equal access to optimal medical health prevention and early intervention services.

Ideally, the doors to the school are open to two-way traffic; that is, community members are invited as mentors, tutors, or advisors to help develop technical education curricula, and students are brought into the community for enriching service learning opportunities and work-related experiences. An indirect advantage of increased community involvement is community support for local schools, as well as improved understanding of school challenges. When the school is the hub of the community and serves as a community center for learning, sports, arts, and physical and mental health for all ages, everyone benefits.

SUMMARY

Given that the dropout problem is complex, the solution must be comprehensive. Although school reform is essential and the focus of this book, these challenges cannot be overcome within the walls of the school alone. Rather, the national dropout crisis requires a far-reaching systematic approach that brings our schools, families, and the larger community together to provide the multiple tiers of prevention and early intervention support that our youth need to be actively engaged and successful in school. To facilitate an open and non-defensive partnership that is focused on success for all children, school personnel must embrace a culture of shared partnership and power. Parents and community members are more likely to become involved when they understand that they should be involved, feel capable of making a contribution, and feel invited by the school and their children to actively participate in school events and decision making.

BIG IDEAS

- Dropout prevention takes a village: schools, parents and families, and community partnerships.
- Small, personalized learning environments are associated with higher student achievement, attendance, promotion, and graduation rates.
- Parents need to be empowered as consumers and to be kept informed of how their children are doing, what their children need, and how to access needed resources and support.
- Community partnerships can contribute numerous important services to students and families.

CHAPTER 3

Academic and Behavior Links to Inform Dropout Prevention Methods

A strong correlation exists between academic skills and prosocial behavior, and both are equally essential for school success. The dropout prevention literature emphasizes the need to identify academic and behavior skill needs simultaneously, and to intervene as early as possible and as intensively as needed to demonstrate progress. When viewing dropout as a process that begins as early as the prekindergarten years, these dropout prevention components align with the well-established schoolwide public health model of prevention and intervention known as MTSS. A unique feature of MTSS is the integration of academic and behavior supports, with the promise that prevention and intervention in each area may lead to improvements in both areas. To illustrate this relationship, see the case example in Box 3.1.

ACADEMIC AND BEHAVIOR LINKS

As research on outcomes of RTI and PBIS evolved, the importance of an integrated approach to universal screening with a systematic review of both academic and behavior data to inform effective interventions emerged. An extensive body of research provides evidence that academic problems are often linked to behavior problems (McIntosh, Horner, Chard, Dickey, & Braun, 2008; Fleming, Harachi, Cortes, Abbott, & Catalano, 2004; Nelson, Benner, Lane, & Smith, 2004); furthermore, improvements in social behavior can be achieved through academic interventions and improvements in attention, and academic performance can be achieved through strategic behavioral and clinical interventions (Kamps et al., 2003; Lane & Menzies, 2002; Lane, 2007; Lee, Sugai, & Horner, 1999; Nelson, Stage, Epstein, & Pierce, 2005).

In a recent study to examine the relationship between academic achievement and social behavior, Algozzine, Wang, and Violette (2011) showed that the link between young

---

BOX 3.1. Case Example: Mia

Mia, a 6-year-old student in the first grade, was referred to the problem-solving team by her teacher due to defiant, argumentative, and noncompliant behavior in the classroom setting. She also had difficulty getting along with peers and making friends. A universal screening in January showed that Mia was well below grade-level benchmarks on all early literacy skills, adversely affecting her ability to learn to read. In response to an initial hypothesis that Mia's delays in reading were contributing to behavior problems, she began receiving additional small-group, evidence-based reading instruction. Initially, it took behavior prompting, planned ignoring of verbal protests, and positive reinforcement procedures to increase Mia's attention to the reading instruction. She was encouraged to participate in graphing her progress data, a suggestion that was met with initial resistance, but as her performance improved, Mia became more cooperative. Meanwhile, periodic observations during the intervention period indicated that Mia's attention and participation had improved and her disruptive behavior decreased. At the third progress monitoring session, Mia entered the room, spontaneously and cheerfully segmenting words exchanged in greeting. She eagerly participated in the early literacy tasks and progress monitoring process, delighted by her graph that showed continued progress toward the benchmark goal. Simultaneously, the literacy specialist observed positive changes in Mia's classroom behaviors and interactions with peers. After 6 weeks of the reading intervention and steady increases in weekly progress monitoring data, the classroom teacher noted that she had observed a remarkable change in Mia's behavior in the classroom setting. Interestingly, at that time Mia continued to be well below spring benchmarks for reading; however, her progress data showed that she had achieved proficiency in phonological awareness and that she was making steady progress in decoding fluency. Perhaps most important, Mia now perceived herself as an emerging reader, with the progress data to prove it!

Practical Application to Dropout Prevention

As shown in Figure 3.1, Mia was not responding to Tier 1 alone; therefore, a Tier 2 reading intervention was put in place. This case demonstrates that effective methods to improve literacy skills can yield improvements in school behavior as well. Clinical observations and weekly progress monitoring indicated that Mia was keenly aware of her reading abilities compared with those of her peers, and these difficulties were likely contributing to disruptive classroom behavior.

---

boys' reading achievement and their antisocial behavior is mediated by environmental factors, such as teacher perceptions and behavior. The researchers demonstrated a strong positive relationship between student behavior measures and teacher ratings of academic competence. These findings indicated that teachers are more likely to rate well-behaved students highly on academic competence and to hold higher expectations of these students. Well-behaved students were believed to be academically competent because they received higher ratings on cooperating with others, asserting themselves, and displaying more self-control in class. Conversely, students who demonstrated more social problems, such as those evidenced with externalizing, internalizing, and hyperactive behaviors, were believed to be less competent academically. This study illustrates that when academic achievement and behavior are viewed as outcomes, explicitly teaching academics and behavior to young children in school is an essential primary prevention strategy.

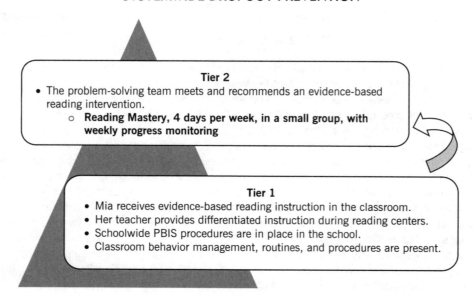

FIGURE 3.1. Tier 1 and Tier 2 supports for Mia.

The interrelationship between academics and behavior has been shown to occur early, with evidence that kindergarten early literacy skills can predict behavior problems at the end of elementary school (McIntosh, Horner, Chard, Boland, & Good, 2006). As in the case of Mia, illustrated in Box 3.1, students who begin school with reading skill deficits are at a greater risk for developing future problem behavior. McIntosh et al. (2006) showed that students identified as being at risk in a brief screening measure of phonemic awareness at the end of kindergarten were more likely to develop future behavior problems. Essentially, kindergarten students low in phoneme segmentation skills had heightened risk of receiving multiple office discipline referrals (ODRs) in fifth grade. These findings demonstrate the symbiotic relationship between early literacy skills and behavior as early as kindergarten. If academic delays are unresolved, the presence of academic and behavior problems is likely to continue in middle school and high school, significantly increasing the risk for high school failure. The compelling research evidence shows that strategic instruction and intervention targeting reading achievement and antisocial behavior as early as preschool is likely to positively influence the development of both early literacy skills and prosocial behaviors.

Research to Practice

The decision to drop out of school is typically the result of multiple and often ongoing risk factors that begin as early as preschool or elementary school, then crystallize at the secondary level (McIntosh, Horner, et al., 2008; Balfanz & Herzog, 2005; Balfanz et al., 2007). Simultaneously, research continues to demonstrate that the older the student, the more difficult it is to successfully and quickly intervene; thus an evidence-based systemic model for dropout prevention that is applicable at all educational levels is needed (Glover & Vaughn,

2010; Vaughn & Fletcher, 2010, 2012). The evolving paradigm shift toward utilizing a multi-tiered system of student supports within general education has extensive research support for prevention and early intervention methods at the elementary levels (Brown-Chidsey & Steege, 2010; Chafouleas et al., 2007), with a growing body of evidence to support similar methods at the secondary levels (Burns et al., 2012; Glover & Vaughn, 2010).

Student Engagement

The reciprocal relationship between academics and behavior can be viewed through the lens of student engagement. Successful school completion is dependent on student engagement and a student's perceived sense of belonging. Conversely, dropping out of school is a process of disengagement and of the development of negative attitudes toward school over time. It is intuitively understood and supported by research that students who are engaged attend school, complete schoolwork, participate in co-curricular activities, and tend to pass their classes. Likewise, positive school performance reinforces a sense of belonging in the school.

Although attention to dropout risk factors increases at both the middle school and high school levels, traditionally the primary focus and intensity of dropout prevention efforts have been at the high school level, at which for the first time earned course credits and course performance directly affect a student's ability to progress with his or her peers and meet high school graduation criteria. Although criteria for graduation are based on the number of credits earned, a review of historical dropout risk patterns shows significant evidence that dropping out is a process of disengagement from school and learning that occurs over many years (Christenson, Sinclair, Lehr, & Godber, 2001). Numerous studies have shown that many students become increasingly disengaged as they progress through school (Anderman, Maehr, & Midgley, 1999). By middle school, a lack of interest in schoolwork and poor attention, task initiation, and work completion become increasingly observable. By high school, the process of disengagement from education and educational pursuits far too frequently results in dropping out. Students who are disengaged often develop a pattern of inconsistent attendance and poor academic performance that perpetuates aversive school experiences. They have more negative interactions with adults, perceive their academic classes as irrelevant, and report a lack of satisfaction and discontent during their high school years (Bridgeland et al., 2006).

Although academic engagement is very important for school success and high school completion, student engagement is multifaceted and includes components that extend beyond academic engagement (Appleton, Christenson, & Furlong, 2008). As seen in Figure 3.2, observable academic and behavioral indicators of student engagement include classroom behavior, attendance, positive social interactions, and work completion, among others. The diagram also lists components of internal engagement, such as cognitive and affective skills. Cognitive engagement encompasses the perceived relevance of a high school diploma for a student's future, as well as a student's ability for self-regulation and goal-directed persistence. In the school setting cognitive engagement requires the development of executive function skills, such as time management, organizational, and study skills to prioritize, initiate, and complete academic tasks successfully (Guare & Dawson, 2009; Guare, Dawson, &

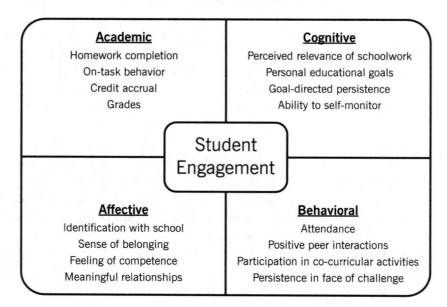

FIGURE 3.2. Elements of student engagement. Based on Appleton, Christenson, and Furlong (2008).

Guare, 2013). Affective components of school engagement, including a sense of belonging, have been shown to be critical components of school success and are contingent on the ability to develop positive relationships with teachers and peers. Essentially, all of these components are equally important, and when students experience all forms of engagement, the likelihood that they will complete school increases.

Focus on Reading

> **Literacy skills are highly correlated with behavior, academic achievement in other subject areas, and school completion.**

Literacy has been identified as a critical academic skill for school success, highly correlated with on-time high school graduation and postsecondary experiences. Consequently, effective literacy instruction is an essential component of dropout prevention planning. Current research shows that reading comprehension of secondary students is so low that it not only impedes school success and postsecondary learning opportunities but also precludes preparation for increasingly competitive employment options (Biancarosa & Snow, 2006; Kamil et al., 2008).

Previous employment options for high school graduates, such as retail or service industries, often did not have significant literacy demands; however, with advances in technology, the ability to comprehend complex text, as well as fluent technological skills, have become basic job prerequisites. Literacy achievement also presents a significant challenge for students with learning problems and learning disabilities, as literacy skills cross all content areas, such as science and social studies, as well as technical education courses. Delays in the development of grade-level literacy skills as early as kindergarten have the potential to adversely affect students' success across multiple courses, often within a single school day. Over time, these academic difficulties frequently manifest as internalizing and/or externalizing behavior problems, which contribute to a student's risk for disengagement and dropping out of school.

A longitudinal study examining the relationship between third-grade reading skills and high school completion found that students who were not reading proficiently by third grade were four times less likely to graduate than proficient readers. Third graders who had not mastered basic literacy skills were six times less likely to earn a diploma (Hernandez, 2012). This study also found that third-grade reading performance was a stronger predictor of high school graduation than poverty. Importantly, the research evidence from these studies highlights the early opportunity to intervene, which can be accomplished with early identification and evidence-based reading instruction within an MTSS framework.

DROPOUT PREVENTION AND MTSS

RTI is well established as an evidence-based, multi-tiered framework for identifying and meeting the academic needs of all students (Brown-Chidsey & Steege, 2010). Likewise, PBIS is generally recognized as the evidence-based multi-tiered framework for effective prevention of and intervention for behavior problems (Chafouleas et al., 2007; Brown-Chidsey & Steege, 2010). Schoolwide positive behavioral interventions and supports (SWPBS) have been identified as an efficient and effective system to promote prosocial behavior and decrease violent behavior in schools (McIntosh et al., 2006).

As academic and behavior problems frequently overlap, and because analysis of both academic and behavioral difficulties is required to inform effective intervention, there is growing research support and recognition for the need to integrate academic and behavioral prevention and intervention methods into MTSS, as depicted in Figure 3.3. The key components of this model are universal, high-quality, research-based academic and behavioral instruction, multiple tiers of research-based interventions that increase in intensity and/or frequency based on individual student needs, and continuous progress monitoring. Academic and behavioral interventions are two sides of the same triangle; RTI and PBIS should not be separate entities. Rather, research for both evidence-based models (RTI and PBIS) supports an *integrated* approach, with teams providing both academic and behavioral support through the same systems, which may lead to better academic and behavioral outcomes for more students (McIntosh et al., 2006; O'Shaughnessy, Lane, Gresham, & Beebe-Frankenberger, 2003). As emphasized in Box 3.2, the focus of MTSS is on prevention and early intervention.

Effective MTSS methods increase student performance and school success. These methods can be applied to dropout prevention, as both academic skills and prosocial skills are important for school completion. The effort to decide which of these should be emphasized or taught "first" can be conceptualized as a "chicken or egg" question. What we know from extensive research is that a reciprocal relationship exists between academic and prosocial skills and that both are essential for school success (Brown-Chidsey & Steege, 2010; Burns et al., 2012; Chafouleas et al., 2007). A weakness in either academic or behavioral

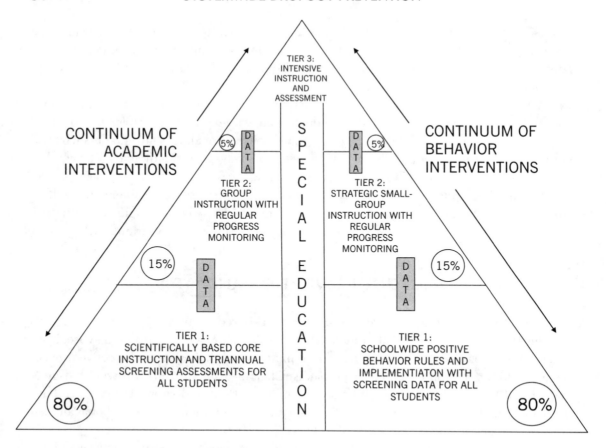

FIGURE 3.3. MTSS model. From Brown-Chidsey and Steege (2010). Copyright 2010 by The Guilford Press. Reprinted by permission.

skills has the potential to adversely affect the other. Similarly, when both academic and prosocial behavior skills are taught explicitly, student outcomes improve. Essentially, when students have learned and can demonstrate appropriate prosocial skills, their receptivity and ability to learn academic skills increases, simultaneously increasing school engagement. Likewise, teaching appropriate behavior skills across settings improves opportunities to learn other skills (Massetti & Bracken, 2010; Haydon et al., 2010). This cycle is illustrated in Figure 3.4. The school setting presents a special opportunity to nurture social, emotional, and academic success for all children. Research shows that children will do as well as the learning environment allows; thus when we improve learning environments, we improve outcomes for children (Brown-Chidsey & Steege, 2010; Brown-Chidsey et al., 2009; Coyne, Carnine, & Kame'enui, 2010).

As in the case of Mia (see Box 3.1), effective instruction of academic skills has the power to also improve students' prosocial behaviors and reduce problem behaviors. Additionally, when academic instruction is at a student's skill, or learning, level, fewer problem behaviors occur (Partin, Robertson, Maggin, Oliver, & Wehby, 2010; Spaulding et al., 2010). Determination of the appropriate instructional level is essential for academic and behavioral success, as all students, including those receiving special education services and those in gifted and

---

BOX 3.2. The Importance of Early Intervention

We know from previous research that signs of antisocial behavior emerge as early as school entry in kindergarten (Hamre & Pianta, 2001; Walker, Kavanagh, et al., 1998). Simultaneously, research shows that both academic and behavioral interventions increasingly lose effectiveness after third grade (Juel, 1998; Kazdin, 1987; Walker & Severson, 1992; Vaughn & Fletcher, 2010), resulting in the need for more intensive intervention with slower gains, particularly at the secondary level. This evidence highlights the importance of early intervention to avert more severe academic, social, and emotional challenges and reinforce school completion (Good, Simmons, & Kame'enui, 2001; Sugai & Horner, 2002).

---

talented programs, need an appropriate level of challenge. If the instruction is too easy, it won't lead to new learning, and students are likely to feel bored. When instruction is too difficult, students are likely to give up and disengage. Disengagement, whether in the form of internalizing inattentive behavior or externalizing disruptive behavior, often serves the function of avoiding or escaping academic activities that are too difficult, too easy, or simply don't seem relevant and should signal the need to make instructional changes. The "Goldilocks rule" is a guideline for determining the appropriate instructional level: Instruction needs to be delivered at the "just right" level of challenge for all students in order for optimal learning to occur.

> **Matching instruction to a student's skill level is a Tier 1, or universal, intervention that leads to gains in academic skills, behavior, and student engagement.**

As mentioned in Chapter 1, post hoc research suggests that students who leave school most often cite push-out factors as reasons for dropping out (Dynarski et al., 2008). These

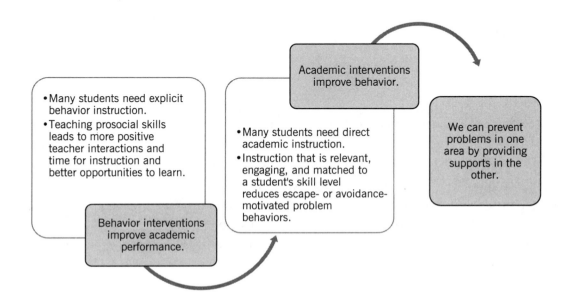

FIGURE 3.4. The academic–behavior link.

variables, such as course content and activities, or school discipline practices, which can leave students feeling unmotivated or isolated, are within the school's realm of influence. Expanding the MTSS model to include integral components of student engagement, family and parental involvement, and community supports provides an evidence-based framework that aligns with dropout prevention research and mediates the myriad of push and pull effects in the early stages of a problem to support school success for all students.

SUMMARY

This chapter highlights research evidence that consistently points to a link between academic achievement and social behavior. This body of research highlights the importance of explicitly teaching prosocial behavior skills, as well as academic skills, as part of our national efforts to improve school success and high school completion for all students. Poor literacy achievement as early as kindergarten can predict the subsequent development of disruptive behavior problems, and reading achievement by third grade correlates with high school completion. The reciprocal relationship between literacy and behavior, and ultimately with on-time high school graduation, provides a compelling rationale for proactive prevention and early intervention systems change.

Current dropout prevention research supports the foundation, or infrastructure, of a multi-tiered pyramid of continuous academic and behavioral supports for all students. As MTSS evolved at the elementary school level, the need to identify effective methods for prevention and early intervention at the secondary level emerged. Simultaneously, dropout prevention research has identified key indicators and predictors of dropout risk, along with protective variables that facilitate school success. Outcomes from converging prevention, early intervention, and dropout prevention research support expanding the MTSS framework to include the essential components of student engagement and family and community partnerships.

BIG IDEAS

- Academic skills and prosocial behaviors are interrelated and equally essential for school success.
- Effective instruction targets academic *and* behavioral skills.
- Dropping out is a multifaceted process that often begins early in school experiences.
- Student engagement is a key component of successful school completion and encompasses academic, behavior, cognitive, and affective engagement.
- Early identification of academic and behavioral problems is pivotal to effective dropout prevention.

PART II

DROPOUT PREVENTION AT THE ELEMENTARY LEVEL

CHAPTER 4

A Process, Not an Event
Early Identification of Dropout Risk

Understanding the current dropout rates is an important initial step in gauging the magnitude of this national educational problem and in beginning to identify the risk factors and variables that contribute to a student's ultimate decision to drop out. The sobering statistic that approximately 25% of students in the United States do not graduate from high school fuels a sense of national urgency about obtaining more accurate, consistent, and sensitive data to identify both system variables and individual student variables that contribute to this critical decision. Once the risk factors are identified, effective dropout prevention strategies can be developed, implemented, and monitored. The case example in Box 4.1 illustrates how some of these early indicators of risk can be present in the elementary grades.

RISK INDICATORS

Key factors in the early grades that researchers have identified as highly predictive of a student's increased risk for dropping out of school include academic, attendance, and behavior problems, retention, and school disengagement, or a lack of connectedness to the school. These major indicators can assist educators in developing powerful early interventions and directing resources to the students most at risk of dropping out of school. We have known for some time that students show signs of disengagement long before they actually drop out.

Early detection of learning challenges; careful attention to behavioral indicators, such as low attendance and disruptive behavior; and appropriate responses and targeted supports are critical for keeping students engaged in school and on track to graduate (Allensworth & Easton, 2005; Neild & Balfanz, 2006).

Early Risk Factors
- **Student engagement**
- **School readiness**
- **Academic performance**
- **Attendance**
- **Behavior**
- **Retention**

BOX 4.1. Case Example: Justin

At the beginning of the school year, the school principal noticed that Justin, a boy in the third grade, was often accompanied by his mom from the parking lot into the school. At first, she would drop Justin off inside the doorway to continue down the hallway with his sister, but as the school year progressed, Justin's mom had to escort him directly to his third-grade classroom, with frequent episodes of tears and tantrum behaviors. The classroom teacher reported that once Justin's mother left the room, he generally settled down quickly, joining friends and easily transitioning to the morning circle time and classroom activities. Both the principal and the classroom teacher observed that, with the exception of school refusal behaviors upon arrival, Justin demonstrated positive behaviors with peers and adults after he arrived. Academically, his teacher reported that based on universal screening data and classroom assignments, Justin was demonstrating above-average reading skills with some difficulties in math. An attendance review showed an increase in late arrivals (tardies) and absences over the preceding 2 months. Further investigation showed a pattern of somatic complaints after lunch, resulting in multiple visits to the nurse with fervent requests to call his mother so she could pick him up early. A review of the daily classroom schedule showed that math was scheduled after lunch. This data review showed that Justin had missed a total of five opportunities for math instruction and practice over the last 3 weeks. Following a particularly difficult dropoff in the morning, the principal approached Justin's mother to express encouragement for her efforts to consistently bring Justin to school on time and to offer assistance and support at school to ease his transition and improve attendance. In consultation with the school psychologist, a number of strategies were implemented to improve Justin's transition to school and consistent attendance for the entire day. The morning schedule was adjusted so that Justin's on-time arrival would be reinforced by access to educational games on the computer; a preference assessment revealed that this was highly motivating. The opportunity to engage in this activity with a peer had the added benefit of fostering positive social interactions and friendships. Justin also met with the school psychologist for a therapeutic intervention with Coping Cat, a cognitive-behavioral approach for teaching coping skills. Finally, additional math support helped boost Justin's skills and confidence.

Practical Application to Dropout Prevention

Even as early as elementary school, we can identify behavioral indicators of risk for future school problems and dropout, and attendance is one of the most powerful predictors. Justin demonstrated avoidant and noncompliant behavior, such as somatic complaints and refusal to enter the classroom, which not only affected his learning opportunities but also suggested the presence of other problems that, if left unresolved, might intensify throughout the years. By acting early and collaboratively, the principal, parent, and school psychologist had the best opportunity to provide Justin with needed supports.

School Engagement

Students at risk for dropping out show signs of disengagement and resistance to attending school long before they actually leave. The causes of disengagement are multifaceted, and include negative interactions with adults and peers, combined with a lack of active participation, attention, and interest in classroom learning activities. Over time, these difficulties increase the severity of current academic problems or the likelihood of developing academic problems due to a lack of opportunity to learn and practice new skills. As a result, disengaged students are more likely to experience negative interactions, receive low grades, engage in passive escape and avoidance behaviors, and display disruptive behaviors. This dual pathway for academic and behavioral problems perpetuates a downward spiral of disengagement. Eventually, these students often experience conflicts with adults, peer rejection, and pessimistic attitudes toward school. They often perceive their potential for school and future success as limited and believe that their teachers and peers share these views. An awareness of this negative cycle can help educators identify the early signs of disengagement and put needed supports in place (see Box 4.2).

School Readiness

Conceivably, one of the biggest hurdles for our educational system is school readiness, or the lack of school readiness for a significant number of children attending schools in the United States. National data estimate that nearly 50% of students from low-income communities are not ready for school by age 5. According to findings reported by the Brookings Institution, by the time children from low-income families enter kindergarten, they are typically 12–14 months below national norms in language and prereading skills (Isaacs, 2012). However, when children receive quality preschool educational opportunities, they are more likely to achieve academic success, graduate from high school, and go on to college or to seek career training. School readiness has effects beyond the first few months of kindergarten; children with higher levels of school readiness at age 5 are generally more successful in grade school, are less likely to drop out of high school, and likely to earn more as adults, even after adjusting for differences in family background (Duncan et al., 2007, Duncan, Ziol-Guest, & Kalil, 2010). With the gap between prosperity and poverty widening, these statistics present real challenges for our nation and early education needs.

Why Preschool Matters

Positive relationships with caregivers and teachers, modeling and direct instruction of social skills, and positive reinforcement for desirable behaviors represent important prevention methods in early childhood. The preschool years provide an influential opportunity to

---

BOX 4.2. Research to Practice: Teachers Matter

As educators and practitioners continue to seek effective interventions to prevent dropout, they must focus on identifying, monitoring, and addressing those risk factors that can be influenced by teachers (e.g., academic performance, peer and adult interactions, attendance, and behavior). As a result, teachers' roles in dropout prevention are critical. Teachers have the opportunity to intervene naturally and frequently within their classrooms each day. Teachers can provide support and opportunities for students that buffer "push effects" that lead to dropout (e.g., academic failure, feelings of alienation and isolation, negative attitudes toward school, poor relationships with teachers and peers, and antisocial behavior).

assist children in the development of prosocial skills and social competencies, and relationships and interpersonal experiences in these years affect future relationships with adults and peers. Findings from prevention and behavior intervention research underscore that unresolved problem behaviors and social–emotional difficulties in young children are likely to continue in elementary school. When challenging behaviors persist and/or escalate, the likelihood of atypical social–emotional development, school failure, and social maladjustment increases (Lane, Barton-Arwood, Nelson, & Wehby, 2008; Lewis, Hudson, Richter & Johnson, 2004; Sutherland, 2000).

Continued advances in behavioral research validate that a multi-tiered framework with a continuum of prevention and intervention methods—such as PBIS, which includes explicit social skills instruction and practice across settings and early identification of problematic behaviors before they escalate—offers promising outcomes for young children. Additionally, improvements in academic outcomes in the early years are often associated with improvements in prosocial behavior. Providing behavioral supports when preschoolers transition to kindergarten and public school expectations enhances a child's opportunity to experience social–emotional health, continuous engagement in school activities, and positive interactions with peers and adults, which are shown to foster long-term school success (Campbell, 1995; Fox, Dunlap, Hemmeter, Joseph, & Strain, 2003; Huffman, Mehlinger, & Kerivan, 2000; Walker, Kavanagh, et al., 1998).

Academic Performance

Reading

According to Cooney and Bottoms (2002), more than 15 million students have graduated from high school reading below the basic level over the past 15 years. The correlation between graduation rates, juvenile delinquency and incarceration, and literacy rates is alarming. The National Assessment of Adult Literacy reports that 19% of students who drop out are able to perform only at basic or below-basic levels when presented with prose literacy tasks such as reading editorials, news stories, and instructional materials (Kaestle, Campbell, Finn, Johnson, & Mikulecky, 2001).

With the implementation of RTI and universal screening to detect risk in the early stages of a problem and the evolution of brief and sensitive curriculum-based screening measures, educators are beginning to recognize and identify large numbers of students as early as prekindergarten who have not developed fluency or automaticity of basic early literacy skills needed for independent reading. Research shows a strong correlation between the lack of mastery of these essential reading skills and poor academic performance, course failures, disengagement, and behavior problems. Ultimately, this combination often results in decreased motivation and lower feelings of self-efficacy.

Torgesen (1998) showed that children who are poor readers at the end of elementary school probably failed to develop early literacy skills during preschool and kindergarten. Extensive research evidence shows that delays in early literacy skills at the beginning of kindergarten that are not resolved early on tend to grow during elementary school, creating an ever-widening gap that becomes more and more difficult to remediate. Because reading skills and vocabulary development progress with reading practice and proficiency, this gap between struggling readers and typical readers, known as the Matthew effect, becomes a chasm for struggling readers by middle school (Foorman, Francis, Fletcher, Schatschneider, & Mehta, 1998; Gettinger & Stoiber, 2007; Juel, 1988; Snow, Burns, & Griffin, 1998; Neuman & Dickinson, 2011; Stanovich, 1986; Reschly, 2010; Whitehurst & Lonigan, 1998, 2001). The emphasis on scientifically based reading instruction from prekindergarten through third grade is based on overwhelming evidence that a child who cannot read at the end of second grade has only a 25% chance of reading at grade level by the end of elementary school without significant intervention (Snow et al., 1998). For more information on early reading instruction, see Box 4.3 and Chapter 6 in this volume.

Another compelling reason to focus on reading at the elementary level is that the older the student, the more difficult remediation becomes (Vaughn et al., 2010; Vaughn & Fletcher, 2012). Although progress can happen, it typically requires more intensive intervention methods, and progress rates are invariably slower. The majority of students with reading delays that persist in fourth grade continue to have reading problems through high school; this increases the probability that they will experience course failures, which in turn increases their risk for dropping out of school (Scarborough, 2001). Resolving the dropout crisis will require improvement in literacy instruction and achievement in the early grades as a vital prerequisite to foster a child's future academic success.

Mathematics

In an increasingly technological global economy, math skills are no longer optional. Once considered a cultural elective, math skills are now essential for school and life success. Just as in reading, low achievement in mathematics can be identified early in elementary school, and persistent low achievement in mathematics has been found to be a significant predictor

---

BOX 4.3. Research to Practice: Direct Instruction and Early Intervention Work

A body of research shows that literacy skill development as early as preschool is highly predictive of continuing development of literacy skills and reading achievement. Decades of research reviewed by the National Reading Panel has identified the essential components of evidence-based reading instruction for all ages, as well as important emergent literacy skills that develop progressively during the preschool years. Achieving proficiency in these skills in preschool is highly predictive of future reading ability (Burns, Griffin, & Snow, 1999; Casey & Howe, 2002; Foorman et al., 1998; Gettinger & Stoiber, 2007; Neuman & Dickinson, 2001; Whitehurst & Lonigan, 1998, 2001). When children begin school without these essential early literacy skills, they encounter significant learning challenges. As a result of a growing body of compelling research, including findings that children as young as 3 years old benefited from early literacy instruction, NCLB (2002) included a subsection that focused on the importance of scientifically based early literacy instruction (Gettinger & Stoiber; 2007; Snow et al., 1998).

of future dropout. Math calculation fluency, which is taught in the elementary grades with expected proficiency by later elementary and middle school, is highly correlated with future math achievement and successful completion of algebra, a high school graduation course requirement.

Effective math instruction is just as important as effective reading instruction for all students, and particularly for students at risk for dropping out of school. Students who are successful in acquiring proficient mathematics skills in elementary school are more likely to continue making expected gains in mathematics achievement. Conversely, students who experience persistent skill deficits in math are more likely to wind up in an adverse cycle involving escape and avoidance behaviors, missed opportunities for instruction, and even wider skill gaps.

A history of low math achievement outcomes has fueled national interest in improving math instruction, instigating a growing body of research to guide effective teaching practices, measurement tools, and future curricular development (National Mathematics Advisory Panel, 2008). When these methods (described in more detail in Chapters 6 and 9) are implemented, struggling students often make measurable gains that set them back on track in math and on course for on-time high school completion and postsecondary options.

Attendance

Attendance has been identified as a key indicator to predict school success (Balfanz & Herzog, 2005), and one of the most important factors in preventing dropout is increasing student attendance. Regular school attendance is a necessary component of student achievement beginning in elementary school. If students are not in school, then they are missing multiple opportunities to actively participate, respond, and gain proficiency in important academic and social skills. Elementary school years provide the foundation for higher level thinking and reasoning skills, and without these basic skills, students fall behind academically as they progress through their educational careers. Peek (2009) found that kindergarten students who were identified with chronic absenteeism, which means missing at least 10% of the school year, exhibited the lowest general knowledge in mathematics and reading on entering first grade. A study completed by Loeber and Farrington (2000) revealed that elementary school students with poor attendance are more likely to exhibit serous delinquent behavior by age 12 and are at higher risk for dropping out of high school. The authors advocated for early identification of chronic truancy and for schools to put forth interventions, including parent involvement, in an attempt to get students to school.

High rates of absenteeism and tardies signal an early process of disengagement highly correlated with future school failure and dropout. From the time school begins, frequent review of attendance data is a critical element of early intervention for absenteeism, as well as early detection of potential separation anxiety, school refusal, social anxiety, depression, or academic problems that may be contributing to a child's emerging attendance problems. Parents, teachers, office personnel, and nurses are often the first to become aware of students' attendance problems, patterns of late arrival or early dismissal, and somatic complaints. Parents and caregivers are important informants about the reasons their children are missing school; however, initial reported absentee information is often incomplete and simply identified as a stomachache or headache or classified as a common sick day. In the early years it is often difficult to distinguish between anxiety-related and depression-related symptoms, noncompliant behaviors, and true illness. Direct and sensitive contact with parents and caregivers in the beginning stages of an attendance problem can help school personnel determine whether the absences involve more than physical illness. Home–school collaboration and problem solving may be required to better understand the function or basis of these behaviors and to design interventions for increasing attendance and student engagement. Consistent school attendance has been identified as a protective factor; thus developing healthy school attendance patterns in early childhood is an important prevention method (Christenson & Thurlow, 2004; Balfanz & Herzog, 2005; Balfanz et al., 2007).

Behavior

As stated earlier, as early as preschool, students who demonstrate behavior problems that persist or escalate in elementary school are at significant risk for disengagement, school failure, and social maladjustment (Lane, 2004; Lewis, Hudson, Richter, & Johnson, 2004; Sutherland, 2000). Because academic difficulties may be contributing to behavior problems, it is important to determine the function of the behavior and to intervene as early as possible to resolve both behavioral and academic concerns simultaneously, before they spiral into more complex and intervention-resistant problems. Also, because behavior problems often result in missed instruction, students without previous academic difficulties are at heightened risk to develop gaps in academic skill development; thus their academic performance should be monitored closely to prevent delays.

Retention

Retention is not an intervention, but it is one of the most powerful predictors that a student will drop out of high school. In fact, the decision to retain a student places that student at greater risk for school failure and dropout. For students who are retained multiple times, the probability that they will drop out of school is even higher (Jimerson, Woehr, & Kaufman, 2007; Jimerson, 2001; Jimerson, Anderson, & Whipple, 2002). A confusing confound of retention in elementary school is that initially academic improvements may occur during the year the student is retained. However, it is important to understand that a retained student is now being compared with younger academic and behavioral expectations. A body of research shows that these initial achievement gains decline within 2–3 years of retention. The end result is that as the children progress through elementary school, they often do not show higher achievement and may show lower achievement than similar groups of children who were not retained. Most important, research has been unable to identify specific

- **Students who were retained are five to nine times more likely to drop out of school.**
- **For most students, grade retention adversely affects academic achievement and social–emotional adjustment.**

indicators that accurately predict when children might benefit from retention; thus it remains a very-high-risk decision that students have identified as one of the most stressful events they experienced (Jimerson et al., 2007).

EARLY IDENTIFICATION

Although the dropout challenge is not new, utilizing data and technology to keep students on track for graduation is a relatively new phenomenon in most school systems. Following a review of available research, the Institute of Education Sciences' dropout prevention guide (Dynarski et al., 2008) clearly identifies the need to develop and implement data systems that accurately identify the number of students who drop out to inform system intervention needs, as well as diagnostic data to determine individual students at high risk of dropping out in the early stages when intervention is likely to be most effective.

Given the predictive function of reading and math data in determining risk for school problems and dropout, academic assessments are important tools for early identification and problem solving. Still, academic achievement tests are a source of much controversy and confusion in current educational reform. The phrase "teaching to the test" is frequently expressed and debated among educators, the public, and public officials. Because the role of assessment is essential in determining individual, local, and national educational progress and outcomes, a thoughtful reexamination of the sentiment "teach to the test" to improve the purpose, reliability, and validity of educational assessments may prove to be a better allocation of expertise and resources. For example, further analysis of this phrase raises the question, Shouldn't we be designing tests that measure what we consider the priority skills and content our students are expected to learn? And, if so, shouldn't we be teaching these skills and content and measuring the extent to which these high-priority skills and content are learned? When assessment and teaching are reciprocal and closely intertwined, the results can provide educators, parents, and students with accurate data to determine the status of current skills, future learning needs, and the efficacy of the instructional methods utilized.

A defensible argument in this debate is that in our national efforts to increase educational accountability, schools may be engaged in administering more assessments than necessary or utilizing assessments that do not accurately answer these questions. With this premise in mind, an area of common ground is the need to know a student's current skill level in order to design effective instruction. This requires assessments that accurately measure what we have identified as priority educational skills and content.

As previously stated, research has shown that student learning is optimized when instruction is targeted at students' current skill levels, maximizing their opportunities to respond and receive immediate feedback (Brown-Chidsey & Steege, 2010; Coyne, Carnine, & Kame'enui, 2010). When instruction is delivered above a student's current skill level, it is too hard, impeding the ability to benefit from the instructional opportunity. Ongoing instruction that is too hard results in ever-widening skill gaps, inevitably resulting in increased frustration and decreased student engagement. A collection of these experiences is likely to increase a student's risk for developing social, emotional, and/or behavior problems that contribute to disengagement. Likewise, when instruction is too easy, a student is often not engaged in instruction, resulting in a loss of critical learning time. Lack of student engagement due to boredom or frustration can increase a student's risk for attention, behavior, and attendance problems. "Student engagement across the school years depends on the degree to which there is a match between the student's characteristics and the school environment so that the student is able to handle the academic and behavioral demands of school" (Christenson & Thurlow, 2004, p. 38).

> **Student engagement and learning are optimized when instruction is targeted at a student's current skill level, maximizing opportunities to respond and receive feedback.**

Summative and Formative Assessment

To determine a student's current instructional level and needs, it is important to understand the difference between summative assessments and formative assessment measures. Generally, summative assessment is characterized as assessment *of* learning, and formative assessment is characterized as assessment *for* learning. As identified in the RTI literature, summative and formative assessments are essential components of multi-tiered systems for effective dropout prevention. The data gleaned from both assessment methods must be analyzed frequently to inform both system-level and instructional needs. The characteristics and benefits of each type of assessment are provided in Table 4.1.

TABLE 4.1. Summative and Formative Assessment

Summative Assessment	Formative Assessment
	Purpose
• Evaluate the effectiveness of instruction. • Evaluate student learning at the end of an instructional unit by comparing it against a standard or benchmark.	• Quickly identify student's current instructional level. • Monitor student learning. • Provide ongoing feedback that can be used to improve student learning.
	Characteristics
• Measure of content mastery. • Formal measure. • Measures student learning. • Minimal effects on student learning.	• Student involvement is encouraged. • Measure of skill performance across time. • Brief and standardized, with multiple measures. • Drives instruction and intervention.
	Benefits
• Determine adequate yearly progress. • Determine the effectiveness of the curriculum and instruction.	• Allows teachers to adjust instruction quickly, while learning is in progress. • Provides immediate feedback to students so they can adjust their focus and improve learning. • Identifies students in the at-risk to above-average range. • Strong and sustained effects on learning.

By definition, summative measures are one-time assessments administered at a designated point in time, such as the end of the school year or a specific grade level, that are designed to monitor global educational outcomes. Summative measures assess content knowledge, or a student's mastery of previous learning, and answer the question, What did the student learn and retain for later retrieval and application? Examples of summative assessments are end-of-year statewide tests, final exams, and entrance exams (e.g., SATs). These assessments are generally administered to evaluate a student's acquisition, or competency with material at a specific point in time. The results are often used to evaluate the effectiveness of curricula and services at the end of the instruction period. Did the students benefit from the current curriculum? Were there any identified instructional gaps? Does the curriculum meet the needs of most of the students?

Formative assessments are brief measures designed to provide immediate feedback about student skill or content acquisition during the instruction and learning process and are considered one of the most powerful methods for improving outcomes (Shinn, 2012). A distinguishing feature of formative assessment is *how* it is utilized to enhance instruction. Formative measures are administered in real time to determine a student's response to the instruction. The student's response serves as immediate feedback to the teacher and

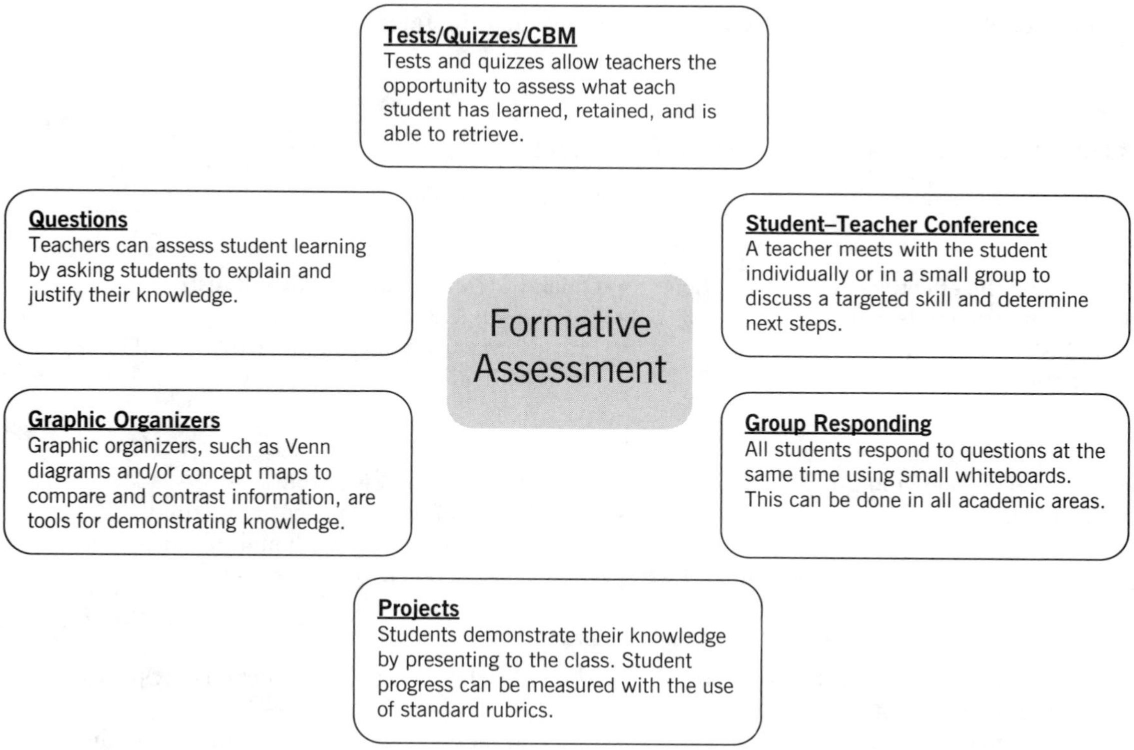

Tests/Quizzes/CBM
Tests and quizzes allow teachers the opportunity to assess what each student has learned, retained, and is able to retrieve.

Questions
Teachers can assess student learning by asking students to explain and justify their knowledge.

Student–Teacher Conference
A teacher meets with the student individually or in a small group to discuss a targeted skill and determine next steps.

Formative Assessment

Graphic Organizers
Graphic organizers, such as Venn diagrams and/or concept maps to compare and contrast information, are tools for demonstrating knowledge.

Group Responding
All students respond to questions at the same time using small whiteboards. This can be done in all academic areas.

Projects
Students demonstrate their knowledge by presenting to the class. Student progress can be measured with the use of standard rubrics.

FIGURE 4.1. Examples of formative assessment.

facilitates a process of fine-tuning the instruction to enhance learning. It is this symbiotic relationship that helps establish effective teaching practices and priorities.

Examples of formative assessments, as shown in Figure 4.1, include curriculum-based measures, quizzes, and diagnostic tests. The immediate feedback derived from formative assessments answers the important questions: Is the current instruction working? Is the student mastering the content and needed skills? If the formative assessment results show that the student is making expected progress, then the current instruction methods can be considered effective and should be maintained. If the data show that the student is not making expected gains, a change is needed. Involving students in the review of formative assessment data, combined with evidence of progress (or not), provides the behavioral momentum to continue the intervention with confidence or to implement the changes needed to boost student progress and, ultimately, school success.

UNIVERSAL SCREENING RECOMMENDATIONS

The next important question for schools engaged in assessment planning is *when* to use *what*. Additionally, this requires evaluation of *how often* assessments should be administered throughout a student's educational career, as the individual student's needs and educational expectations change across the school years. Current research (Glover & Vaughn, 2010) indicates that when meaningful assessment data are gathered on the "big three" shown to be highly predictive of school success—academics (literacy and math), behavior, and attendance—at the early stages of skill acquisition in the elementary grades, fewer assessments are needed at the secondary levels. Vaughn and Fletcher (2012) highlight that careful and frequent review of these assessment data to inform instruction as a student progresses through elementary school provides a wealth of information about instructional needs at the middle school and high school levels. Thus duplication of assessment can be avoided at the secondary levels to more effectively invest in resource allocation of needed instructional supports when MTSS methods are simultaneously more critical and difficult to achieve for effective dropout prevention. Research continues to support the idea that middle school and high school transition years are critical periods during which to review prior assessment data to inform instructional needs, a topic further explored in Chapter 7 (Dynarski et al., 2008).

The National Center for Response to Intervention (NCRTI) and the National Center on Intensive Intervention (NCII) evaluate assessment measures and publish their findings. Ratings and reports of various universal screening and progress monitoring assessments can be located by curriculum and grade level. The reports provide information on the publisher, assessment products, purpose, and cost of each universal screening and progress monitoring tool. Most important for the consumer, products reviewed on the NCRTI and NCII websites must meet specific research-based criteria to be reviewed. More detail on the following assessment measures can be found at *www.rti4success.org* and *www.intensiveintervention.org*.

Academic Screeners

Curriculum-Based Measurement

Curriculum-based measurement (CBM) is a type of formative assessment developed over 30 years ago to meet the need for brief, valid, standardized, cost-effective measures that are sensitive to very small increments of progress (Deno, 1985, 1986). Because CBM has multiple forms, it can be utilized for multiple functions. CBM can be used to screen, assess, and monitor a student's current fluency, or automaticity in basic academic skills shown to be highly predictive of future academic achievement. Extensive research has confirmed the utility of these measures to quickly identify a student's current academic skill level, which reveals his or her instructional needs. Alternate forms allow educators to administer CBM probes as frequently as needed (daily to monthly), providing discrete skill data in minutes that can be easily graphed to monitor a student's rate of progress toward grade-level benchmark goals. Because CBM is curriculum-independent, measuring skills that all students should master regardless of what curricula are used, it provides an excellent research-based method to determine whether students are achieving automaticity and generalization of academic skills.

When CBM is administered as recommended at the elementary levels for universal screening (three times per year, in the fall, winter, and spring), schools can promptly determine whether students are responding to the core instruction. The data can be analyzed to indicate schoolwide, grade-level, class-level, and individual-student response. In this way CBM results inform curricula effectiveness and Tier 1 differentiated instruction needs. Another important feature of CBM is the identification of students above grade level, who are in need of alternative instructional methods and enrichment, and those students below grade level, who, without additional instruction and practice opportunities (Tier 1 + Tier 2), are at risk for ongoing academic difficulties.

Curriculum-based measures have been developed in early literacy, reading, early numeracy, mathematics, spelling, and written expression. A number of different CBM products are available for free download or purchase, including:

- AIMSweb (*aimsweb.com*).
- Dynamic Indicators of Basic Early Literacy Skills (DIBELS; *dibels.uoregon.edu*).
- EasyCBM (*easycbm.com*).
- EdCheckup (*www.edcheckup.com*).
- Get It! Got It! Go! (*ggg.umn.edu*).
- Helping Early Literacy with Practice Strategies (HELPS; *www.helpsprogram.org*).
- Monitoring Basic Skills Progress (*www.proedinc.com*).
- Yearly Progress Pro (*www.ctb.com/Yearly/ ProgressPro*).

For an extensive review of valid and reliable universal screening and progress monitoring assessments identified by grade level and content area, see the NCRTI website (*www.rti4success.org*).

Academic Achievement Tests

Standards-based achievement tests are given to students nationwide to assess individual performance and collect districtwide and state data. Importantly, few of these state assessments are given every year or in the early grades, and this fact limits their use as universal screening measures. Increasingly, schools are turning to other group-administered academic assessments, which can be given annually or three times per year, as screening tools. For example, the Discovery Education Predictive Assessment and the Group Assessment and Diagnostic Evaluation are standards-based assessments that predict performance on high-stakes tests, identify students at risk, and determine skill gaps and instructional needs. Computer-based assessments can also be administered to groups of students to gather individual and schoolwide academic achievement data, identify academic skills, and develop targeted instruction for individuals and groups. The Measures of Academic Progress (MAP) and STAR are examples of computerized adaptive tests, meaning that the difficulty of each item is adjusted to the individual student.

Behavioral Screeners

Collecting attendance and office discipline referral (ODR) data is an effective method for universal screening of behavior at the elementary school level. With data management systems such as the School-Wide Information System (SWIS), schools collect schoolwide data to assess their Tier 1 behavior instruction and practices and to monitor progress toward desired schoolwide behavior outcomes. Objective ODR data are collected and frequently analyzed to monitor the type, location, date, time, frequency, and interpersonal variables of problem behavior that occurs at school. Analysis of these data, particularly when academic performance is also incorporated in the review, often illuminates previously unrecognized triggers for problem behaviors to inform schoolwide, grade-level, class-level, and individual-student interventions. ODRs are often associated with disruptive or inappropriate physical or verbal behaviors. Many behavior problems that merit an ODR at the elementary level occur in unstructured and/or less supervised settings, such as the bus, playground, cafeteria, and hallways. Understanding the setting events helps schools design appropriate schoolwide and/or individual interventions. The main objective of behavior screening is to identify problems early and prevent them from developing into more entrenched and interfering behavior patterns.

A TEAM APPROACH

MTSS and dropout prevention efforts are best achieved with a team approach. To foster collaborative problem solving and shared responsibility, schools have developed many types of school teams that vary in purpose, membership, and member roles. Although the organization of teams will vary according to the size and structure of the school, clarity about the types of teams in the school and the school district is often needed. Examples of school teams include student assistance teams (SATs), professional learning communities (PLCs), grade-level teams (GLTs), problem-solving teams (PSTs), and crisis teams.

GLTs are the backbone of MTSS decision-making and prevention efforts. GLTs typically meet on a weekly basis to review universal screening and/or progress monitoring data and collaborate on providing differentiated instruction at the classroom and grade levels. At Tier 2, PSTs provide support to teachers and develop strategies for students who are struggling at school. The aim is to help teachers integrate the core elements of MTSS—assessment, intervention, and monitoring—into their practices. Initially, PSTs often represented academic (RTI) or behavioral (PBIS) goals but, although they shared a common mission, they rarely had the opportunity to communicate and truly collaborate with one another. Given the links between academics and behavior (see Chapter 3), a highly recommended format is for schools to form one integrated problem-solving team that serves school- and district-identified priorities for ongoing MTSS methods, with active participation from school leaders.

SUMMARY

Compelling evidence from MTSS and dropout prevention research shows that a student's decision to drop out of school typically follows a long process of disengagement. Left undetected, problems with school engagement, attendance, academics, and/or behavior tend to evolve over time, culminating in critical dropout risk factors by middle school and high school. Research conclusively shows that data about the big three—academics, behavior, and attendance—are all readily accessible in schools, provide educators the best prevention and intervention data available to intervene effectively at the elementary levels, and scaffold a successful school experience for all students.

BIG IDEAS

- Dropout prevention begins early—as early as prekindergarten.
- Consistent attendance, fluent academic skills, and prosocial behaviors are key protective factors for all students.
- The purpose of early risk identification is to resolve academic and behavior problems at a young age when intervention is most effective.
- Both summative assessment and formative assessment provide important data to identify academic risk and inform effective intervention.
- Attendance and behavior data are important for recognizing emerging internalizing and externalizing behavior problems.
- District and school leadership in an integrated team-based approach is essential to analyzing schoolwide data and allocating resources effectively.

CHAPTER 5

Tier 2 and Tier 3 Problem Solving at the Elementary Level

Are We Closing the Gap?

As early as elementary school, problem-solving methods within a framework of MTSS provide an effective approach to identifying and addressing the needs of all students, including those at risk for dropping out of school. The problem-solving model has both research and legal support and is still gaining a foothold in U.S. schools. In order to make informed decisions to help support students at risk for dropping out, we need valid and reliable methods for collecting data and a system in place for interpreting and responding to those data. Chapter 4 provided information and resources about early identification of students at risk; this chapter builds on those methods in describing the ways that we respond to and monitor students in need of Tier 2 or Tier 3 supports.

Tier 2 interventions and supports are supplemental to the core instructional practices of Tier 1. Tier 3 is more intensive than Tier 2, meaning that it may involve more time or more targeted or individual instruction. Importantly, decisions about when to intervene at Tier 2 or 3 are made on the basis of student data. This process is illustrated in the case example in Box 5.1.

THE PROBLEM-SOLVING MODEL

Since Stanley Deno's (1985, 1986) early application of the problem-solving model and standardized progress monitoring methods to school-based assessment and intervention, it has become widely known as a best practice for improving instruction and service delivery for students (Brown-Chidsey & Andren, 2012). Deno (2012) described a problem as a discrepancy between a student's perceived behavior or skill level and that which is expected. Problem solving occurs when efforts are made to reduce those discrepancies. Thus we are

BOX 5.1. Case Example: Diego

A review of first-grade benchmark screening data showed that Diego was at risk in his development of early literacy skills. The grade-level team confirmed these findings with his teacher and learned that Diego also displayed a high level of physical activity, impulsive behavior, and inattention in the classroom. He was referred to the problem-solving team, which determined that Diego would benefit from additional evidence-based reading instruction. Diego was placed in a Tier 2 supplemental reading intervention group with five other children who were at the same literacy skill level. A review of weekly progress data indicated that he was responding to the intervention with small gains, but his performance remained below the weekly goals and expected rate of improvement. Concerns remained about Diego's high level of activity during classroom instruction and intervention time. He often appeared off-task and easily distracted by the lesson materials, suggesting that he was often not attending to instruction. The problem-solving team determined that although other students were making adequate progress, Diego did not appear to be benefiting from this particular reading intervention. As a result, a change in intervention was made. This time, Diego participated in a reading intervention group that used Reading Mastery, an evidence-based curriculum that focuses on sequential, systematic, and explicit instruction. After 4 weeks of supplemental Tier 2 instruction with Reading Mastery, progress monitoring data showed that Diego had made significant improvement, achieving above expected gains. At the next monthly problem-solving team meeting, Diego's progress data showed that he had demonstrated proficiency on the first-grade literacy measures. The school psychologist continued monitoring his weekly progress, and within 2 months, Diego demonstrated above-average first-grade reading skills. The problem-solving team agreed that Diego had demonstrated sufficient progress to begin phasing out the Tier 2 intervention but would continue with regular progress monitoring. When the school psychologist asked Diego whether he had noticed his improvement in reading, he stated enthusiastically, "Everybody's noticed!"

Practical Application to Dropout Prevention

This example illustrates the problem-solving process, which often continues in a circular fashion. In this case, when the problem-solving team reviewed progress monitoring data, they determined that the current intervention was not leading to expected gains and therefore that a change was needed. By responding promptly and selecting a reading curriculum that better fit Diego's instructional needs and captured his attention, significant gains in reading skill were achieved.

engaged in problem solving when we take systematic action to assess a student's risk of dropping out and implement interventions to enhance protective factors and reduce the risk of dropping out of school.

Collecting data on students at risk is not new. Providing targeted interventions to students in need is not new. The key to doing this successfully and reducing the number of students who drop out of school is in understanding the early signs of risk and responding at the primary level (e.g., at the first signs of a literacy problem) rather than at the critical care level (e.g., when a middle school student has missed more than 20 days of school or received multiple detentions). Because rapid response is a critical component of MTSS and effective intervention, we must have efficient

> **The key to successful dropout prevention efforts is understanding the early signs of risk and responding at the earliest opportunity.**

progress monitoring tools, methods for collecting, displaying, and interpreting data, and procedures in place for making timely and data-based decisions. The following sections describe how these practices fit into the five stages of the problem-solving model, displayed as an ongoing process in Figure 5.1.

Identify and Define the Problem

The first stage of the problem-solving process is problem identification. Identifying the problem involves determining the student's present level of performance, as well as current expectations—for example, by examining the match between a student's skill level and classroom instruction. The second stage, defining the problem, will lead to a more detailed description of behavior in observable, measurable terms. This may involve collecting data on the student's academic skills, attendance, and discipline referrals. As in the case example of Diego (Box 5.1), information gathered at these stages will help inform decisions about whether to intervene at Tier 2.

The team can also analyze these data to determine whether a problem exists at the school, the classroom, or the Tier 2 level. Using the MTSS model as a guide (see Chapter 3, Figure 3.3), the percentage of students receiving supports and services at each tier should approximate 80% at Tier 1, 15% at Tier 2, and 5% at Tier 3. In a school with high-quality core academic instruction and behavioral supports, 80% of its students will make adequate progress within Tier 1; 15% of students are likely to need additional Tier 2 supports; and if Tier 2 is made up of effective programs, only 5% of students would require the intensive interventions characteristic of Tier 3. If the problem-solving team analyzes schoolwide data and finds that these indicators of school health are not present, problem solving may need to continue at the school level by examining the core curriculum and Tier 2 practices.

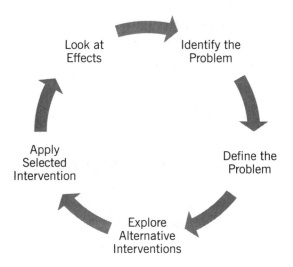

FIGURE 5.1. The problem-solving model. Based on Deno (2012).

Explore Alternative Interventions

Once a student has been identified as being at risk for disengagement and future school problems, the next stage of the problem-solving model is aimed at exploring individual, school, and home variables in order to identify both protective and risk factors and how these help inform possible solutions. This is an essential component of problem solving and forms the link between assessment and intervention. For example, in the case study presented earlier in this chapter (see Box 5.1), the grade-level problem-solving team considered individual variables, such as Diego's reading skills and inattentive behavior, as well as environmental variables, such as the classroom setting and type of reading instruction, when designing an intervention. As outlined in Table 5.1, teams must consider a number of intervention variables to maximize fit and effectiveness.

Apply Selected Intervention

With growing research in the area of dropout prevention, educators have more and more information on what works. Importantly, there are numerous interventions with an evidence base indicating that they are effective for keeping students in school and increasing high school completion rates. These are presented in more detail in the next chapter.

Look at Effects

An important component of dropout prevention methods within a problem-solving model is formative assessment. In contrast to summative assessment, which measures the extent to which an outcome has been attained (e.g., a final exam or high-stakes standardized test), formative assessment procedures measure progress at regular intervals along the way and assess the effectiveness of an intervention. Progress monitoring within MTSS is analogous to practices within the medical model. Children make regular visits to a pediatrician to monitor health and development. Physicians routinely check patients' blood pressure because it is an indicator of overall health or risk for health problems. Blood pressure can also be used to gauge improvement. For example, a patient who has begun a diet and exercise regimen to reduce the risk for heart disease may routinely need to monitor his or her blood pressure to ensure that the diet and exercise changes are having a positive effect. In educational terms, this is a general outcome measure because it predicts more general performance. For

---

TABLE 5.1. Questions to Ask in the Exploring Solutions Stage

- Is the selected intervention evidence-based?
- Does the intervention target the identified area of need?
- Do we have trained personnel available to implement the intervention?
- How will we maximize and monitor attendance, student engagement, and treatment fidelity?
- How will we notify, involve, and support parents?

---

example, oral reading fluency is a general outcome measure because it is a strong predictor of overall reading achievement; it can be used to measure progress toward reading goals and, in turn, to assess the extent to which an intervention is working. We should pay attention to reading performance and attendance rates, because they not only identify students at risk for dropping out but also let us know whether we are closing the gap with the chosen intervention(s).

The problem-solving process does not end with the fifth stage. As shown in Figure 5.1, the process continues in a circular fashion. When looking at the effects of an intervention, the team must decide whether a problem still exists. Do the current data still indicate a discrepancy between what is perceived and what is expected? If so, those data are used to redefine the problem and explore alternative solutions. If the data suggest that the student closed the achievement gap and a problem no longer exists, the team may wish to continue monitoring relevant data but provide core instruction within Tier 1. Table 5.2 provides recommendations for the general steps involved in collecting and using data to inform dropout prevention strategies.

> The problem-solving process continues in a circular fashion. Data gathered in the Look at Effects stage often lead the team back to the first stage.

DATA MANAGEMENT SYSTEMS

Most schools already collect and maintain student data. One more measure could easily seem like a burden. Schools are not necessarily encouraged to do more but to be wiser about what data are collected and how they are used. There are numerous methods and systems for schools to choose from. Chapter 4 described various universal screening tools appropriate for identifying students who are at risk for academic and discipline problems and ultimately for dropping out. Importantly, these screening measures are in place so that students can receive needed support. At Tiers 2 and 3, many of the same measures are used, but the purpose shifts from early identification to progress monitoring for instructional planning. It is

TABLE 5.2. Steps for Developing Dropout Prevention Strategies

1. Use longitudinal, student-level data to get an accurate read of graduation and dropout rates.
2. Use data to identify incoming students with histories of academic problems, truancy, behavioral problems, and retentions.
3. Continually monitor the academic and social performance of all students.
4. Review student-level data to identify students at risk of dropping out before key academic transitions.
5. Monitor students' sense of engagement and belonging in school.
6. Collect and document accurate information on student withdrawals.

Note. From Dynarski et al. (2008).

important that progress monitoring assessment methods are valid and reliable, efficient and cost-effective to administer, and sensitive to student growth. The NCRTI (*www.rti4success. org*) and the NCII (*www.intensiveintervention.org*) websites are helpful resources for locating universal screening and progress monitoring assessment measures that meet these standards. This chapter describes a limited number of data management systems, which focus on academic skills or student behaviors that have been identified as key indicators of risk, that meet NCRTI and NCII standards as progress monitoring measures in Tiers 2 and 3.

> **Schools don't necessarily need to collect more student data but must carefully plan which data are collected and how they are used.**

Academic Assessments: Curriculum-Based Measurement

CBM is a method of formative assessment within a problem-solving model that utilizes brief standardized tests of basic academic skills. CBM is one tool for gathering universal screening and progress monitoring data that meet requirements for validity, reliability, efficiency, and sensitivity (Deno et al., 2009; Stecker, Lembke, & Foegen, 2008). Teachers' use of CBM within a data-based decision-making model has been associated with improvements in student achievement, providing evidence for its utility in guiding instructional decisions (Deno et al., 2009; Stecker, Fuchs, & Fuchs, 2005).

As described in Chapter 4, specific CBMs differ according to grade level. For kindergarten students, CBM targets early literacy skills, such as letter identification and phonemic awareness, and early numeracy skills, such as number identification and counting. Other assessments, which can often be administered through eighth grade, include measures of oral reading fluency, silent reading comprehension, spelling, writing, and mathematics concepts and computation. For more information on CBM tools and methods, see Hosp, Hosp, Howell, and Allison (2014).

Behavioral Assessments

Like progress monitoring measures for academic skills, instruments for gathering data on student behavior should be reliable, valid, efficient, and sensitive to change. Chapter 3 identified student behaviors that are key indicators of risk for dropping out and that are evident as early as elementary school. These include disengagement, attendance problems, and behavior requiring disciplinary action. The assessment systems and procedures described here can be used to gather data on these behavioral indicators for intervention planning and monitoring purposes.

School-Wide Information System

As described in Chapter 4, SWIS is a data management system that allows schools to track and analyze individual student-level and schoolwide behavioral data. In Tiers 2 and 3, SWIS can also be used to monitor student participation and progress with interventions.

Check-In, Check-Out (CICO) is a structured behavioral intervention that connects students to a positive adult every day and emphasizes goal setting, feedback, and positive reinforcement (Crone, Hawken, & Horner, 2010). Figure 5.2 is an example of a CICO point card, used daily to keep track of goals, provide opportunities for feedback and reinforcement, and document progress toward goals. These data can be recorded in SWIS and graphed to display the total number of CICO points earned each day or the percentage of points earned in each period of the day. In the same graph, these data are viewed relative to individual student goals and changes in the intervention. The option of tracking schoolwide data allows teams to measure progress and problem-solve on a systems level (School-Wide Information System, 2012b). See Chapters 6 and 9 for more information on CICO.

Direct Behavior Ratings

A useful and customizable system for progress monitoring of student behavior is direct behavior ratings (DBRs), also known as performance-based behavior ratings (Steege & Watson, 2009) or behavior report cards. This method involves specifying a target behavior and assigning a rating system, such as a checklist or scale, to measure changes in the behavior over a period of time (Chafouleas et al., 2007). DBRs can be used to track academic or social behavior in a variety of settings and by different informants. Because there is so much flexibility in how they are created, DBRs can be used to track progress with numerous types of interventions. For example, given the importance of student engagement, an intervention aimed at increasing active participation in class could include operational definitions of the specific behaviors (e.g., raising hand, responding to questions, or initiating and completing tasks) and a checklist to record the number of times the student demonstrates the behavior

CICO Point Card

Student: _____ **Date:** _____

Check-In: _____ **Check-Out:** _____

	☐ **A** ☐ **B** Day	1	2	3	4	5	**Total**
	Teacher Initials						
Respect	Use appropriate language.	2 1 0	2 1 0	2 1 0	2 1 0	2 1 0	
	Use a calm voice.	2 1 0	2 1 0	2 1 0	2 1 0	2 1 0	
Integrity	Follow directions.	2 1 0	2 1 0	2 1 0	2 1 0	2 1 0	
	Ask for help if I need it.	2 1 0	2 1 0	2 1 0	2 1 0	2 1 0	
Perseverance	Finish my work.	2 1 0	2 1 0	2 1 0	2 1 0	2 1 0	
	Do my best.	2 1 0	2 1 0	2 1 0	2 1 0	2 1 0	
	Total						
	Accuracy Check						

FIGURE 5.2. Check-In, Check-Out Point Card. From School-Wide Information System (2012). Copyright 2012 by Rob Horner. Reprinted by permission.

per class period. These data are useful for defining the problem, tracking progress, and informing intervention needs (Chafouleas et al., 2007).

Can't Do/Won't Do

In the Explore Alternative Interventions stage (see Figure 5.1), it can be useful to determine whether academic and behavior problems are a function of skill deficits (*can't do*) or performance deficits (*won't do*) or, perhaps, a combination of both. These distinctions are not always evident, but they can be clarified with a brief assessment of the child's current skills by offering a pre-identified and highly valued reinforcer for successful completion of the task(s). If the student's performance does not change in the reinforcement condition, the problem is likely due to a skill deficit. If the student is capable of completing the task when reinforcement is offered, the team should look at environmental and behavioral factors that may be contributing to the problem. Results of this assessment provide valuable information to inform effective academic and/or behavioral interventions. When a child lacks the skills necessary to perform the task(s), explicit instruction is needed at the child's skill level to remediate gaps. When a child can exhibit the desired skills with preferred reinforcement, this suggests that other behavior is affecting the child's consistent performance of the acquired skill and that strategic behavioral interventions are indicated. It is not uncommon for a student to demonstrate a combination of both performance and skill deficits, as attention and behavior problems are often linked to difficult academic tasks (VanDerHeyden & Witt, 2008).

Single-Subject Experimental Design

Within the problem-solving model, particularly the Look at Effects stage (see Figure 5.1), single-subject experimental design is useful for evaluating individual performance and the effectiveness of an intervention by collecting and analyzing data before, during, and after the intervention. Academic or behavioral data from any of the previous assessments described in this chapter can be applied to single-subject design procedures. For example, for a student displaying disruptive behavior in the classroom, DBRs and ODRs may be monitored to evaluate the effects of a Tier 2 behavioral intervention. Essentially, the data gathered during a baseline phase are graphed and compared with the same types of data after an intervention has been implemented with treatment integrity. If the data do not reflect a change in the target behavior from baseline to intervention, the problem-solving team can return to the Explore Alternative Interventions phase and make changes to the intervention. If the student demonstrates a stable baseline and then makes progress during the intervention phase, the team could conclude, in the absence of confounding variables, that the intervention has a positive impact on the student's behavior. The data would then be analyzed in light of specific goals, the presence of other risk factors, and ongoing student needs. For more information on single-subject methods and progress monitoring graphs, the reader is referred to two other volumes in the Guilford Practical Intervention in the Schools series: *Evaluating Educational Interventions: Single-Case Design for Measuring*

Response to Intervention (Riley-Tillman & Burns, 2009) and *Response to Intervention: Principles and Strategies for Effective Practice* (2nd ed.; Brown-Chidsey & Steege, 2010).

DATA-BASED DECISION MAKING

In addition to deciding what types of data will be collected and which progress monitoring measures will be used, teams must have procedures in place for interpreting those data and making programming decisions, such as when to intensify, replace, or discontinue an intervention, accordingly. Although specific recommendations may differ according to the student and the target behavior, problem-solving teams should review data every 3–4 weeks. As a general decision-making rule, three data points are required to establish a trend. In other words, at least three CBM assessments or behavioral observations should be made before determining whether they represent a pattern of behavior. Similarly, 6–8 data points are recommended to establish consistency of skills or behavior once the student's performance reaches the benchmark level. That is, interventions and supports that promoted skill improvement should not be withdrawn until consistent performance has been maintained for six trials or intervals. At Tier 2, when there is evidence of 6–8 consistent data points at grade-level benchmark goals, the current intervention is phased out and monthly progress monitoring is continued to ensure maintenance of skills at the Tier 1 level until the team determines that Tier 1 universal screening (three times per year) is sufficient to monitor progress. Table 5.3 illustrates the problem-solving team's process of data-based decision making.

Rates of Progress

When analyzing universal screening data, teams focus on the presence of certain behavioral indicators or the level of students' academic skills to identify students at risk and to gauge the effectiveness of the core curricula. At Tiers 2 and 3, progress monitoring data are used to track these skills while focusing on the rate of progress. A student could be making improvements with a given intervention, evidenced by growth in oral reading fluency scores, for example; however, the *rate* of progress is a key indicator as to whether the student is likely to close the gap. Additionally, because rapid response is important for tailoring interventions and improving outcomes, the best instruments to measure rate of progress are sensitive to small changes in performance.

The graph in Figure 5.3 illustrates progress monitoring data for a first-grade student who is receiving Tier 2 reading instruction. Universal screening data in September indicated that her reading fluency scores were below grade-level benchmark goals. The square data point on the far right of the graph shows the spring benchmark goal, indicating the rate of progress this student would need to make in order to be reading on grade level by the spring. When a trend line is created in the graph, it becomes clear that at her current rate of progress, this student is not on track to meet spring benchmark goals. A review of these progress monitoring data informed the current problem definition and led the problem-

TABLE 5.3. Tier 2 and Tier 3 Data-Based Decision-Making Process

Review progress. Review all data used in assessing Tier 2 or Tier 3 intervention (e.g., CBM, group-administered achievement test, classroom assessments).

Evaluate effectiveness of the intervention. Determine whether the intervention was implemented with fidelity and whether gains are linked to the intervention.

Make decisions. Determine whether to continue the intervention, discontinue the intervention, or implement a Tier 3 intervention (if the student is currently at Tier 2) or whether a referral to special education is needed (if the student is currently at Tier 3).

Set measurable goals. Set an observable, measurable goal to be achieved by the next benchmark assessment.

Select the intervention. Select the intervention that best matches the student's identified area of need.

Determine and plan for the intervention. Identify the intensity and frequency of the intervention, the person who will deliver the intervention, and the space in which it will take place; and plan for monitoring treatment fidelity.

Plan for progress monitoring. Decide which skills will be measured (e.g., reading, math, social skills); determine what assessment(s) will be used to monitor progress, how often and when progress monitoring assessments will be given, and by whom.

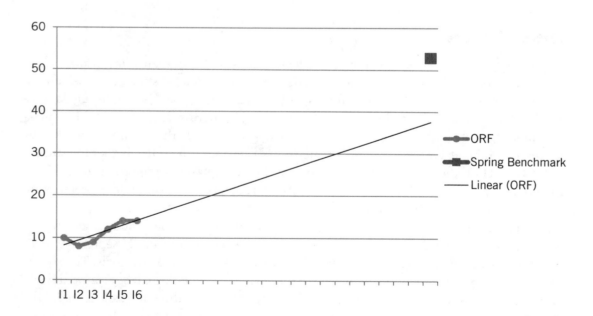

FIGURE 5.3. Progress monitoring graph for a first-grade student.

solving team back to the Explore Alternative Solutions stage. After considering criteria such as the time, frequency, and integrity of the intervention, the team determined that a more intensive reading intervention targeting reading fluency skills would be implemented.

Benchmark Scores

As in the previous example, academic skill data are often compared with national or local benchmark norms. National averages by assessment type, grade level, and time of year are provided by publishers such as AIMSweb and DIBELS. After a school or district has a history of its own screening data, it may wish to establish local norms against which to compare individual student performance; however, it is still important to keep in mind national averages and expectations. In the following scenario, Figure 5.4 represents progress monitoring data for a fifth-grade student who was struggling with grade-level mathematical computation. After a review of classroom and universal screening data, which indicated that he was scoring below local grade-level norms, he began receiving additional math instruction in the math lab at school. AIMSweb CBMs of mathematics computation (M-COMP) were administered as weekly progress monitoring probes and show that this student responded to the intervention, making significant gains in the first 3 weeks and showing consistent performance at or above the grade-level benchmark for the next 6 weeks. Given this progress, the problem-solving team determined that the additional math instruction could be withdrawn, but they would continue to monitor his math skills monthly to make sure that these gains were maintained.

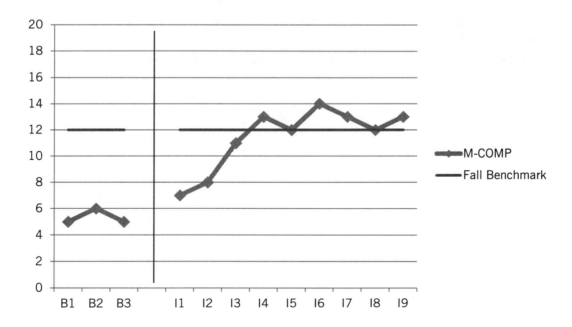

FIGURE 5.4. Progress monitoring graph for a fifth-grade student.

SUMMARY

A cornerstone of problem solving within MTSS is a technically sound method for gathering data on student progress paired with a process for analyzing the data in order to identify students in need of additional instruction and to determine whether the instruction is effective. The elementary grades present the most advantageous time to provide supports for students who demonstrate risk for disengagement and school problems, because the earlier we help students acquire the skills they need to be successful in school, the best chance we have at closing achievement gaps. Students with grade-level academic achievement are more likely to remain engaged and complete school with the skills needed to be successful in life.

BIG IDEAS

- The five stages of the problem solving model are:
  - Identify the problem.
  - Define the problem.
  - Explore alternative interventions.
  - Implement the intervention.
  - Look at effects.
- Students at risk are referred to the problem-solving team, which is responsible for targeting interventions and monitoring integrity of interventions.
- CBM, ODR data, DBRs, and single-case-study designs are valuable tools for progress monitoring at Tiers 2 and 3.
- Problem-solving teams monitor the rate of progress toward identified goals and follow data-based decision-making guidelines.

CHAPTER 6

Early Intervention
Elementary Evidence-Based Resources

with Jennifer L. Robert

As emphasized in earlier chapters, one of the very first strategies for preventing dropout is early intervention from preschool through the elementary school years. To reduce the number of dropouts and increase student graduation rates, schools need to make system-wide changes. Educational factors such as grading policies, school size, assignments, course content, school climate, and teacher–student relationships can all have an impact on whether students continue with their education or drop out of school. Because these factors exist long before a student enters middle school or high school, school improvement strategies that help increase students' engagement and sense of belonging in school through meaningful curricula and effective instruction have proven to be effective methods of preventing at-risk students from dropping out of high school. Shannon and Bylsma (2003) reported on critical school improvement strategies that have been important for the success of all students. Following is a list of some of the school improvement strategies that have shown promising results for keeping children in school:

- Making efforts to increase students' sense of belonging in schools.
- Providing a strong, rigorous, and research-based core of academic instruction.
- Personalizing schools.
- Improving relationships between teachers and students.

Jennifer L. Robert, PsyD, is a 2013 graduate from the doctoral school psychology program at the University of Southern Maine. She graduated from the University of Southern Maine with her master's degree in school psychology in 2000, after which she worked as a school psychologist/specialist for the Lewiston Public Schools. As a school psychologist, she worked on the development and implementation of a schoolwide RTI model. She has also consulted with schools implementing Tier 2 and Tier 3 interventions, including supporting teachers to improve the link between assessment and instruction.

- Improving school climate.
- Building resiliency.
- Revising school discipline.
- Revising school attendance policies.
- Improving student engagement.

Given the growing awareness of diminishing educational resources and the need for proven effective methods that achieve positive outcomes as quickly as possible, this chapter highlights the importance of early intervention. A comprehensive review of elementary evidence-based resources applicable at each tier is given, with an emphasis on their relevance to dropout prevention. The case example in Box 6.1 demonstrates some of the important considerations in planning and providing interventions.

THE IMPORTANCE OF *EARLY* INTERVENTION

Early intervention matters because students who fall behind their grade-level peers early in their school careers may never catch up and tend to fall further behind year after year. As previously discussed, dropping out of school is a process of disengagement that often begins long before a student is in high school. By the time students enter high school, they have accumulated a history of school experiences, home characteristics, and personal values that predict future behavior. The warning signs that a student is at risk for dropping out may be clearly evident in middle school and high school, but they are often present in elementary school. Students who have learning disabilities or emotional disturbances, Hispanic and African American students, students from low-socioeconomic-status backgrounds, students who are poor readers, students with poor attendance, and students who have been retained are at a higher risk of dropping out of school (Denti & Guerin, 1999). As in public health, for school health, a focus on early intervention and prevention, rather than treatment after a problem has developed, is both socially and economically more effective in the long term. Prevention will have the greatest impact on a student's education because it starts the developmental trajectory of children in a positive direction at an early age.

As described in Chapters 3 and 4, the framework through which schools address prevention, early identification, and intervention has been an MTSS model for academics and behavior. Prevention in education draws upon the research through the public health model and distinguishes three kinds of prevention. Primary prevention is aimed at reducing the number of children identified with academic or behavioral difficulties to keep the problems from appearing in the first place. Secondary intervention strives to remediate the problem as soon as it surfaces, and tertiary prevention further individualizes and increases the intensity of interventions for students with persistent and more critical care needs. At all three tiers, teaching methods, interventions, assessments, and communications must take into account the cultural and linguistic needs of students and their families.

Sylva and Evans (1999) reviewed the effects of four early education interventions aimed at preventing school failure: preschool programs for disadvantaged children, a Tier 2 read-

---

BOX 6.1. Case Example: Mariana

Mariana was in second grade, and she had struggled with learning to read since she enrolled in her elementary school in kindergarten. Her first language was Spanish, and she received English as a second language (ESL) services. Mariana spoke and comprehended English, but she hadn't been making adequate progress in reading. Her regular education teachers had not had specific professional development in evidence-based reading practices for English language learners (ELLs) and believed that Mariana just needed more time to learn English to improve her early literacy skill development. Mariana had been observed to have reading delays compared with her classmates, and her second-grade teacher was concerned because Mariana had already missed 3 days of school during the first few weeks of the school year. Following a phone call home after the third school absence, Mariana's mother stated that Mariana did not want to come to school this year.

Mariana was referred to the problem-solving team when she continued to score in the at-risk range in a universal screening of reading skills. Team members reviewed results of language and reading assessments and quickly learned that the primary language spoken in Mariana's home was Spanish. Mariana could speak Spanish fluently and often interpreted English for her parents. ELL reading assessment results showed that she demonstrated above-average Spanish reading skills. The team decided to begin with a Tier 2 direct-instruction reading program to be provided daily during the RTI intervention block to facilitate her English reading development. Weekly progress monitoring data revealed immediate improvements in Mariana's phonological awareness and decoding skills. At the next monthly problem-solving team data review, Mariana's teacher reported that the improvement in Mariana's reading skills and progress data, as well as attendance, were evident in the classroom.

Practical Application to Dropout Prevention

As an ELL student with Spanish as her primary language in the home, Mariana was not responding to Tier 1 English reading instruction alone; therefore a Tier 2 reading intervention was initiated. This case demonstrates that evidence-based reading instruction designed to improve English literacy skills is an effective intervention for teaching reading to ELLs as well.

---

ing intervention, a Tier 1 focused literacy program, and a parent involvement program. The review concluded that early intervention is more effective and economical than responding to problems after they develop. Early intervention can help prevent future academic and social problems as early as preschool, especially for disadvantaged children. By advocating for early intervention and making early literacy a priority in teacher and administrator training programs, dropout prevention can be a goal for preschool, kindergarten, and first- and second-grade teachers (Denti & Guerin, 1999). Effective instruction and evidence-based interventions for elementary school students are well researched and documented as being beneficial and necessary to help accelerate all students, beginning at Tier 1.

WHY EVIDENCE MATTERS

An increasing emphasis on accountability in education, as well as our desire and responsibility to provide our children with a high standard of care in education and the best chance to be successful in school, call for evidence-based instruction and support to maximize positive outcomes for our children. Evidence-based, or research-based, interventions are those that have empirical support as being effective in achieving desired outcomes. It is important that a system of evidence-based strategies and interventions is available to all educators, along with a plan for intervening with students who do not respond to instruction (Jones, Yssel, & Grant, 2012). NCLB has required schools and educators to be more accountable for the academic and social–emotional growth of all students. Recent educational initiatives have emphasized the critical role of early evidence-based reading instruction in the prevention of reading difficulties. Students who read proficiently in early elementary school typically make expected gains in reading achievement. Because reading achievement is highly correlated with academic performance and school success, their risk for dropping out of school is minimized. Alternatively, students who do not learn to read adequately in the primary grades typically have persistent reading difficulties throughout their school years, placing them at greater risk for multiple academic problems and school failure. The percentage of students who perform below the average range in basic reading skills at the end of first grade may be reduced dramatically through the provision of high-quality instruction in the classroom (Denton, Fletcher, Anthony, & Francis, 2006). Providing quality classroom instruction with evidence-based programs can make a big difference for all students.

The What Works Clearinghouse (WWC) is a website that provides educators with information they need to make evidence-based decisions, including practice guides for addressing challenges in the classroom and reviews of intervention reports. A search feature in WWC makes it possible to focus on a specific area of interest, such as math interventions, reading interventions, and dropout prevention programs. The Best Evidence Encyclopedia (BEE) provides unbiased reviews of research-based educational programs. BEE, created by the Johns Hopkins University School of Education's Center for Data-Driven Reform in Education (CDDRE), weighs the evidence for a variety of K–12 programs. The American Institutes for Research (AIR) provide research in the areas of education, educational assessment, health, and human development. Research is available on evidence-based practices for ELLs, as well as disadvantaged youth. Table 6.1 lists these online resources.

The following sections include information about evidence-based resources applicable at each tier of the MTSS framework. The resources and interventions described here should be part of a comprehensive dropout prevention strategy. In other words, these strategies will be most effective if they are implemented within the framework of the problem-solving model, MTSS, and data-based decision making.

TIER 1

The first tier consists of universal strategies, including a high-quality core curriculum in combination with a positive school climate, research-based teaching strategies, schoolwide screening to identify students at risk for difficulty, and the design of academic and behavior supports within the regular education classroom. Tier 1 provides opportunities for instruc-

TABLE 6.1. Online Resources for Identifying and Evaluating Evidence-Based Programs

What Works Clearinghouse (WWC)
http://ies.ed.gov/ncee/wwc

WWC reviews the research on the different programs, products, practices, and policies in education. By focusing on high-quality research, it tries to answer the question "What works in education?" The goal is to provide educators with the information they need to select evidence-based practices.

Best Evidence Encyclopedia (BEE)
www.bestevidence.org

BEE presents reliable, unbiased reviews of research-based educational programs to help policy makers use evidence in their decisions, principals to choose proven programs to meet state standards, teachers use the most powerful tools available, and researchers to find rigorous evaluations of educational programs.

American Institute for Research (AIR)
www.air.org

AIR helps practitioners and policy makers at all levels improve teaching and learning, with a special emphasis on children who are disadvantaged. The information on this website provides research that will help improve learning in the classroom, at home, online, and in other environments through evaluation, research, evidence-based technical assistance, and technology solutions.

tional differentiation and schoolwide routines and procedures. Using the MTSS triangle as a guide, approximately 80% of students should be making adequate progress in Tier 1. This is an indicator of school health and effective core curricula. Universal screening data are collected, usually, three times per year to identify the students who are at risk for failure. The results from the universal screening will indicate what percentage of students are on track given current Tier 1 practices. If that percentage is lower than 80%, a schoolwide intervention, or changes to the core instruction, are indicated. Tier 1 will be most effective when a comprehensive school improvement plan is put in place to target schoolwide behavior and academic performance.

One of the key components of sustainable Tier 1 instruction is professional development. Professional development should be ongoing and based on the results from research findings, such as those from the National Reading Panel (National Institute of Child Health and Human Development, 2000). Professional development that changes teacher behaviors in ways that lead to improvements in student performance is critical to an effective and sustainable Tier 1 system. Teachers need to be provided with the opportunity to acquire and practice new skills over time and to receive coaching support and feedback relative to their progress. If it is best practice to instruct, model, provide multiple opportunities to practice, and give feedback in order for our students to gain skills, then teachers should be provided with this same model when receiving professional development.

Harwell (2003) reported that a lack of professional development is not typically the problem, but, rather, that many professional development opportunities stop short of delivering their intended results. Many professional development activities point out what is wrong with the education occurring in the classrooms but do not provide the teachers with opportunities to practice what they learn. Harwell (2003) presents some characteristics of high-quality professional development, including buy-in from the administration; settings that support professional development; agreement among teachers that change is needed; strong content that addresses gaps in student achievement; sound educational practices; and cooperative learning activities. When teachers are given the opportunity, via high-quality professional development, to learn new strategies for teaching to rigorous standards, they report changing their teaching in the classroom (Harwell, 2003). Additionally, when professional development provides opportunities for participants to interact, cooperate, and serve as peer resources, what they learn transfers to behaviors that are observable in the classroom (Harwell, 2003). Teachers who are trained in effective teaching practices will reach more of their students, thereby reducing the number of students at risk for dropping out of school in the future.

> **Teachers who are trained in effective teaching practices will reach more of their students, thereby reducing the number of students at risk for dropping out of school in the future.**

Core Instruction

The Institute of Educational Sciences' *Dropout Prevention: A Practice Guide* (Dynarski et al., 2008) recommends rigorous and relevant instruction as a central element of a comprehensive dropout prevention strategy. Direct instruction is a key component of effective instruction in all academic areas. Many children, including those who have been characterized as slow learners or learning disabled, respond to explicit, structured, and sequential instruction, paired with frequent review, performance feedback, and opportunities to practice. Importantly, the instruction must be designed and delivered at the students' academic skill level and include checks for understanding and progress monitoring. Carnine, Silbert, Kame'enui, and Tarver (2009) reported on the research done by Rosenshine (1986) on direct instruction. Direct instruction refers to general teaching techniques that have produced gains in learning for at-risk students (Carnine et al., 2009). Rosenshine (1986) reviewed research on teacher effectiveness variables that were associated with students' academic success. The key components of effective teaching of all students at all ages include:

- High levels of student engagement.
- Academic focus.
- Teacher direction.
- Carefully sequenced and structured materials.
- Clear goals.
- Sufficient time allocated for instruction.
- Extensive content coverage.

- Monitoring of student performance.
- Immediate, academically oriented feedback to students.
- Structured, but not authoritarian, teacher–student interactions.

Tier 1 Reading Instruction

The National Reading Panel (National Institute of Child Health and Human Development, 2000) critically examined decades of research on reading and identified five key components to reading instruction:

1. Phonemic awareness.
2. Phonics.
3. Fluency.
4. Vocabulary.
5. Comprehension.

All five reading components are equally essential and should be systematically and explicitly taught within core reading curricula. Systematic instruction has several important characteristics (Learning Point Associates, 2004):

1. Skills and concepts are taught in a planned, logically progressive sequence. For example, certain sounds (those that are easier to learn or those used more often in the words students will read) are taught before other sounds.
2. Lessons focus on clearly defined objectives that are stated in terms of what students will do.
3. Multiple practice opportunities are purposefully scheduled to help students master and retain new skills. Students work on carefully designed tasks that give them opportunities to apply what they have been taught.
4. Assessments are designed and used in a timely fashion to monitor skill acquisition, as well as students' ability to apply new skills, retain them over time, and use them independently.

"Explicit instruction means the teacher states clearly what is being taught and models effectively how it is used by a skilled reader" (Learning Point Associates, 2004, p. 2). The five elements of effective reading instruction identified by the National Reading Panel were synthesized in a review by Learning Point Associates (2004). Table 6.2 provides a list of these strategies, which are appropriate at Tier 1 and which can also be applied to small-group targeted instruction in Tiers 2 and 3.

This is not an exhaustive list of effective instructional practices; however, it highlights the key aspects for each of the five key components of effective reading instruction. Many teachers have not received extensive preparation in scientifically based reading instruction and will benefit from ongoing professional development, coaching, and PLCs in this critical curricular area.

TABLE 6.2. Effective Reading Strategies

Phonemic Awareness

- Focus on one or two phonemic awareness skills at a time.
- Emphasize segmenting words into phonemes.
- Working with three to four children may be more effective than one-to-one tutoring. The research shows that students learn from observing other students and listening to the responses of other children.
- Use manipulatives when teaching about phonemes.
- Connect phonemic awareness instruction to reading and writing.
- Use manipulatives to help students acquire phonemic awareness.

Phonics

- Phonics instruction should be systematic and explicit.
- Explain clearly and directly that certain letters or letter combinations represent certain sounds.
- Follow the predetermined sequence of letter–sound relationships rather than teaching them randomly as students encounter them in stories.

Fluency

- Repeated reading has proven to be an effective practice in improving student fluency. For repeated reading, the student rereads instructional-level text with immediate feedback until a predetermined reading fluency goal is met.
- Guided repeated oral reading differs from repeated reading in that students receive direct support from others. Guidance or support is provided through modeling fluent reading or telling students unfamiliar words instead of having them sound them out.

Vocabulary

- Preview new vocabulary and preteach these words.
- Identify, prioritize, and explicitly teach vocabulary.
- Use examples and nonexamples.
- To help students learn new words as they read, teach students word learning strategies, such as how to use a dictionary, word parts or root words, and context clues to determine what unfamiliar words mean.
- Repeated exposure to new vocabulary is critical.
- Active engagement with new vocabulary improves learning.
- Associate new words with known words.
- Use new words in a sentence.

Comprehension

- Activate prior knowledge. Help students connect what they are reading with relevant background knowledge.
- Teachers should explain, model, and provide practice in generating questions. Generating questions leads to better monitoring of comprehension and provides better identification of main ideas.
- Cooperative learning strategies are helpful for increasing comprehension.
- The use of graphic and semantic organizers is an effective way to help students remember what they are reading.

Note. Based on Learning Point Associates (2004).

Tier I Math Instruction

Although we have less available research in effective math instruction, two major research reviews have been conducted to inform current best practices in math instruction: Adding It Up (Kilpatrick, Swafford, & Findell, 2001) and Foundations for Success (National Mathematics Advisory Panel, 2008). Similar to the National Reading Panel, the National Mathematics Advisory Panel (2008) reviewed a body of research in mathematics and developed recommendations for effective math instruction and policy changes needed to facilitate improved mathematics instruction and outcomes for all students. Also, the Trends in International Mathematics and Science Study (TIMSS) provides additional information to guide instructional priorities.

One of the many challenges in mathematics instruction identified by the National Mathematics Advisory Panel report (2008) is that current mathematics curricula tend to focus on breadth versus depth, introducing many mathematical concepts in a single school year. This has the unintended and unfavorable consequence of limiting opportunities to practice content and skills, which most students need to achieve skill proficiency. When skills are mastered, they are more likely to be encoded into memory for later retrieval and to facilitate learning more difficult mathematical concepts. Additionally, teachers often report that they do not have sufficient time to complete the breadth of curricula as designed. A primary conclusion of the current mathematics research findings is that the essential priority skills need to be identified, prioritized, and explicitly taught to mastery.

The characteristics of effective math instruction parallel the features of direct instruction already described. A growing body of research has shown that multi-tiered math instruction produces gains in math achievement test results and individual student progress. Differentiated instruction, an important feature of MTSS, is essential to reducing gaps in essential mathematics skills. Additionally, using a variety of instructional strategies helps students who are struggling in math (Baker, Gersten, & Lee, 2002; Bryant, Bryant, Gersten, Scammacca, & Chavez, 2008). As with reading, fluency is important for math proficiency. Teaching math fluency helps all students and can make a significant difference for those who are struggling. When students achieve fluency in math calculation, it frees working memory and allows the mind to concentrate on comprehension of concepts. In other words, automaticity with math calculations allows students to focus on application and problem-solving strategies.

Math achievement generates continued progress and facilitates student engagement and interest in math activities. This is especially important for students who are caught in the cycle of low math achievement, which occurs when widening skill gaps lead to increased errors, discouragement, disengagement, and reduced effort (Axtell, McCallum, Bell, & Poncy, 2009; National Mathematics Advisory Panel, 2008). Box 6.2 summarizes some of the research-based recommendations for math instruction.

Positive Behavioral Interventions and Supports

Because of the link between disruptive behavior and dropout, researchers (Dynarski et al., 2008) recommend implementing programs to improve students' classroom behavior and

---

**BOX 6.2. Research to Practice:
Recommendations for Tier 1 Mathematics Instruction**

- Streamline the curriculum to emphasize the most critical skills and topics.
- Provide explicit and sequential instruction of math facts and concepts, with teacher modeling.
- Provide sufficient time for explicit math instruction (1 hour daily) to introduce and practice new skills toward mastery. Students also need multiple opportunities to practice with immediate feedback.
- Review and compare student assessment data to allocate instructional time effectively.
- Monitor math calculation fluency and implement supplemental fluency-building interventions.
  - Computer software programs
  - Classwide tutoring
  - Peer-assisted learning strategies

---

social skills. Evidence supporting the use of positive behavior management strategies dates back to Skinner's development of operant learning theory (Maag, 2001). Since that time, a robust body of evidence has demonstrated the effectiveness of positive classroom environments, direct instruction, and various methods of positive reinforcement for improving student behavior (Simonsen, Fairbanks, Briesch, Myers, & Sugai, 2008). PBIS is a three-tiered problem-solving model that incorporates a continuum of strategies to teach and reinforce appropriate behavior. Tier 1 PBIS strategies, such as positively stated expectations for behavior (see Figure 6.1 for an example of a school-wide behavior matrix), instructional practices that maximize opportunities to engage, public acknowledgment of demonstration of desired behaviors, and group contingencies, are able to reach large numbers of students. Interventions delivered in the regular education setting have the greatest potential to enhance student behavior by altering the classroom environment to support all students, including students who are isolated or rejected by their peers.

> **Interventions delivered in the regular education setting have the greatest potential to enhance student behavior by altering the classroom environment to support all students.**

Given the impact of early problem behavior on children's future health, academic, social, and emotional development, school-based strategies should be considered a critical component of prevention. Table 6.3 provides a few examples of evidence-based classroom behavior programs that have shown positive effects on preventing problem behavior.

Through implementation of evidence-based schoolwide and classroom behavioral programs, the overall school climate will feel safer for students. When a safe learning environment is provided in schools, students who are experiencing difficulty may be more likely to take risks in their academic engagement. A positive school climate promotes academic success and predicts the degree to which students actively participate in learning, including how consistently they attend school, how attentive they are in class, how carefully they complete

> **Classroom climates can be enhanced when teachers model respect, empathy, and collaboration.**

	HALLWAY/STAIRS	PLAYGROUND	BATHROOMS	CAFETERIA	LIBRARY
BE SAFE	✓ Face forward ✓ Hands at side ✓ Walk ✓ Maintain physical space	✓ Follow playground procedures ✓ Stay within playground boundaries ✓ Use playground equipment properly	✓ Follow bathroom pass rules ✓ Wash hands ✓ Go directly back to class/activity	✓ Chew and swallow before talking ✓ Stay seated while eating ✓ Walk	✓ Walk ✓ Follow library space procedures (e.g., one person in a chair; three people in a library nook)
BE RESPECTFUL	✓ Voice level 0 or 1 ✓ Quiet steps ✓ Walk on right side	✓ Include others ✓ Share playground equipment ✓ Hands, feet, bodies in control	✓ Voice level 0–1 ✓ Knock on door ✓ Flush ✓ Wash hands	✓ Voice level 1 ✓ Use utensils to eat ✓ Practice good table manners	✓ Use voice level 0 or 1 ✓ Treat books, computers, and materials carefully ✓ Share library spaces and materials
BE RESPONSIBLE	✓ Go directly to your destination ✓ Follow hallway procedures	✓ Play safely ✓ Put litter in garbage/recycling containers ✓ Follow playground/game rules	✓ Practice good bathroom manners ✓ Keep bathroom clean ✓ Follow bathroom procedures	✓ Clean up table ✓ Table conversation ✓ Put litter in garbage/recycling containers	✓ Return books/materials on time ✓ Replace books in their proper place ✓ Follow library procedures

FIGURE 6.1. Schoolwide behavior matrix.

TABLE 6.3. Evidence-Based Behavior Programs for the Classroom

Good Behavior Game

This game uses team competition and group incentives to reduce disruptive behavior in the classroom. Features include specific performance criteria for winning, immediate behavior feedback, and group-based reinforcement.

Three Steps to Self-Managed Behavior

In this intervention, a three-part self-monitoring procedure is paired with a token economy to reduce disruptive behavior and improve academic productivity.

Positive Peer Reporting

The purpose of this program is to enhance prosocial behavior and positive peer relationships and to reduce inappropriate social behaviors by systematically encouraging and reinforcing peer compliments.

their class assignments, and how committed they are to staying in school and doing well there. A key component of positive school climate is the relationship between teachers, students, families, and the community. Teachers must show high expectations for their students and have confidence that their students will be successful. Students who feel connected to their schools are more likely to graduate from high school. PBIS is about providing behavioral supports to ensure that all students have access to the most effective and accurately implemented instructional practices and interventions possible (*www. pbis.org*).

Family Involvement

When schools and families have frequent contact, share information, and work together to promote learning and prosocial behavior, their efforts will be more successful than when they work independently. Regular communication with parents, sharing information about learning activities and how parents can support their children's learning at home, is an important preventative measure. Schools should communicate with parents regularly and clearly about information important to student success. This can be done through newsletters, phone messages, and websites. Parent–teacher conferences, open houses, literacy and math nights for students and parents, and home visits are all ways that schools can engage families to become involved with their children's schools and become invested in their children's educations. Schools can provide family nights as an opportunity for students and families to share information about their cultural and community values. Strengthening the school–family partnership through sharing information about cultural differences is an essential investment for schools. Translations should be provided to ensure that non-English-speaking parents are fully informed about standards, curriculum, assessments, school programs, discipline policies, and student progress.

If Tier I instruction is effective, then it should reach 80% of the student population in any given school. If schools are successful at reaching 80% of their students through Tier 1

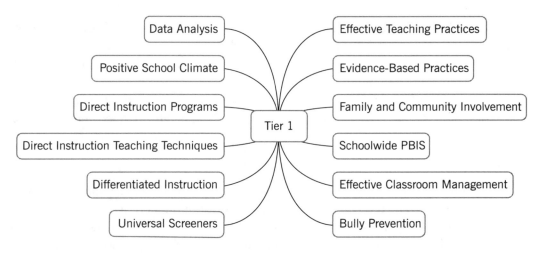

FIGURE 6.2. Tier 1 early intervention.

instruction, there will be more availability to meet the needs of the other 20% of students, who are more at risk. There will always be students who need additional support, different instruction, and more individualized plans. MTSS provides a framework for schools to provide effective differentiated instruction for all students and additional, more targeted instruction for those at-risk students. To summarize, Figure 6.2 lists some of the important components of Tier 1 dropout prevention.

TIERS 2 AND 3 TARGETED INTERVENTIONS

For students who are not making adequate progress with Tier 1 instruction alone, or who fall within the "off-track" range of the MTSS triangle, additional instruction with more intensive Tier 2 or Tier 3 supports may be needed. Evidence-based practices for these students are often very similar to the best practices within Tier 1 but are more individualized, take place in smaller groups, or involve more time and practice. Typically, Tier 2 interventions involve small-group instruction in the identified area(s) of need and are supplemental to Tier 1 instruction (Tier 1 + Tier 2). At Tier 3, students who do not respond at Tier 2 are likely to participate in more intensive and individualized interventions and may see a change in the type or frequency of instruction.

As discussed in previous chapters, students at risk for dropping out show one or more signs of disengagement, including poor attendance, low grades, disinterest in academic, social, or co-curricular activities, poor relationships with teachers and/or peers, disruptive behavior, and low expectations for success. Early intervention and identification are critical for supporting students before they reach that point. Students who have failed to respond or to progress adequately with good classroom instruction require more intensive instruction and intervention. The following sections describe evidence-based interventions for improving reading, math, executive functioning skills, behavior, and social–emotional development at the elementary school level. The most effective programs are those that focus on changing the family, school, and/or community environment in a long-lasting and positive way. Quality staff training in program philosophy, strategies, and materials is critical to program effectiveness (Hammond et al., 2007). For a more thorough discussion of targeted interventions for students at risk, the reader is referred to *Academic and Behavior Supports for At-Risk Students: Tier 2 Interventions* (Stormont, Reinke, Herman, & Lembke, 2012).

Attendance

As discussed in Chapter 4, attendance is a critical factor in school engagement and success, and it is just as important at the elementary school level as at the middle and high school levels. Peek (2009) identified several reasons for poor attendance, including family, economic, school, and student variables. In considering interventions for improving attendance, it is important to understand these reasons so that strategies are tailored to fit the individual needs of the student and family. The research on poor attendance suggests the importance of developing family and community partnerships. "Interventions to any attendance process must be comprehensive, flexible, responsive, and persistent. Trained professionals, working to support a family's needs, while building positive relationships between the family and school, are invaluable when implementing interventions to increase attendance" (Peek, 2009, p. 11). Strategies for increasing attendance in elementary school are provided in Table 6.4. "The most promising interventions to reducing excessive student absences are increased parent involvement, having an on-going process of steps within the attendance policy, using incentive programs for students, involving community resources, and incorporating consequences for truancy" (Peek, 2009, p. 14).

Academic Interventions

The Institute of Education Sciences' *Dropout Prevention: A Practice Guide* (Dynarski et al., 2008) recommends providing academic support and enrichment to improve academic

TABLE 6.4. Strategies for Improving Attendance

- Increase parents' knowledge of school attendance policy.
- Create uniform attendance rules.
- Strengthen community knowledge of the importance of regular attendance.
- Reach out to parents when student has had three or more unexcused absences.
- Incorporate home visits by school personnel.
- Establish a student incentive program, in which students who have perfect attendance are recognized each month, quarter, or semester.
- Schedule highly preferred activities for the first period of the day and at frequent yet unpredictable times.

performance and school engagement. By the fourth grade it is very important for children to have mastered the skills required to learn to read. As students enter third grade, the expectation is that they are reading to learn rather than learning to read. If students who are below grade level in reading in second and third grade are to catch up, they need more strategic instruction targeted at their current skill levels. Although these students are sometimes held back, retention is not a recommended intervention (see Box 6.3). Getting these students to grade level requires an evidence-based reading program that is designed to accelerate students through the most important elements of basic reading skills identified by the comprehensive National Reading Panel research. Further information and guidance on supplemental reading interventions can be found in *Interventions for Reading Problems: Designing and Evaluating Effective Strategies* (Daly, Chafouleas, & Skinner, 2005).

Students who have not yet mastered the skill of reading are at risk for falling further behind each year. This is true for students in the content areas of math and written language, as well. Students who are not fluent with their math facts are at risk for falling behind academically, particularly in math and science, as poor math calculation fluency precludes efficient access to content and application of new concepts. Spelling is a prerequisite skill for

BOX 6.3. Is Retention an Evidence-Based Intervention?

Because it continues to be a common practice, it is worth repeating that retention is not an intervention. For students who are not making expected academic gains or who seem young, immature, or hyperactive compared with their peers, grade retention is often thought to provide the gift of time, which will help the child develop and acquire skills to be successful in school. However, decades of research have consistently shown that grade retention is not an effective intervention for struggling students. In fact, much of the evidence points to disadvantages of retention. Specifically, grade retention has been found to have a negative impact on academic achievement, social skills and behavior, peer relationships, self-esteem, and school attendance, and it is one of the best predictors of dropping out of high school (Jimerson et al., 2002; Jimerson, 2001). Rather than retention or social promotion without additional intervention, educators need to design and implement targeted strategies that promote skill development and school engagement. One question to ask when considering retention is "What will we do differently next year?" If it is more of the same instruction that is currently not working, one should not assume that more of it will be better, nor that it will be able to address the multiple factors that are likely at play.

Teachers and administrators who advocate grade retention in the elementary years may do so because they see short-term gains and are not aware of the negative long-term outcomes associated with the practice. Communication among staff members at different grade levels and coordinated policies are important for establishing a continuum of best practices throughout a child's education. The evidence regarding retention has consistently shown that it is not an effective intervention, and these findings are critical for making informed decisions for students presenting academic and/or behavior delays. This information should be presented not only to teachers, administrators, counselors, and others within the school but also to parents, who may believe that retention is the best option for their child. Professional development and school policies must emphasize evidence-based prevention and early intervention strategies as alternatives to grade retention for students at risk.

fluent writing; thus students who are not fluent in spelling are at a significant disadvantage in their ability to express their ideas in writing.

To address these academic delays, academic support need not be limited to the hours of the school day. Students may benefit from extended days, homework help, or summer school to catch up on basic academic skills. Interventions aimed at preventing dropout primarily incorporate academic and behavioral support components in two ways: with more intensive in- or out-of-school programs and through homework assistance or tutoring programs, which may include family participation. Interventions can be presented in many different formats, such as direct instruction, technology, direct instruction tutoring, and small-group and one-to-one instruction. Appendix B in this book is an Academic Intervention Record Form, a checklist that can be used to keep track of important intervention elements and steps at each stage of the problem-solving model. Some specific evidence-based interventions that have been shown to increase student skills and to close the gap for struggling students are listed in Tables 6.5 (reading) and 6.6 (mathematics).

> **Direct instruction emphasizes small-group or one-on-one instruction using carefully planned and articulated lessons. Skills are broken down into smaller units, taught explicitly, and sequenced deliberately.**

Executive Functioning Skills

Executive functioning are those skills that are required to organize, plan, and execute activities, including task initiation and follow-through, working memory, sustained attention, performance monitoring, inhibition of impulses, and goal-directed persistence. Dawson and Guare (2010) suggest there are two broad domains of support for students with executive functioning deficits. In the classroom, teachers can intervene at the environmental level by making changes to the physical or social environment, to adult–student interactions, to the nature of the task(s), and to how cues are provided; at the individual student level, they can provide specific strategic instruction and directions, monitor performance, engage in problem solving, and provide motivation, encouragement, and feedback.

Our success at achieving any task is largely dependent on our use of beneficial strategies. We all develop or learn strategies to approach many different tasks. The more routinely we apply a strategy and succeed at the task, the easier it becomes. Students identified as at risk often have deficits in their executive functioning skills. This negatively affects their ability to take notes while participating in class discussion; to complete classwork on time; to get their assignments accurately written into their agenda books; to bring home the materials required to complete their homework; and then to return it the next day. Dawson and Guare (2004) presented a six-step process for teaching children executive functioning skills, which is presented in Table 6.7. The research on executive functioning recommends that students be explicitly taught executive functioning skills, just as they are taught reading and math. All students can benefit from explicit instruction and practice in developing organizational, note-taking, and study skills that are needed to execute school demands at the secondary level and beyond.

TABLE 6.5. Examples of Tier 2 and Tier 3 Evidence-Based Reading Interventions

Reading Mastery

Reading curricula covering phonological awareness, phonics and word analysis, fluency, vocabulary, and comprehension for students in grades kindergarten through fifth grade. Students receive intensive, explicit, and systematic instruction in small groups or one-to-one settings.

Early Interventions in Reading 2012

Reading intervention that builds mastery of essential skills, including phonemic awareness, letter–sound correspondence, word recognition and spelling, fluency, and comprehension, through explicit, systematic instruction in the five critical strands of reading.

Corrective Reading Program

Reading intervention program for students in grades 3–12. Students receive intensive, explicit, and systematic instruction in small groups or one-to-one settings in the skill areas of decoding, fluency, and comprehension.

READ 180

A blended model of direct reading instruction and computer activities that focus on all reading skill areas in small groups or one-to-one settings. Designed for students in grades 4–12.

Scott Foresman Early Reading Intervention

Direct reading intervention that builds mastery of essential skills through explicit, systematic instruction in the five critical strands of reading in small groups or one-to-one settings.

Success for All

Direct reading instruction and intervention that builds mastery of essential skills through explicit, systematic instruction in the five critical strands of reading in small groups or one-to-one settings.

PALS Reading (Peer-Assisted Learning Strategies)

A peer-mediated reading activity for students in preschool through the sixth grade, which covers letter identification, letter sounds, decoding, phonological processing, sight words, fluency, and comprehension. Students are divided into pairs; one is the coach, and the other is the reader. A variety of activities, including partner reading, are incorporated into the PALS reading program.

Phonological awareness and word analysis

Lexia Reading

Individualized, adaptive learning of discrete reading skills aligned with progress data through computer instruction and practice activities.

Phoneme Segmentation

Students orally segment words using counters or Elkonin boxes. Students work in pairs. They draw a card with a picture on it and orally segment the sounds in the word to match the picture. Student 2 repeats the sounds while moving a chip into a box that represents one of the sounds.

(continued)

TABLE 6.5. *(continued)*

Phonological Awareness Training (PAT)

A program that teaches children to read, spell, and write phonetically regular single-syllable words by making analogies. This program includes interventions for segmenting words, blending sounds, decoding and encoding words.

Word Analysis

Direct and explicit instruction in the six types of syllables with identification of root words, prefixes, suffixes, and word endings.

Fluency

Partner Reading (PR)

Research-based activity that has been demonstrated as being effective in boosting students' reading fluency. During a PR session, a more capable, fluent reader is typically paired with a less capable peer. While one student reads, the listening partner provides feedback and alerts the reader when an error has been made.

Quick Reads

Develops fluency by repeatedly using high-frequency words and words with common phonetic and syllabic patterns. It builds background knowledge by clustering multiple passages around high-interest topics, allowing the student to explore a subject in depth through a series of short focused readings.

Repeated Reading

An evidence-based reading fluency intervention that requires the student to read a preselected passage aloud to a trained teacher, tutor, or peer partner. The student rereads the passage three times, with immediate corrective feedback as needed. This process may be continued until the student reaches his or her fluency goal.

Listening Passage Preview (LPP)

LPP is an evidence-based reading fluency intervention that begins with a student following along silently as a trained teacher, parent, adult, or peer tutor reads a preselected passage aloud. Then the student reads the passage aloud, receiving immediate corrective feedback as needed.

Great Leaps

A reading fluency intervention that focuses on individual letter sounds, words, phrases, and short stories.

Helping with Early Literacy with Practice Strategies (HELPS)

The HELPS program integrates instructional strategies specifically designed to improve students' reading fluency. Incorporates (1) repeated readings of ability-appropriate text, (2) listening to model reading, (3) systematic error-correction procedures, (4) verbal cues for students to read with fluency, (5) verbal cues to read for comprehension, (6) goal setting, (7) performance feedback, and (8) systematic praise and structured reward system.

(continued)

TABLE 6.5. *(continued)*

Read Naturally

This program uses three main strategies: repeated reading of text, teacher modeling of story reading, and systematic monitoring of student progress.

Phrase Drill Error Correction

Feedback is given on oral reading miscues by modeling the correct reading of a word and having the student reread the phrase that contains the word error three times. Students repeat the reading of the entire passage after practicing reading all phrases that contained word errors.

Vocabulary

Graphic Organizers

The use of graphic organizers is an evidence-based method for improving student vocabulary. The student places the vocabulary word at the center and includes additional cells connected to the central word or concept. Graphic organizers facilitate higher level thinking, and they serve as retrieval cues to promote learning.

Logic and Prediction

A teacher asks the students to predict the meaning of the words in isolation and then in context helps them to use their problem-solving skills to examine the roots or origins.

Synonyms and Antonyms

Ask students to identify words that have similar or opposite meanings.

Word Sorting

Students sort words by those they (1) know, (2) have heard but don't know the meanings of, and (3) have not heard and do not know. This increases word awareness.

Peer Tutoring in Vocabulary

Pairs of students practice vocabulary words together, with reward contingent upon the combined academic performance of both students.

Comprehension

Collaborative Strategic Reading (CSR)

A comprehension strategy that teaches students to practice and eventually assume responsibility for implementing appropriate strategies to enhance reading and concept knowledge before, during, and following reading.

"Get the Gist"

Students summarize paragraphs or a page of reading content in one sentence, using 10 words or less. This process continues until the completion of the reading content. Then the sentences are reviewed for a final "Get the Gist" sentence to summarize the main idea of reading material. Comprehension strategies such as "Get the Gist" require active engagement with the reading

(continued)

TABLE 6.5. *(continued)*

material, as well as synthesis of the reading content to extrapolate the main idea, which facilitates encoding important points into memory for later retrieval.

Know, Want to Know, Learned (K–W–L)

This strategy is intended to guide students in reading and understanding a text. This strategy is composed of three stages including what we *know*, what we *want* to know, and what we *learned*.

Story Mapping

Aims to increase comprehension by providing a method of identifying the main elements of the story. Story mapping is a reading comprehension intervention in which the student creates a visual representation of the story by writing the important elements (character, setting, problem, etc.) on a graphic organizer.

Soar to Success

A reading intervention program that helps students learn to apply comprehension strategies (summarizing, clarifying, questioning, predicting) across the curriculum. The systematic instruction includes fiction and nonfiction trade books, a daily, five-step lesson plan (rereading, reviewing, rehearsing, reading/reciprocal teaching, responding), graphic organizers, and ongoing assessment.

Behavioral Interventions

The research on dropout prevention shows that student needs differ and that interventions need to be tailored to the individual student. Like students who receive Tier 2 academic support, some will benefit from more intensive behavioral support, such as social skills instruction, Check-In, Check-Out (CICO), alternative educational placements, or individual behavior plans based on the results from functional behavioral assessments. Others will need a combination of academic and behavioral interventions. For a more comprehensive review of evidence-based behavioral interventions, the reader is referred to *Managing Challenging Behaviors in Schools: Research-Based Strategies That Work* (Lane, Menzies, Bruhn, & Crnobori, 2011).

Check-In, Check-Out

CICO is designed for use in schools in which schoolwide PBIS are already in place. Students who consistently require more adult support than the average student may benefit from CICO (Crone et al., 2010). As discussed in Chapter 5, students who participate in CICO check in with the CICO coordinator in the morning, receive positive reinforcement, discuss their goals for the day, and then continue to receive feedback throughout the day from their classroom teacher(s). The student then checks out with the coordinator at the end of the day. Daily progress reports are brought home each night to be shared with parents and signed, and then returned to school the next day. The evidence for CICO suggests that it is effective for students who have low-level problem behavior that is maintained

TABLE 6.6. Examples of Tier 2 and Tier 3 Evidence-Based Math Interventions

Time Practice, Practice, Practice

This strategy helps build fluency with basic computation skills.

Flashcards and Folding in New Items

This method builds and maintains a student's fluency with computation facts.

Cover, Copy, Compare (CCC)

CCC is a method to provide students with independent practice with math calculation, vocabulary, and/or concepts. CCC prepares a worksheet with accurately completed math problem models that students review for instruction. Students then Cover the model and Copy and solve the math problem independently. The final step is to Compare the calculations and student answers with the original model for immediate feedback (Skinner, McLaughlin, & Logan, 1997).

Peer-Assisted Learning Strategies (PALS)

PALS is a peer-mediated math activity for students in preschool through the sixth grade. Students are divided into pairs; one student is the coach and the other is the student.

Accelerated Math

This is a software tool that customizes assignments and measures progress. It is aligned with state math standards and generates feedback to teachers and students.

Reciprocal Peer Tutoring in Math

Students work in pairs using flashcards to solve math computation problems. Pairs add up their total points and then compare their team score with their team goal. Students receive reinforcement if they meet their goal.

Great Leaps Math

Great Leaps is a math fluency intervention that focuses on fact fluency for addition, subtraction, multiplication, and division.

TABLE 6.7. Steps for Teaching Executive Skills

1. Describe the problem behavior.
2. Set a goal that relates directly to the problem behavior.
3. Establish a procedure or set of steps to reach the goal.
   a. Create a checklist that outlines the procedures.
4. Supervise the child through the procedure.
   a. Walk the child through the entire process and provide reminders, prompts, and feedback.
5. Evaluate the process and make changes if necessary.
   a. Monitor the child's performance and identify areas that need improvement.
6. Fade the supervision.
   a. Decrease the number of prompts and level of supervision once the child can perform the skill independently.

Note. Based on Dawson and Guare (2010, p. 40).

through attention (Todd, Campbell, Meyer, & Horner, 2008). CICO provides students with an opportunity to have adult attention frequently throughout the school day. See Chapter 9 for a more complete discussion of CICO.

Check and Connect

Check and Connect is a comprehensive intervention that has been proven to enhance student engagement through relationship building, problem solving and capacity building, and persistence. There are four components to Check and Connect, including mentoring, systematic monitoring, timely and individualized interventions, and enhancing home–school communication (Alvarez & Anderson-Ketchmark, 2010). For more information on Check and Connect, see Chapter 9.

Promoting Alternative Thinking Strategies

Children who demonstrate signs of behavior problems require an intensive intervention to stop the emerging problem behaviors from escalating and leading to further problems. The Promoting Alternative Thinking Strategies (PATHS) preventative program focuses on the importance of the developmental integration of affect, behavior, and cognitive understanding as they relate to social and emotional competence (Kam, Greenberg, & Kusche, 2004). Research on child development suggests that children undergo a major developmental transformation, including changes in responsibility, independence, and social roles. The PATHS curriculum incorporates 60 lessons about self-control, feelings, and social problem solving that are targeted to elementary school children. Research completed by Kam et al. (2004) showed positive results for the long-term effects of the intervention on student behavior and social problem-solving skills.

Mentoring Programs

Mentoring is a community development program for at-risk students and is an effective strategy for keeping students in school. One of the key factors of effective mentoring programs is the relationship between the mentor and the mentee. This is largely achieved through the following mentor qualities and behaviors:

- Involving youth in deciding how the pair will spend their time.
- Committing to being consistent and dependable.
- Taking responsibility for keeping the relationship alive.
- Respecting the student's viewpoint.
- Seeking advice from program staff when needed.

VanderVen (2004) listed numerous benefits for children and youth who have participated in mentoring programs such as Big Brothers Big Sisters. Mentoring programs have led to improved grades, better attitudes toward school, avoidance of drug and alcohol use, fewer incidences of violence, increased attendance at school, and decreased aggression toward others. Given the fact that mentoring programs can lead to many positive outcomes for at-risk youth, it is critical that these programs provide adequate training to mentors and ensure consistency and commitment.

Social–Emotional Interventions

Research on dropout prevention has found that social–emotional learning enhances academic achievement, helps students develop self-management and self-control, improves relationships at all levels of school and community, reduces conflict among students, improves teachers' classroom management, and helps young people to be healthier and more successful in school and life (Durlak, Dymnicki, Taylor, Weissberg, & Schellinger, 2011). Unfortunately, many students lack social–emotional competencies and become more disengaged from school as they progress from the early elementary grades through high school. Social and emotional learning integrates interventions aimed at reducing risk factors and fostering protective mechanisms for positive adjustment. Strong Kids, Skillstreaming the Elementary School Student, Coping Cat, and cognitive-behavioral therapy for anger management have all been proven effective in teaching

> **Cognitive-behavioral interventions have achieved effective outcomes across educational environments, disability types, ethnicity, and gender.**

students appropriate coping strategies and replacement behaviors. Although not an exhaustive list, descriptions of these evidence-based interventions applicable to elementary school students are listed in Table 6.8.

Alternative Education Settings

Students in elementary school who are struggling behaviorally and academically may require an alternative placement that has a therapeutic and family component to their education. These classrooms should provide flexible and personalized learning environments that focus on community-building skills, life skills, and working as a team. Other features of high-quality alternative programs include specially trained teachers, effective classroom management, parent and community collaboration, and high expectations for students (Quinn & Poirier, 2006). Table 6.9 presents sample characteristics of an alternative placement program for elementary school students with significant behavioral and emotional concerns.

Progress Monitoring

Frequent formative evaluation procedures, such as CBM or review of ODRs, DBRs, and CICO data, are important for monitoring the effectiveness of Tier 2 and Tier 3 interventions, so that necessary instructional changes can be made in a timely fashion. Student support teams, or problem-solving teams, regularly review these data in light of individual

TABLE 6.8. Evidence-Based Interventions for Social–Emotional Learning

Second Step

A universal prevention program designed to reduce aggression and promote social competence, Second Step focuses on skills such as empathy, impulse control, problem solving, and anger management. Teachers use discussion, role play, homework, and video to support the curriculum.

Strong Kids

Strong Kids is designed to provide direct instruction in prosocial skills, and helps promote social–emotional competence and resilience.

Skillstreaming the Elementary School Child

Skillstreaming the Elementary School Child is a social skills program that employs a four-part training approach. Students are taught age-appropriate social skills through modeling, role playing, performance feedback, and generalization. This intervention addresses the needs of students who display aggression, withdrawal, and other antisocial behaviors.

Coping Cat

Coping Cat is a cognitive-behavioral therapy program that helps the child and family recognize the physiological aspects of heightened levels of anxiety and how to manage those symptoms in a calm manner. The child learns new ways to challenge anxiety-provoking thoughts and resolve conflicts.

Cognitive-behavioral therapy for anger management

During this performance-based cognitive-behavioral intervention, the client is exposed to cognitive reframing, relaxation training, modeling, and role playing to enhance the ability to cope with problem situations. Cognitive-behavioral therapy can be done in a small-group format or can be provided as more intensive individualized therapy.

academic and behavioral goals and make determinations or recommendations for intervention accordingly.

SUMMARY

Dropout prevention research suggests that student disengagement is multifaceted and that many of the most effective methods for keeping children in school incorporate multiple interventions. School programs that focus on social, emotional, and academic learning and that engage families and develop community partnerships from kindergarten through high school have been found to improve school attitudes, behavior, attendance, and academic performance (Zins, Weissberg, Wang, & Walberg, 2004). To implement effective early intervention, schools must invest in high-quality professional development for teachers in the areas of evidence-based instruction, effective teaching practices, educating non-English-speaking students, and resources available to students who are at risk.

TABLE 6.9. Case Example of an Elementary-Level Alternative Treatment Program

Demographic information

- Serves students in grades K–6.
- Located in a public school.
- Behavioral specialist, clinicians, and school psychologist are connected to the program.

Classroom features

- Maximum of 13 students per class.
- One teacher and three paraprofessionals.
- Small-group academic instruction matched to students' skills.
- Direct instruction in reading and math with evidence-based curricula.

Supports and services

- Highly supervised and interactive free time with opportunities to teach appropriate social skills.
- Daily, evidence-based social skills training.
- Individual counseling for students.
- Daily life skills training, including study skills, learning strategies, perseverance training, and community-building activities.

Other program components

- Programwide behavior plan in which students can earn rewards.
- Monthly parent education meetings.
- Continuing professional development for staff.

BIG IDEAS

- Early intervention can remediate skill gaps to foster engagement, academic, and behavioral success for children at risk.
- Components of Tier 1 instruction include empirically based, rigorous, and relevant academic instruction; universal strategies, procedures, and routines; research-based teaching strategies; and schoolwide screening to identify students at risk.
- Interventions aimed at preventing dropout primarily incorporate academic and behavior support components in two ways:
  - More intensive in or out of school programs
  - Homework assistance or tutoring programs
- Interventions can be presented in many different formats, such as through direct instruction, technology, direct instruction tutoring, and small-group and one-to-one instruction.
- Efforts to prevent dropout incorporate family and community partnerships.

PART III

DROPOUT PREVENTION IN MIDDLE SCHOOL AND HIGH SCHOOL

Time Is of the Essence
Early Warning Systems for Middle School and High School

The focus of the previous three chapters was on the elementary grades in terms of prevention and early intervention, recommendations for assessment, problem solving, and student supports. At the secondary level, the opportunity for prevention and early identification has passed, and time is of the essence. At this point, MTSS and dropout prevention strategies emphasize transition years, ongoing identification of risk, strategic intervention, and remediation, with a goal of keeping students on track for high school graduation with their cohorts. The case example in Box 7.1 highlights the importance of transition years for recognizing and responding to warning signs that a student is at risk of dropping out.

AT-RISK INDICATORS

In a research effort to find what Balfanz (2009) termed "high-yield indicators" that identify students with a 25% or lower probability of graduating based on current school data, the researchers discovered key indicators highly predictive of a student's likelihood of dropping out as early as sixth grade. This research points to several critical risk factors, or high-yield indicators, and to steps that schools can take to identify students unlikely to graduate from high school on time. Key indicators include poor grades in core subjects, poor attendance, grade retention, disengagement in the classroom, and behavior problems. Most students at risk for dropping out of school can be identified as early as sixth grade, and many can be identified even earlier in elementary school. This marks the beginning of middle school as a critical period for effective dropout prevention efforts (Balfanz et al., 2007).

Balfanz (2009) found that students in sixth grade often had only one risk indicator. Notably, one indicator appears to be sufficient to significantly predict a higher probability of

---

BOX 7.1. Case Example: Michael

Michael was an adolescent boy in the eighth grade who had a history of chronic absenteeism, multiple ODRs, and a recent episode of juvenile criminal behavior. In elementary school, he experienced learning difficulties and received Tier 2 and 3 academic interventions. Michael demonstrated gains in basic literacy and math skills, but he continued to receive reading and study skills support due to poor course performance. He was brought to the attention of the problem-solving team due to concerns about escalating behavior. A review of school data indicated that Michael had been absent 5 days in the first 20 days of school and had completed less than 50% of homework assignments in his math and reading classes. His teachers reported that he rarely participated in learning activities, school events, or extracurricular activities. The team quickly determined that Michael presented a high risk for dropping out of school and planned numerous and intensive interventions to help him get back on track for graduation as quickly as possible. Current interventions, including academic and study skills support, were intensified at Tier 3. Michael was referred to a psychologist at school for individual counseling. He also began participating in Check and Connect, a structured mentoring program that improves student engagement and success by emphasizing consistent and caring relationships, problem-solving skills, personal responsibility, family involvement, and monitoring of progress. Over the next months, the mentor helped Michael identify personal goals and competencies, provided guidance, feedback, and encouragement, and worked with his parents on providing after-school supervision and supporting homework completion.

Practical Application to Dropout Prevention

Michael demonstrated clear signs of disengagement from school, including two specific risk factors that are highly predictive of dropout risk in middle school and high school: a greater than 20% absentee rate and multiple ODRs. Given the high level of risk and need for support, the team selected intensive academic supports, mental health services, and a mentoring program that would provide a positive role model and opportunities to engage in interesting and enriching activities that would help Michael build the skills to be successful in school.

---

persistent school problems and eventual school dropout. These research findings translate to evidence that failing a single class, poor attendance patterns, or misbehaving as early as sixth grade increases a student's risk for becoming off track for on-time graduation. Further analysis of these behaviors indicates a pattern of escape and avoidance of frequently unidentified academic or behavior problems that manifest as absenteeism, disruptive behavior, or inattention and lack of engagement in classroom activities.

Three Key Indicators Predict Student Success
- **Attendance**
- **Academics**
- **Behavior**

Research consistently points to the "big three" critical risk factors: course performance, attendance, and behavior. Balfanz and colleagues (2007) found that more than half of sixth graders who met these at-risk criteria eventually dropped out of school. If they attended school less than 80% of the time, received a low final grade from their teachers in behavior, or failed either math or English, their risk for dropping out of school doubled. Researchers Neild and Balfanz (2006) reported that 78% of eighth-grade students who attended school less than 80% of the time—equivalent to missing at least 5 weeks of school—eventually dropped out of high school; 77% of the eighth graders who failed either mathematics and/or English dropped out of high school. Additionally, this study found that gender, race, age, and achievement test scores do not have the strong predictive power that attendance and course failures do for future dropout. These findings support the idea that monitoring attendance and course failure data as early as middle school can predict dropout risk with high accuracy.

Attendance

Extensive research has demonstrated a relationship between truancy or high rates of absenteeism and school dropout, and some of these findings are highlighted in Table 7.1. Consistent variables that appear to contribute to truancy and eventual dropout include a lack of active participation in school activities, lack of a positive identification with school, and student-reported feelings of alienation from teachers and peers (Finn, 1989). Additionally, high absentee rates, truancy, and school dropout have been associated with high rates of retention in previous grades (Kortering, Hess, & Braziel, 1997). Accurate rates of school refusal and truancy are difficult to calculate, because the true reasons for absences are often not given. What is known is that poor attendance as early as the first 20 days of school is highly correlated with disengagement, poor course performance, and increased risk for school failure. Early and frequent review of attendance data is a critical element of proactive intervention for attendance problems at the secondary level.

International research on school refusal behavior shows that school attendance problems are worldwide, with extensive research evidence coming from England, Australia, France, Sweden, and Venezuela and an increasing trend in school refusal behaviors being shown in countries such as Japan, which has historically lower rates of absenteeism than the United States (Wimmer, 2003). In a comprehensive study, Kearney (2008) reviewed data on four broad-based components of school refusal behavior and concluded that up to one-quarter of children and adolescents display some aspect of school refusal behavior. This concerning statistic alone has significant implications for school-based efforts to improve attendance and school engagement, with direct relevance to improving academic achievement outcomes.

TABLE 7.1. Links between Attendance and Dropout

- Ninth-grade attendance of less than 80% of the school year is a better predictor of school dropout than eighth-grade test scores.
- Even moderate absences (5–10 days) in the first semester of ninth grade indicate risk for dropout.
- Students who miss more than 10% of the first 20 days of school (2 days) are particularly at risk for high school dropout.
- Any student missing more than 10% of instructional time (at 20-day mark or at each quarter) should be flagged for intervention.

Academic Performance

Balfanz and colleagues (2007) found that course grades and failure rates are highly predictive of which students will or will not graduate from high school. Students who fail one or more courses in middle school or high school are significantly more likely to drop out. In fact, even one failed grade in math or English in middle school places a student at risk for dropping out. Figure 7.1 shows data from Chicago Public Schools indicating that with each failed course during ninth grade, the risk of dropping out increases.

Literacy

The adverse impact of poor literacy skill development becomes a critical risk factor at the middle school and high school levels. Eighth-grade students with reading achievement scores in the lowest quartile (< 25th percentile) are 3.5 times more likely to drop out than students in the next highest quartile (> 25th percentile), and they are 20 times more likely to drop out than students with above-average academic achievement (Alliance for Excellent Education, 2007). As discussed in Chapters 3 and 4 of this book, numerous research studies have established a link between literacy skills and other measures of school success, including high school graduation. Reading skills as early as kindergarten are correlated with later school achievement and behavior (McIntosh et al., 2006), and third-grade reading achievement is highly predictive of dropout (Hernandez, 2012). Torgesen (1998) showed that delays in reading achievement at the secondary level could be traced to delays in early literacy skill acquisition in preschool and elementary school. Because literacy is a critical factor related to school success and because delays become increasingly more difficult to remediate at the

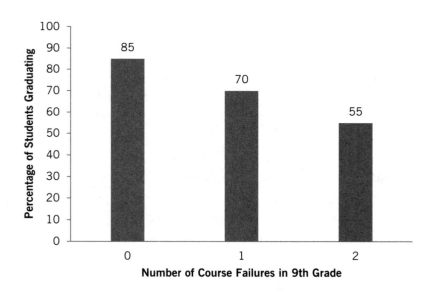

FIGURE 7.1. Percentage of students who graduate in 4 years by number of course failures in ninth grade. Based on Allensworth and Easton (2007).

secondary level, transition-year data for entering students, literacy achievement screening data, and students' English course grades are critical elements of effective early warning systems. Because literacy skills are required for school success across multiple courses, intensive and strategic evidence-based reading interventions, matched to individual student skills and informed by frequent progress data, are needed to maximize reading skills during the pivotal middle school and high school years.

Academic Achievement Assessments

State assessments and other academic achievement tests provide another measure of academic performance that can be incorporated into early warning systems. Generally, at the secondary level, there are many prior years of data to indicate academic risk. Unfortunately, academic risk factors often go undetected, particularly for new students, transient students, and well-behaved students who complete their class and homework assignments, so results of academic achievement assessments should not be overlooked. Students who perform at partially proficient levels or below proficiency standards should be flagged for further analysis so that these scores can be corroborated with other academic indicators.

Retention

Students who are held back in elementary school are at significant risk for eventual school failure. Retention in middle school and ninth grade poses an equally high risk that students will not finish high school. Alexander, Entwisle, and Horsey (1997) found that repeating a grade in elementary school increases the risk of dropping out of school to 64%, with retention in middle school grades increasing a student's risk for leaving school to 63%. In a more recent longitudinal study, Alexander, Entwisle, and Kabbani (2001) followed a sample of first graders in Baltimore through high school and extended these findings to show that retention in any grade had a negative impact on a student's odds of making it through the ninth grade but that retention in the middle grades posed even higher risks. For these reasons, effective early warning systems incorporate retention data as one risk indicator to monitor closely (Jimerson, Reschly, & Hess, 2008).

> **64% of students repeating a grade in elementary school eventually drop out of school. 63% of students held back in middle school eventually drop out (Alexander et al., 1997).**

Behavior

Most students check out of school emotionally before deciding to drop out, and there are numerous signs of disengagement at this stage. Attendance and behavior data are key indicators of disengagement. Social, emotional, and academic problems often manifest as behavior problems, and one of the primary ways they are identified and quantified at the secondary level is by ODRs. Typically, ODRs are associated with disruptive behavior, often classified as major behavior problems; however, schools are encouraged to also monitor minor behavior infractions, such as tardiness, absences, and dress code violations, to identify students at risk in the early stages of a problem. Proactive early warning systems monitor both minor and major ODR data to identify students in need of strategic intervention. In terms of tracking data, three minor ODRs are considered equal to one major ODR. When schools intervene at the minor level, a more critical level of student disengagement can be prevented. Conversely, when behavior problems escalate, other risk factors, including absences, poor course performance, suspension, and disengagement, are likely to intensify.

A lack of engagement with school can set in motion a cycle with other risk factors. A student who demonstrates attendance, academic, or behavior problems in middle school is at risk for continued problems and disengagement in high school. Upon transition to high school the student may be well behind in core academic skills, which adversely affects access to and comprehension of core content and the likelihood of earning the needed credits to graduate. This situation is likely to activate a spiral of negative attitudes toward school, decreased motivation, avoidant behaviors, and attendance problems. At this point, student engagement becomes an even more significant risk factor (Reschly & Christenson, 2006). This combination is compounded by a decrease in self-confidence and self-esteem as the gaps between students at risk and their peers widen. Simultaneously, as these challenges persist into tenth grade, the student often reaches the legal age for dropping out of school. Recognition of this negative spiral, depicted in Figure 7.2, and the prevailing lack of self-correction for these events in adolescence is key to understanding the need for schools to proactively intervene as early as possible (Jimerson et al., 2008).

Signs of Disengagement
- **Attendance problems.**
- **Inattention in the classroom.**
- **Poor relationships with teachers and peers.**
- **Inappropriate classroom behaviors.**
- **Poor social skills.**
- **Lack of involvement in classroom and co-curricular activities.**

EARLY WARNING SYSTEMS

Now that dropout prevention research has clearly identified high-yield indicators, early warning systems (EWS) can be implemented to detect these difficulties in the early stages. Frequent review and analysis of EWS data, combined with effective interventions that reduce the number of students exhibiting these difficulties as early in their middle and high school years as possible, holds great promise for high schools to improve their graduation rates.

- **Students enter secondary school with years of data indicating whether they are on track for graduation.**
- **Assessing risk across multiple variables allows more accurate predictions and targeted interventions.**

As one high-yield indicator is highly predictive of a student's risk for becoming off track for high school graduation, a combination of high-yield at-risk indicators significantly increases a student's risk for dropping out. EWS have been developed that are designed to detect a student's attendance, behavior, or core academic difficulties as soon as the student begins demonstrating

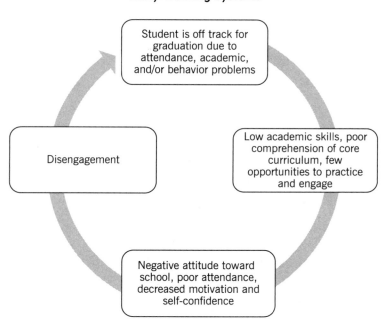

FIGURE 7.2. The negative spiral of disengagement.

problems. We now know that a student who misses 2 or more days of school in the first 20 days of a school quarter is at risk. We have state testing data at our fingertips, along with course performance and ODR data. Frequent review of these accessible sources of information can highlight students who are at risk in attendance, behavior, and course performance and allows for strategic interventions to be put in place.

Early Warning Systems within MTSS

The key to effective intervention is the link between early detection through EWS data and the implementation of MTSS. The goal of MTSS in dropout prevention is to respond to EWS data, utilizing a team approach and the problem-solving model to make data-based decisions regarding the type and intensity of intervention needed. Shown in Figure 7.3, the well-known MTSS triangle has been adapted to reflect on- or off-track status for high school graduation. Being on track for graduation corresponds to Tier 1, or universal instruction. The three risk factors discussed in this chapter and listed in Table 7.2 are defined as off-track indicators and are predictive of dropout. A student who is on track displays none of the risk factors listed in Table 7.2 and is more than 3.5 times more likely to graduate from high school in 4 years than students who are off track (Allensworth & Easton, 2005, 2007). In contrast, students with evidence of just one off-track indicator are at a higher risk for school failure (Balfanz, 2009; Balfanz & Herzog, 2005; Balfanz et al., 2007). Researchers have found that the off-track indicator more accurately predicts graduation than students' middle school achievement scores or their background characteristics (Allensworth & Easton, 2005).

FIGURE 7.3. On or off track for graduation.

For students who have been identified as off track for graduation, the problem-solving team continually monitors and evaluates their attendance, behavior, and course performance data to adjust the type and intensity of strategic supports in response to student needs. This process continues until the students are back on track academically and/or behaviorally, with evidence of increased school engagement. Interventions should be considered effective for students who move back on track for graduation *or* who show a decrease in risk level. Students who continue to be identified as off track for graduation may require more intensive dropout prevention efforts.

TABLE 7.2. Risk Factors

---

1. Attendance
   - ≥10% absenteeism
   - 2 or more absences in first 20 days of each school quarter

2. Academics
   - Course failure in English or math
   - GPA below 2.0
   - Failure to accrue enough credits for promotion
   - Failed state assessment

3. Behavior
   - Signs of disengagement
   - Multiple ODRs
   - Suspension
   - Social and emotional challenges

Early screening is pivotal to the accurate identification of all at-risk students to inform needed interventions prior to their transition years. Academic, behavior, and attendance data should be reviewed for all incoming students to identify those who display any off-track indicators. This will allow schools to prepare to intervene as early as possible, to develop systemwide interventions, and to allocate school resources effectively.

In middle school, EWS should be used to target students who show signs of disengagement or who fail their math or English courses. Students who display both disengagement and academic failure should be identified as at high risk. High school EWS pay close attention to attendance, particularly during the first 20 days of each quarter, the number of course failures, credits earned, and grade point average (GPA). For example, to calculate risk with course performance data, problem-solving teams should monitor data at the end of each quarter and academic year, particularly in ninth grade, and flag those students who fail even one course *or* earn a GPA of 2.0 or lower. Combining these two indicators, two or more F's in core academic courses or failure to earn enough credits to be promoted to tenth grade indicate that a student is at high risk of dropping out (Allensworth & Easton, 2005; Kennelly & Monrad, 2007).

Developing EWS

The National High School Center (NHSC), funded by a U.S. Department of Education grant, developed Early Warning Intervention and Monitoring System (EWIMS) data management tools that are available to educators and school districts online to download for free (*betterhighschools.org/ews.asp*), with training webinars on implementation of the EWIMS and EWS tools, as well as a discussion forum, technical support, and professional collaboration. The NHSC grant ended in 2013, but updated middle school and high school EWS tools are still available for free download through the American Institutes for Research (AIR; *www.early warningsystems.org*). There, schools can also find system design and implementation support.

The EWIMS tools assist staff at the district, high school, and middle school levels identify and focus on the same key indicators that research shows predict school success: attendance, course performance, and behavior. Students who have reached a specific benchmark in these areas are flagged to receive more intensive interventions and supports. Educators across the United States have been bridging the research-to-practice gap by using the EWIMS tools to monitor high-yield indicators and identify early dropout prevention needs. NHSC developed a seven-step process to support district and school implementation of EWS. A checklist of these steps is provided in Table 7.3, and a more complete description of these steps can be found in Appendix C in this book.

The EWS tools can be customized to fit the local context, and benchmarks and risk indicators can be modified based on ongoing longitudinal school and district data analysis. Data on absences, course failures, GPA, and course credits per grading period are readily available. Districts and schools can also import student-level data from other existing data systems. Beyond identifying students who are at risk, the EWS tools allow educators to document intervention options, assign and group students for intervention, and monitor student progress and RTI over time. In addition to tracking individual progress, the EWIMS

TABLE 7.3. Steps to Build an Early Warning System

1. Develop an EWS data collection system.
2. Determine on-track and off-track criteria for high school graduation.
3. Monitor attendance data monthly.
4. Monitor behavior data (ODRs and/or suspensions).
5. Monitor academic performance quarterly (course failures, GPA, credit accrual).
6. Identify and monitor students who are retained in ninth grade.

Note. Based on *www.betterhighschools.org.*

tool helps high schools and middle schools evaluate the success of current interventions and monitor potential system issues such as school culture, low achievement areas, and problematic courses that may contribute to dropout risk.

The EWS tools include four report options that clearly and graphically illustrate students' at-risk status at the individual and school levels. First, reports with customizable features can assist with current and longitudinal data analysis and data-based decisions. School-level reports summarize schoolwide trends in the key at-risk indicators. For example, they could show the number of students flagged for attendance problems during each grading period. Second, student-level reports provide information about which students in the school have been flagged for certain at-risk indicators. This not only provides a list of students who may be at risk but also highlights which indicators each student has met. Third, detailed student reports can be generated for individual students and include all of the student data that have been entered into the tool, including a history of interventions that have been implemented. Finally, the Student-Level Intervention Summary Report lists each student, his or her at-risk indicators, and the type(s) of intervention he or she receives. The case example in Box 7.2 illustrates how one high school uses the EWS tool.

SUMMARY

To increase every student's chance of graduating from high school, educators must attend to the early warning signs that predict a student's risk for disengagement, course failure, and behavior problems. By planning for transition years and routinely monitoring the big three—attendance, behavior, and course performance data—schools establish the best opportunity to mediate a student's risk for dropping out. Early identification and intervention that successfully moves a student from off-track to on-track status as early as middle school significantly increases the likelihood that he or she will graduate from high school on time.

BOX 7.2. Case Example: Mountainview High School's Early Warning System

Using the National High School Center's template (found at *www.betterhighschools.org/docs/EWStool.xls*), administrators at Mountainview High School developed a customized EWS tool to track relevant data on their first-year students. The template is set up to record student information, number of absences in the first 20 days of school, number of days absent by quarter, number of course failures, and GPAs. After this information is entered, the tool automatically calculates the data and creates a report listing each student, with an alert if the student is flagged for any of the at-risk indicators. An example of how these data may look in an Excel file is shown in Figure 7.4. This tool tracks attendance and course performance data, but it could easily be expanded to include credits earned and behavioral indicators.

According to first-quarter reports, 45% of ninth-grade students at Mountainview High School were identified as being at risk for off track, off track, or extremely off track for graduation, exhibiting at least one of the at-risk indicators. The problem-solving team examined the data for schoolwide patterns and found that 39% of students had failed Algebra I, indicating a need for improved core instruction in math and student intervention support. Additionally, they followed up on those individual students who had been flagged as at risk. Figure 7.4 shows examples of three students who met these criteria. Alex was flagged for absences in the first 20 days of school; however, the team learned that he had been sick in September, and there were no concerns about his attendance or course performance for the rest of the quarter. Deena was flagged due to a course failure in Algebra I, but she did not show signs of risk in the other indicators. The problem-solving team determined that Deena was struggling in a specific academic area, and she was offered additional math instruction support. Christopher was selected for more intensive intervention, as he exhibited problems with attendance and course performance, indicative of high risk for eventual dropout. The team took a comprehensive approach, providing academic support, promoting parent involvement, and initiating efforts to reengage Christopher in school activities. The following two chapters provide more information on how these interventions would be selected, implemented, and monitored.

BIG IDEAS

- Powerful signs of risk for dropout can be seen during the first year of middle school and of high school.
- The "big three" risk indicators are attendance, course performance, and behavior.
- EWS provide a systematic way to detect the presence of risk indicators so that interventions can be implemented as soon as possible for students who are not on track to graduate.
- The key to effective dropout prevention is the link between early detection through EWS data and the implementation of MTSS.

Relevant student data are recorded each quarter.

First Quarter Student Data							
Last Name	First Name	Student ID	Grade	First 20 Day Absences	Quarter 1 Absences	Number Course Failures	GPA
Austin	Alex	11111	9	2	2	0	3.0
Baltimore	Bryson	22222	9	0	3	0	3.2
Chicago	Christopher	33333	9	4	5	1	2.0
Denver	Deena	44444	9	1	2	1	2.5
Eugene	Emily	55555	9	1	4	0	2.9

The data for each indicator are automatically converted in MS Excel to show at-risk status.

First Quarter At-Risk Indicators									
Off-Track Alert	Last Name	First Name	Student ID	Grade	Flag for First 20 Day Attendance	Flag for Q1 Attendance	Flag for Course Failures	Flag for GPA
✓	Austin	Alex	11111	9	Yes	No	No	No
	Baltimore	Bryson	22222	9	No	No	No	No
✓	Chicago	Christopher	33333	9	Yes	Yes	Yes	Yes
✓	Denver	Deena	44444	9	No	No	Yes	No
	Eugene	Emily	55555	9	No	No	No	No

FIGURE 7.4. Sample EWS tool.

CHAPTER 8

Tier 2 and Tier 3 Problem Solving at the Secondary Level

There are many similarities between the problem-solving process at the elementary level and at the secondary level. In middle school and high school, efforts are still focused on identifying key risk indicators, attending to academic, social, and emotional needs in selecting effective interventions, ongoing progress monitoring, and data-based decision making. Of course, there are also fundamental differences in what dropout prevention methods look like when time is of the essence. In the secondary grades, there is a shift from prevention and early intervention at the early stages of a problem to a more critical level of care. The need for triage calls for changes in how screening and progress data are collected and interpreted and in how interventions are implemented. Box 8.1 presents a case example in ninth grade, a critically important year for intervention.

PROBLEM SOLVING

Over a decade of research has established that the middle school years, generally defined as fifth grade through eighth grade, play a major role in closing achievement gaps that are highly predictive of a student's likelihood to graduate from high school on time (Balfanz, 2009). Although these research findings are often surprising to educators and policy makers, they also present opportunities to successfully intervene with challenging middle school and high school populations. The literature provides clear direction and priorities for schools to develop proactive strategies to identify students at risk for school failure in the early stages of a problem. Special attention and planning for the transition years for both middle school and high school increases the potential for successful identification and intervention for students off track. The problem-solving model described in Chapter 5 of this book can be applied from prekindergarten all the way through graduation. At each age

BOX 8.1. Case Example: Ashley

Ashley was a 15-year-old girl enrolled in the ninth grade. She had engaged in frequent disruptive behavior at school, including verbal protests to teachers and fighting with peers, which resulted in multiple school suspensions. At a problem-solving team meeting, a review of ODRs showed that the majority of disruptive behaviors occurred during math and were reported by her algebra teacher. In an interview with the school psychologist, Ashley revealed that math was her most difficult subject and that she thought that her teacher did not like her. Ashley recalled that she had had a lot of difficulty with math last year, her eighth-grade year, but that extra teacher support and assistance helped her pass the course. Evaluation of Ashley's math skills with CBM showed significant gaps in basic math calculation skills, particularly fractions, percentages, and decimals. Ashley noted that she had never really learned how to do fraction and decimal problems, so she usually avoided or skipped those problems. Assessment results indicated the need for additional instruction and practice in basic math calculation skills, prerequisite skills for successful completion of algebra, and an assisted study hall with math support.

While speaking with the school psychologist, Ashley also revealed that she had recently experienced the sudden loss of a close relative. Feelings of grief were complicated by anger and fear, and Ashley reported difficulty sleeping and recurring nightmares about violent acts. It was clear to the team that Ashley would benefit from emotional and counseling support. She was referred to a bereavement group for children and began receiving cognitive-behavioral therapy for anxiety symptoms. The school psychologist also helped Ashley explore areas of personal interest to increase her engagement in school activities.

At follow-up, Ashley was benefiting from the additional math instruction and assisted study hall support to complete homework; her math grades improved, and she was now on track to receive her algebra course credit. Her math teacher observed more active participation, positive behaviors, and improved academic achievement in math. Ashley continued to address feelings of anxiety and to work on developing adaptive coping skills in therapy, and she found comfort and friendship through participation in the peer support group. She joined the high school chorus and was looking forward to traveling to a regional high school chorus competition.

Practical Application to Dropout Prevention

This case illustrates one way in which academic, behavior, and mental health concerns overlap. Externalizing behaviors, such as verbal protest or skipping class, often have underlying emotional causes. Feelings of anxiety were interfering with Ashley's ability to be present at school and ready to learn. Math calculation skill gaps were adversely affecting her performance in algebra. The school psychologist and problem-solving team realized that this was a complex problem that required academic, social, and mental health supports.

level, teams participate in an ongoing process of gathering and analyzing relevant data to identify and define the problem, explore alternative interventions, implement the selected intervention, and look at effects (Deno, 2012).

Identify the Problem

When MTSS is in place beginning in kindergarten, a wealth of student data is available by the time students enter middle school. Grade-level or problem-solving teams are encouraged to pay close attention to information about students' previous educational history, as these data are highly predictive of future school achievement and behavior. As described in Chapter 7, EWS that monitor attendance, grades, behavior, and standardized test results provide an efficient and systematic method for identifying middle school and high school students who are at risk. Universal screening of all students with CBM becomes less essential in middle and high school, as existing data are often sufficient to identify students in need of additional attention and support (Reed, Wexler, & Vaughn, 2012); however, selected use of CBM for academic screening is often applicable at the secondary level to quickly assess a student's skill level, as needed.

Academic Performance

At Tiers 2 and 3, CBM is still a valuable tool for measuring skill levels, designing instruction, and monitoring progress at the secondary level, because most middle and high school students who are identified as at risk demonstrate below-grade-level academic skills, even if the primary indicator is attendance or behavior. Selected CBM tools described in Chapters 4 and 5, including AIMSweb and EasyCBM, contain measures that are appropriate for secondary-level students, with standardized probes that assess skills from kindergarten through the eighth grade.

Attendance and Behavior

In addition to academic performance, attendance and behavior are key indicators of disengagement and dropout risk in middle and high school. Many of the assessment methods described in previous chapters of this book are well suited for problem solving at the secondary level as well.

One of these tools is the School-Wide Information System (SWIS; *www.swis.org*). Introduced in Chapters 4 and 5, SWIS is a valuable data management tool for monitoring attendance and behavioral data at the secondary levels. By using SWIS software to collect, summarize, and analyze ODRs, problem-solving teams have access to individual and schoolwide data to assist them in making accurate and responsive data-based decisions. Just as at the elementary level, SWIS data allow educators to identify the different types of problem behaviors that occur at the secondary levels, as well as the location, time, frequency, and participants involved. Examination of these variables helps educators determine the functions and scope of problem behaviors. For example, this analysis helps distinguish a system-level problem, such as the need for more active supervision in hallways or the cafeteria, from an individual behavior problem, such as a student disrupting a specific class. Understanding the topography, setting events, and frequency of problem behavior informs effective system-level solutions and individualized interventions. SWIS data can be generated and summarized in numerical reports and graphs to show the different outcomes listed in Table 8.1. An example is shown in Figure 8.1, in which ODR information is presented by type of behavior.

TABLE 8.1. SWIS Data Reporting Options

- Number of ODRs per month.
- Types of problem behaviors leading to ODRs.
- Locations of problem behavior events.
- Problem behavior events by time of day.
- Names of students receiving ODRs.
- CICO individual and schoolwide progress data.
- ISIS outcome data.

Define the Problem

The variables leading to a student's decision to drop out are complex, and the problem can rarely, if ever, be defined in simple terms. For example, EWS data can easily and promptly alert the problem-solving team to an attendance problem. This serves the important role of identifying the presence of a problem, but a more thorough definition of the problem,

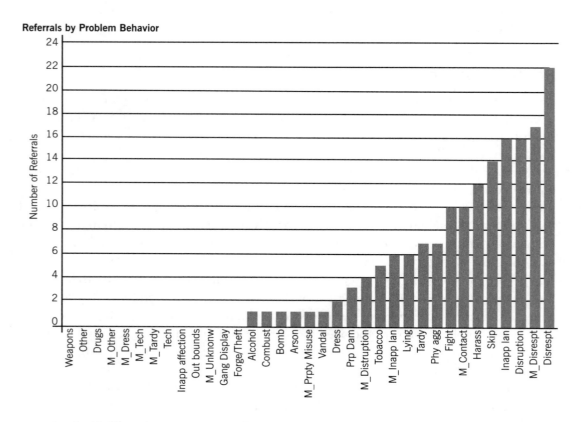

FIGURE 8.1. SWIS graph of ODRs by problem behavior. From School-Wide Information System (2012a). Copyright 2012 by Rob Horner. Reprinted by permission.

including the reasons behind the absenteeism, is needed to inform an effective intervention. As seen in Figure 8.2, there are numerous factors that contribute to poor attendance, and several of them can be present at once.

To better understand the problem and develop appropriate individual or systemwide strategies, problem-solving teams must gather relevant data on individual and institutional variables and supports. This review would likely

> **A thorough definition of the problem considers risk as well as protective factors.**

include an analysis of course performance data, behavior data, and other signs of engagement. Sometimes an analysis of these data reveals a classroom-level or system-level problem (see Box 8.2) that has significant implications for developing solutions.

Explore Alternative Interventions

With few school years remaining, time is of the essence in assisting students who are at risk in academic and/or behavior skills to get back on track to graduate with their freshman cohort. In the secondary grades, when skill deficits are often more pronounced, the emphasis of MTSS shifts from prevention to remediation.

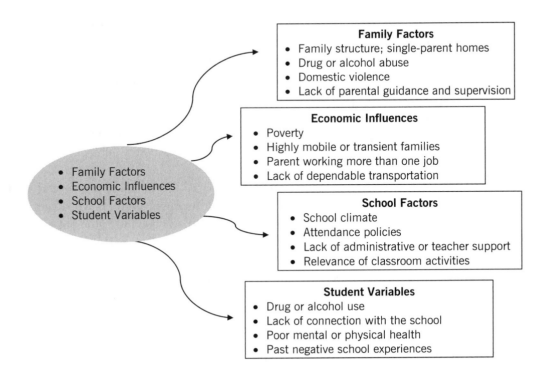

FIGURE 8.2. Reasons for attendance problems.

BOX 8.2. Courses That Fail Students

School teams are tasked not only with identifying individual students at risk for failing courses but also with identifying those courses that fail students. When data show that a particular course has a high failure rate, the course content, classroom setting, instructional practices, and grading procedures must be evaluated. To better understand what variables may be contributing to such a trend, school teams should consider the following questions:

- Is the curriculum evidence-based?
- Do we have evidence of treatment integrity of the instruction in these courses?
- Are students engaged in the current classroom instruction?
  - Attendance problems?
  - Time in instruction?
  - Behavior problems?
  - Assignments completed?
- What are the skill levels of students entering these courses? Do they have the prerequisite skills to access the course content?
- Are students failing all course content? Or certain sections of the course content?

Transition Year

Transition years into middle school and high school have been identified as the best opportunity for identification and successful intervention for middle school and high school students.

> **Attending to behavior challenges, engagement, and attendance with middle school students who are not yet failing coursework may be one key to reaching a group of students who may otherwise drop out later.**

Students with a history of behavior problems are more likely to fail during transition years and eventually drop out. Middle school presents as a window of opportunity to effectively intervene for students who show signs of poor behavior but are not yet failing academic subjects (Balfanz et al., 2007).

Researchers discovered that academic and behavior risk factors often converged as at-risk middle school students got closer to high school. Middle school students who eventually dropped out often showed one risk factor, an academic or behavior indicator but not both off-track indicators, in sixth grade (Balfanz et al., 2007). These findings suggest that attending to attendance, behavior problems, and school engagement as early as middle school for students not already failing core courses may be an important avenue of early intervention for this segment of the identifiable at-risk population. Box 8.3 emphasizes ninth grade as a make-or-break year.

Communication Is Needed to Bridge Transitions

Because it is difficult to intervene successfully in later high school years, the transition to high school is a critical period for proactive and intensive dropout prevention methods. One

---

BOX 8.3. Ninth Grade: A Make-or-Break Year

The transition to high school is often marked by declining school engagement and motivation, particularly for students with low academic performance (National Research Council, 2003). More students fail ninth grade than any other grade level, and retention in ninth grade is associated with greater risk for dropout (Herlihy, 2007). Referring to the on-track indicator, research has found that students performing in the highest quartile on eighth-grade achievement tests but who fall "off track" during their first year of high school are much less likely to graduate than students who scored in the lowest quartile on eighth-grade achievement tests but are "on track" at the end of ninth grade (Allensworth & Easton, 2007).

---

of the key findings from this research is that communication between middle school and high school teachers could reduce dropout risk (Neild, Balfanz, & Herzog, 2007). Since dropping out of school is not an event but a process that begins as early as prekindergarten, effective dropout prevention must incorporate a continuum of systems and services so that the needs of *all* incoming students are met. Communication of student progress data across buildings is crucial to supporting successful transitions and increasing student success. To accomplish this, transition-year teachers, such as eighth-grade middle school teachers and ninth-grade high school teachers, or fifth-grade elementary school teachers and sixth-grade middle school teachers, need to be aligned on academic, social, and organizational school issues (Akos & Galassi, 2004). A key component of this improved communication plan extends beyond teachers and includes students and parents. It is important to help all constituents, students, teachers, and parents, to understand the increased expectations and requirements of high school. Although this seems like a simple task, unfortunately, a lack of communication from building to building within a school district occurs frequently in both small and large districts. The Southern Regional Education Board (SREB) conducted research in more than 60 schools, and over half of the high school teachers surveyed reported never meeting with teachers from sending middle schools to discuss students or curriculum (Cooney & Bottoms, 2002).

> **Effective dropout prevention incorporates a continuum of systems and services requiring regular communication between school and home and among school buildings.**

Apply Selected Intervention

Because it is more difficult to predict dropout risk in later high school grades, it becomes more challenging to identify strategic interventions (Neild & Balfanz, 2006). Box 8.4 presents some of the challenges that educators face when interventions are needed at the high school level. Chapter 9 explores evidence-based interventions for secondary students in more depth. Credit recovery, alternative schools, and alternative pathways to graduation remain important dropout intervention strategies to support at-risk students in high school, and these options are discussed in more detail in Chapter 10.

BOX 8.4. High School Challenge

High school students at risk for dropping out often exhibit a discouraging combination of low academic skills and a long history of limited work completion and opportunities for practice. Teachers are faced with the challenge of simultaneously remediating skill gaps *and* providing students with access to courses needed to achieve high school credits. Also, it is more difficult to keep students engaged when skill gaps are significant.

At the elementary levels, students in need of additional support are provided with increasingly more targeted and intensive interventions until adequate progress is documented. As shown in the MTSS diagram in Chapter 3 (Figure 3.3), student data provide the pathway between tiers. In other words, intervention decisions are made on the basis of the student's response to the intervention, identified through progress monitoring measures. At the secondary level, current academic achievement and dropout statistics indicate that we are not closing the gap for many students. Research consistently shows that academic progress rates are slower at the secondary levels than in the early grades (Glover & Vaughn, 2010; Vaughn & Fletcher, 2012). Unfortunately, middle and high school students receiving additional Tier 2 or 3 supports are often multiple grade levels behind in academic skills and thus less likely than younger students to reach grade-level benchmarks in a single year. As a result, the first response may need to be more intensive for these students. Recent research suggests that flipping the tiers for secondary students and intervening more intensively at first to resolve problems as quickly as possible, rather than relying on low rates of progress to move from one intervention to a more intensive one, may be a more successful approach and a better allocation of resources. With this approach, a student's current performance, or risk level, would determine the level of intervention, even if it means beginning with focused, individualized Tier 3 services (Reed et al., 2012; Fuchs, Fuchs, & Compton, 2010; Vaughn et al., 2010). As in the medical model, patients with advanced illness are in need of more intensive treatment. Similarly, in high school we are past the prevention stage, and more significant support may be needed.

Look at Effects

Academic Progress Monitoring

Whereas numerous CBM are designed and normed for students through eighth grade, few academic progress monitoring instruments are designed specifically for the high school level (Reed et al., 2012). High schools will often use course grades and state assessment data to make Tier 2 and 3 academic programming decisions; however, these measures are not typically as reliable or sensitive to growth as CBM, rendering them less useful for making rapid, data-based decisions.

The on-track indicator, introduced in Chapter 7, is highly predictive of high school graduation and should be monitored across the tiers. In ninth grade, academic indicators that a student is on track for graduation include earning enough credits to advance to tenth grade and passing core courses (Allensworth & Easton, 2007; Balfanz et al., 2007).

Monitoring Behavior

The procedures for measuring a student's RTI that were described in Chapter 5, particularly DBRs and single-subject design, are applicable at the secondary level. Both of these assessment methods are data-driven approaches to looking at the effects of an intervention so that it can be adapted to the student's current skill or performance level and need.

SWIS data management systems can be used at this stage of the problem-solving model to monitor student response to Tier 2 interventions, such as CICO. The Individual Student Intervention System (ISIS) is another feature of SWIS designed to assist problem-solving teams in documenting and analyzing intervention outcomes. ISIS can be used to store and manage individual behavior plans, define behavioral measures, and organize data. Teams can track specific target behavior, such as asking for help and completing assignments, and generate reports to display progress. Figure 8.3 provides an example of an ISIS report that documents a student's response to an intervention in specific behavioral terms.

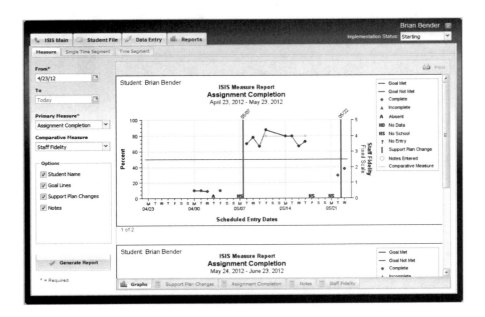

FIGURE 8.3. ISIS measure report. From School-Wide Information System (2012a). Copyright 2012 by Rob Horner. Reprinted by permission.

SUMMARY

As compared with the elementary grades, problem solving at the secondary level is characterized by differences in assessment methods and intervention planning. Still, MTSS and the problem-solving model, with an emphasis on student engagement and on-track status for graduation, serve as a best practice approach to dropout prevention in middle and high school. Particular attention must be given to students at risk during transition years, as the behavior, progress, and school experiences during these years are highly predictive of future outcomes.

BIG IDEAS

- At the secondary levels, the opportunity for prevention has passed, and time is of the essence.
- The transition year is a school's best opportunity to intervene.
- Proactive planning and effective identification of students at risk as they enter middle school and high school is a critical prevention component highly predictive of a successful response.
- In contrast to MTSS procedures in elementary school that focus on prevention by designing increasingly intensive interventions, middle and high school interventions are designed on the basis of current need and are likely to initially be more intensive.

CHAPTER 9

Middle School and High School Evidence-Based Resources

with Jennifer L. Robert

At the middle school and high school levels, time is of the essence, and the need for effective methods that achieve positive outcomes as quickly as possible is paramount. This chapter highlights the importance of focusing resources on the transition year for middle school and high school populations to maximize intervention opportunities and outcomes. A review of effective programs for dropout prevention—including multiple intervention strategies such as building social competency skills; providing academic support, life skills development, and family strengthening; and educating adolescents on issues such as violence and substance use—is provided. Middle school and high school evidence-based resources applicable at each tier are identified, with an emphasis on their relevance to dropout prevention. In the case example in Box 9.1, dropout prevention methods at the secondary level are highly focused on keeping students engaged and on track for graduation.

TIER 1

MTSS has been described extensively in previous chapters. Although the essential components of MTSS still apply at the secondary levels, there is wide agreement that the structural and organizational differences at the middle school and high school levels present unique challenges. For example, middle school and high school students may have four or five different teachers in one day, compared with only one or two teachers at the elementary level.

At the secondary level, the hallmark of Tier 1 continues to be a focus on prevention. High-quality, evidence-based classroom instruction is provided for all students to lower the

BOX 9.1. Case Example: Liam

Liam was a boy in the sixth grade who was struggling academically, socially, and behaviorally. He was reading at a fourth-grade level and demonstrated difficulty reading the social studies text and directions on worksheets. During reading activities, Liam became verbally disruptive by shouting out comments and often refused to participate in paired reading tasks. These behaviors frequently resulted in ODRs and removal from the classroom during reading. Although he gained peer attention by acting out in class, he did not have any close friends at school. Liam's attendance had been poor since the first grade, and he had moved four times since beginning kindergarten. He was retained in the first grade due to academic and social delays, and his teacher felt he was young for his grade. Since that time, he had not been able to catch up and acquire grade-level academic skills, and his mother reported that being held back a year hurt Liam's self-confidence.

The school's problem-solving team met to discuss Liam's strengths and weaknesses and intervention needs. After gathering information on school history, analyzing relevant data, and soliciting teacher and parent observations, the team developed a plan that targeted academic skills and engagement. Liam began receiving supplemental evidence-based reading instruction 4 days per week, in a small group with three other students. He also participated in a CICO intervention to increase attendance, home–school communication, and daily encouragement from a caring adult at school.

Practical Application to Dropout Prevention

Liam presented with four of the common characteristics of a child at risk for dropping out of school: retention, poor attendance, reading below grade level, and display of acting-out behavior. He was in sixth grade, which is a critical opportunity for preventing dropout risk factors from intensifying, while building protective factors such as reading skills and school engagement. Intervening at this point would have the most powerful effect on his middle school and high school years.

incidence of academic or behavior problems. Reed et al. (2012) described features of effective Tier 1 instruction that are applicable for all academic classes, including:

- Communicating clear expectations.
- Modeling expectations.
- Breaking the tasks into small steps and providing feedback.
- Planning for follow-up instruction.
- Engaging students.
- Providing distributed practice.
- Differentiating instruction.

Universal Screening

When MTSS universal screening methods are implemented districtwide, student performance is monitored three times per year in the areas of reading and math as they progress through elementary school. By the time they reach middle school and high school, students typically have a wealth of academic data to inform their current instructional levels. Although it continues to be important to assess and monitor student growth at the secondary levels, state tests or other standardized achievement measures, as well as failing grades, are tools for flagging students at risk. The research on dropout prevention shows that passing ninth-grade algebra and English classes places students on a positive trajectory for on-time high school completion. Conversely, not passing these classes is significantly correlated with negative outcomes and dropout risk. As identified in Chapters 7 and 8, state tests, failing grades, attendance rates, and ODRs are sensitive indicators of dropout risk at the secondary levels. Continuous attention to these signs at the secondary levels, particularly during transition years, allows educators to be responsive to student needs and to intervene at the earliest opportunity (Balfanz et al., 2007).

Effective Teaching Practices

Curriculum and classroom activities that are relevant, interesting, and motivating for students are shown to enhance student engagement (Christenson et al., 2008). Additionally, Kennelly and Monrad (2007) reported on the importance of school climate, academic rigor, effective teachers, and extended learning time as important best practices for increasing student engagement. A positive school climate helps foster student engagement and a smooth transition from middle school to high school. Academic achievement is maximized when teachers scaffold student support within an academically rigorous environment (Kennelly & Monrad, 2007). Cooperative learning groups, frequent opportunities to respond, and immediate feedback also foster high academic rigor, increase student participation, and provide ongoing feedback for teachers on students' level of understanding. Another key to increasing engagement and keeping students in school is highly qualified and effective teachers. Teachers who understand their subject areas and use strategies to reach all students are more likely to help close the achievement gap for students at risk (Kennelly & Monrad, 2007). The research on extended learning time has had mixed reviews; however, outcomes show that extended learning time should be devoted to intensive instruction that includes all of these effective teaching practices.

Reading Instruction

By the secondary level, fluent reading skills are required to access all academic course content. Despite the importance of acquiring proficient literacy skills in the elementary years, many of America's youth lack the necessary basic reading skills to keep pace with secondary-level academic demands. As a result, many students enter middle school and high school with reading skills far below those that are needed to complete the basic graduation requirements (Marchand-Martella, Martella, Orlob, & Ebey, 2000). Older struggling readers often fall further behind their peers and need to achieve large gains to close the achievement gap and meet grade-level benchmarks. Whereas many of these readers are victims of poor early reading instruction, others may have received relatively sound instruction during their early school careers but continue to have difficulty with reading fluency or comprehension (Roberts, Torgesen, Boardman, & Scammacca, 2008). Moats's (2001) research shows that at any age, poor readers as a group exhibit weaknesses in phonological processing and word recognition speed and accuracy. Further complicating the task for older readers is years of labored reading and limited knowledge of the vocabulary, sentence structure, text organization, and concepts of academic language. This leads to a decline in their reading comprehension over

As with interventions for younger students, struggling readers in high school benefit from systematic and explicit instruction in the fundamental skills involved in reading.

time that adversely affects course performance across content areas. Considerably less is known about effective interventions for older students with reading difficulties, particularly those who are English language learners (ELLs). For more information, see Box 9.2.

BOX 9.2. English Language Learners

In 2008, approximately 10.8 million children ages 5–17 in the United States spoke a language other than English in the home (Lawrence, White, & Snow, 2010). August and Shanahan (2006) reported that compared with their native English-speaking peers, language minority students on average have lower reading performance in English.

Using evidence-based interventions in an MTSS model with ELL students can have a significant impact on educational outcomes and reduce the number of students referred for special education. Many ELL students have floundered without appropriate intervention for a number of reasons, including low expectations for their academic performance. Before ELL students are recommended for Tier 2 or Tier 3 interventions, teachers need to ensure that they have had sufficient exposure to high-quality, appropriate teaching that includes academic English instruction in an environment that is supportive of their language development (Echevarria & Hasbrouck, 2009).

Recent research-based recommendations for instruction and academic interventions for ELLs have provided evidence to support the use of explicit, intensive instruction in phonemic/phonological awareness and phonics (Francis, Rivera, Lesaux, Kieffer, & Rivera, 2006). Once ELLs can recognize words automatically, the focus can shift to overall meaning. The research on instruction for ELL students has revealed that many of the same programs that have been found effective for English-only students are the same programs that are successful with ELLs (Slavin & Cheung, 2004; Calderon, Slavin, & Sanchez, 2011; Moats, 2001; Francis et al., 2006). The key features of effective reading instruction for all students are systematic and explicit direct instruction methods focusing on the five key components of reading identified by the National Reading Panel: phonemic awareness, alphabetic principle, fluency, vocabulary, and comprehension (National Institute of Child Health and Human Development, 2000). The ability to decode words is a necessary condition for effective comprehension among all students, yet not all students will develop these skills without explicit instruction. Reading intervention that is grounded in research helps older readers develop the skills they may have missed in primary grades and can bring them to grade level in 1–2 years (Moats, 2001).

Math Instruction

Mathematics achievement becomes highly predictive of on-time high school graduation at the secondary levels. Successful completion of algebra, a high school course requirement typically achieved in ninth grade, is highly correlated with on-time high school completion. Students who complete 2 or more years of high school algebra are more likely to attend college.

The National Mathematics Advisory Panel (NMAP; 2008) identified five strands that should be included in math curricula at all grade levels. These strands provide structure and organization for math instruction. All students need to be able to master the skills associated with each of these five strands in order to develop math proficiency at each grade level (NMAP, 2008). Brown-Chidsey and colleagues (2008) provide examples of skills for each strand. Students of all ages will benefit from effective teaching practices in math, including focusing on basic skills, explicit and systematic instruction, and frequent progress monitoring (Baker et al., 2002). NMAP (2008) showed that early intervention, best practice instructional methods, knowledge of how children learn, and a focus on effort, conceptual understanding, fluency, and automaticity are key components to effective math instruction.

Mentorship and Coaching

Mentoring can have benefits for at-risk youth and adolescents, including increases in positive self-concept, increases in educational attainment, decreases in drug and alcohol use, decreases in violence, increases in student engagement at school, and improvements in social relationships with parents and peers (Osterling & Hines, 2006). The research on mentoring has also demonstrated that the quality, consistency, honesty, and frequency of interactions in the mentoring relationship are critical variables determining whether the mentoring program will be effective. Training and supervision of mentors has been identified as another important factor in strong mentoring programs. All students in elementary school through high school can benefit from developing meaningful and positive relationships with caring teachers and adults in school and community settings, and these important connections enhance student engagement (Christenson et al., 2008). Additional strategies for behavioral support and skill development can be found in *Positive Behavior Support in Secondary Schools: A Practical Guide* (Young, Caldarella, Richardson, & Young, 2011).

TIER 2 AND TIER 3 TARGETED INTERVENTIONS

Hammond et al. (2007) identified several common factors in effective dropout prevention programs. These included multiple interactive strategies for building social competency skills, providing academic support, developing life skills, strengthening families, and educating adolescents about issues such as violence and substance use. The researchers identified 50 exemplar programs and strategies shown to be effective in reducing dropout rates (Hammond et al., 2007). Of these 50 programs:

- 60% included life skills development. Life skills development includes improving communication and social skills, critical thinking skills, conflict resolution, and resistance to peer pressure.
- 46% offered family strengthening strategies. These programs provided parent education on specific parenting skills, family management, communication skills, and strategies to support parents in providing academic assistance to their children at home.
- 26% provided academic support in the form of tutoring, computer labs, homework assistance, or experiential learning.
- 20% added a mental health component, such as cognitive behavioral therapy or individually designed behavior plans.

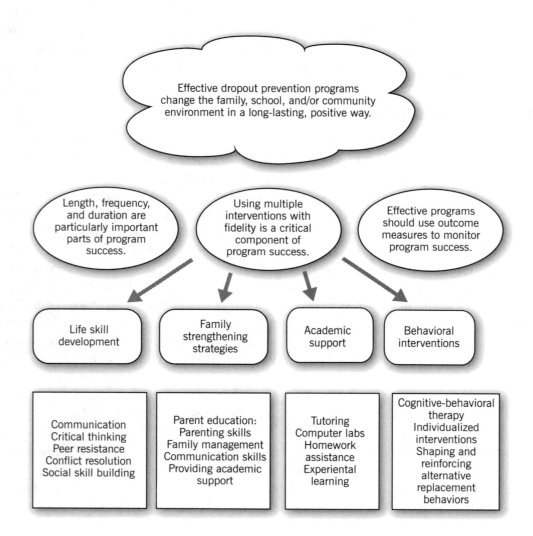

FIGURE 9.1. Characteristics of effective dropout prevention programs. Based on Hammond, Linton, Smink, and Drew (2007).

Figure 9.1 depicts the major components of exemplar dropout prevention programs based on the review of the research done by Hammond et al. (2007).

Academic Interventions

The research has shown that many of the interventions at the Tier 2 and 3 levels that are effective for elementary school students are also effective for students at the secondary level. Interventions such as direct instruction methods and fluency interventions for reading and math, described in more depth in Chapter 6, have proven to be effective with adolescents as well (Moats, 2001; Reed et al., 2012). Appendix B in this book provides a checklist of the key elements and steps in planning and implementing academic interventions at any age level.

Reading Interventions

Chapter 6 provided a sample of some of the evidence-based interventions that have proven effective for improving phonemic awareness, phonics, fluency, vocabulary, and comprehension. Many of those interventions are also successful at the secondary level. Research has shown positive reading outcomes for older students when provided explicit instruction in (1) word study strategies to decode words, (2) word meanings and strategies for deriving meanings of unknown words, and (3) comprehension strategy instruction (Reed et al., 2012). A widely researched intervention for increasing reading fluency is repeated readings. The research on repeated readings for secondary-level students has suggested that this method improves reading fluency but does not consistently lead to improvements in comprehension without the added component of a vocabulary intervention; as reading materials become more complex, fluency and comprehension are less closely related (Hawkins, Hale, Sheeley, & Ling, 2011). Hawkins et al. (2011) suggest that when doing repeated readings, secondary-level students should read longer passages (300–500 words) twice rather than reading 100- to 200-word passages four to five times. Based on previous research with secondary-level students, this may be more efficient and desirable for teacher and students, as well as helping to improve vocabulary and sight word accuracy. Secondary-level reading fluency interventions should incorporate a vocabulary and comprehension component, as research has shown a strong correlation between vocabulary knowledge and comprehension (Hawkins et al., 2011). One common vocabulary-building intervention is previewing vocabulary words prior to having students read the material. Using the reading material and vocabulary from daily instruction could potentially lead to gains not only in reading performance but also in content knowledge (Hawkins et al., 2011).

Math Interventions

The research on Tier 2 and 3 math interventions at the secondary level is scarce; however, just as with the reading interventions, many of the interventions listed in Chapter 6 are effective for use with students at the secondary level. In addition, problem-based learning, peer tutoring, and strategies to improve math problem solving have proven effective for secondary-level students. Problem-based learning is an instructional technique that allows students to work together on a complex math problem. Students seek solutions to real-world-based problems and then work to implement that solution (Bender, 2012). Peer tutoring has been researched as an effective math intervention for students of all ages and abilities. Bender (2012) described reciprocal peer tutoring as a partnership in which each student serves as both tutor and tutee. Peer tutoring provides detailed instructional guidance and immediate feedback. The peer-assisted learning strategy (PALS) is an example of an evidence-based peer-tutoring program. Other math problem-solving strategies include the use of diagrams and the STAR approach. STAR is a strategy that facilitates problem solving by sequencing the solution planning and calculation stages. This process includes the following four steps: (1) Search the problem; (2) translate the words into an equation in picture form; (3) answer the problem; and (4) review the solution (Bender, 2012). These strategies, as well as the evidence-based interventions listed in Chapter 6, will support student growth in math at the secondary level.

Behavioral Interventions

Check and Connect

Check and Connect is a structured mentoring program that closely monitors school performance indicators for students at risk for dropping out. Check and Connect aligns with current dropout prevention research recommendations; it focuses on increasing student engagement in school by targeting risk factors highly correlated with dropout, including poor academic progress, truancy, and discipline problems. A trained mentor is paired with a student who has been identified as at risk and serves as an advocate, resource broker, and bridge between home and school. The mentor agrees to build a long-term relationship with the student and is responsible for reviewing attendance, course performance, and behavioral data with the student on a regular basis; for providing feedback; for discussing educational goals; and for engaging the student in an ongoing process of problem solving (Pohl, 2013). The program uses mentoring, cognitive-behavioral strategies, and family-centered practices to build resiliency, competency, and home–school collaboration. A review of the research shows that the Check and Connect program works best when implemented with universal prevention efforts, such as smaller learning communities and positive behavioral supports (Stout & Christenson, 2009). A brief description of the steps for implementing Check and Connect is provided in Table 9.1.

> A study with at-risk high school students found that compared with controls, students enrolled in Check and Connect were one-third less likely to drop out (Sinclair et al., 2005).

Check-In, Check-Out

CICO is a Tier 2 behavior intervention that addresses mild problem behavior and is appropriate for elementary school as well as secondary students. At the secondary level, CICO combines social and academic supports for students demonstrating mild behavior problems.

TABLE 9.1. Check and Connect Implementation Steps

1. Determine indicators of student disengagement and establish criteria for intervention.
2. Identify participants based on indicators of risk for disengagement or dropout.
3. Select and assign mentors who are willing to be persistent and consistent.
4. Organize existing resources and intervention ideas.
5. Get to know students, teachers, and parents.
6. Use "check" procedures to monitor key indicators of dropout risk.
7. Implement "connect" interventions that are matched to student needs.
8. Strengthen the family–school relationship.
9. Monitor the fit between the student and the environment.
10. Provide mentor support and supervision.
11. Evaluate the fidelity and effectiveness of the program.

Note. Based on *http://checkandconnect.umn.edu.*

This is particularly important for middle and high school students, who need to experience academic accomplishments and avoid public displays of incompetence to stay engaged academically (Crone et al., 2010). CICO is recommended for students in their freshman and sophomore years of high school, when the transition can be overwhelming. The mere size of a high school, along with the increasing academic and social demands, can be difficult for students with higher academic and behavioral needs. The transition period is especially important to manage because students typically decide within the first 2 years of high school whether they will stay in school or drop out (McIntosh, Flannery, Sugai, Braun, & Cochrane, 2008).

The CICO program is structured to provide opportunities for positive reinforcement throughout the school day. Academic supports are designed to reduce barriers and facilitate competencies that result in passing grades, which in turn increase student engagement and motivation to stay in school. In addition to academic and social support, CICO develops resources that help students manage their workload, such as time management and problem-solving skills, early in their high school careers. This program is consistent with the research recommendations reported by Hammond et al. (2007), who emphasized the need for a combination of interventions for students at risk at the secondary level. The daily components of CICO follow:

1. Morning Check-In
   a. Typically takes place during morning homeroom period.
   b. Could be part of the morning routine for students participating in CICO.
   c. Students receive their daily progress note and discuss their goals for the day.
2. Feedback at the beginning and end of each class
   a. Student provides teacher with the daily progress note at the start of the period.
   b. Student collects the daily progress note at the end of the period and receives brief feedback about his or her performance during that class.

3. Check-Out
   a. Student checks out during afternoon homeroom and receives a few minutes of positive adult interaction, reinforcement for daily progress, and a reminder of goals.
   b. Students take their daily progress note home for parent review.
4. Home review
   a. A parent or guardian reflects on the child's daily progress and signs the daily progress note.

A sample CICO progress note is provided in Figure 9.2.

Student Name: _____   Date: _____

GOAL: **80%**

	Be Safe	Be Respectful	Be Responsible	Success comments; teacher initials
Homeroom	0 1 2	0 1 2	0 1 2	
Period 2	0 1 2	0 1 2	0 1 2	
Period 3	0 1 2	0 1 2	0 1 2	
Period 4	0 1 2	0 1 2	0 1 2	
Period 5	0 1 2	0 1 2	0 1 2	
Period 6	0 1 2	0 1 2	0 1 2	
Period 7	0 1 2	0 1 2	0 1 2	
Period 8	0 1 2	0 1 2	0 1 2	
Homeroom	0 1 2	0 1 2	0 1 2	
TOTAL				Total Percent:

PARENT SIGNATURE: _____

EXPECTATIONS	DEFINITIONS
Be Safe	• I kept my hands, feet, and objects to myself. • I used my materials and furniture correctly. • I used my laptop appropriately.
Be Respectful	• I used polite words to students and staff. • I raised my hand and waited to be called on.
Be Responsible	• I followed directions given to me. • I completed work that was assigned to me. • I used the hall pass quickly. • I had materials ready. • I wrote down assignments in my agenda. • I showed up to class on time. • My materials were organized.

FIGURE 9.2. CICO daily progress note.

Targeted Transition Interventions

Transition years from elementary school to middle school and from middle school to high school are times when students may question their own abilities and present with feelings of uneasiness and anxiety. As described in Chapter 7, these years are highly predictive of dropout, and therefore are prime intervention opportunities.

> **Student performance and attendance in ninth grade is highly predictive of on-time graduation.**

School Transitional Environment Program

The School Transitional Environment Program (STEP) is a dropout prevention strategy that assigns students to homerooms with other classmates participating in the STEP program. STEP is modeled on the theory that transitions to middle school and high school can be stressful events and can contribute to academic, behavioral, and social problems that lead to dropping out. The purpose of this transition intervention is to increase student engagement in school by making the transition from elementary school to middle school and middle school to high school less threatening. This is accomplished by increasing peer and teacher support, decreasing student anonymity, and enhancing students' ability to learn school rules and expectations. In addition to making changes in the school community, interventions actively involve the individual, peers, and parents (Gentle-Genitty, 2009). STEP has been proven effective in reducing dropout rates by:

- Building positive and trusting relationships with teachers.
- Involving parents in monitoring their children's progress and planning class schedules.
- Developing positive peer groups and social skills.
- Providing academic support.

Executive Functioning

Many students who struggle at the secondary levels have not acquired the attention, metacognitive, organizational, and study skills needed to complete school assignments independently and successfully. Research has shown that development of this cluster of frontal lobe skills, classified as executive functions, varies widely throughout childhood and adolescence. At the same time, research has shown that the development of executive functions is highly correlated with future academic achievement, school, work, and life success. Often students with global or discrete delays in executive functions appear capable to parents and educators, but they have a long track record of missed assignments and failed tests. They are often asked to redo class assignments and assess-

> **Teaching students with failing grades to monitor their own academic process can increase learning and result in higher levels of achievement (Anderson et al., 2008).**

ments, which results in feelings of frustration and disappointment. Unresolved, these feelings often manifest as internalizing behaviors, such as school avoidance, absenteeism, anxiety, or depression symptoms, and/or externalizing behaviors, such as emotional outbursts, noncompliance with adult requests, and class disruptions (Anderson, Munk, Young, Conley, & Caldarella, 2008; Dawson & Guare, 2012).

Recognition that all students benefit from explicit instruction in organizational, note-taking, study, and metacognitive skills to enhance learning and task performance is an important step in designing effective core instruction across all classes. For students who require additional assistance, direct study skills instruction, active teacher involvement in keeping track of assignments and course status, and weekly monitoring of assignment completion are proving to be important interventions to facilitate executive functioning. Dawson and Guare (2012) provide multiple examples of evidence-based coaching methods that are helpful for improving time management and organizational skills in students with executive function skill delays. Additionally, supervised study halls in subject areas of need, such as a math teacher-directed study hall for students who have difficulty completing mathematics assignments on time, make teachers available for instruction and assistance within the school day. This provides opportunities to preteach and reinforce academic skills before students fall too far behind their classmates.

Community Collaboration
- **School-to-work programs**
- **Drug abuse prevention programs**
- **Teen parenting programs**
- **After-school centers**
- **Parental involvement programs**

Community Collaboration

Initiatives that support dropout prevention efforts through community partnerships include school-to-work programs, drug abuse prevention programs, teen parenting programs, after-school centers, and parental involvement programs.

School-to-Work Programs

School-to-work programs involve rigorous classroom instruction that is linked to workplace experiences and that provides students with the skills needed to identify and prepare for careers. Work-based learning, such as job shadowing and internships, are also essential components of school-to-work programs. The benefits of these arrangements include developing job skills, increasing self-esteem, giving students a sense of ownership over their learning, and keeping students engaged in school. For more information about these programs, see Chapter 10.

Drug Abuse Prevention Programs

Findings from cross-sectional studies provide conclusive evidence of higher rates of cigarette, alcohol, marijuana, and other drug use among dropouts and students at risk for dropping out compared with in-school students or graduates (Townsend, Flisher, & King, 2007).

LiFE SPORTS.

The LiFE SPORTS (Learning in Fitness and Education through Sports) program targets youth workers and parents, as research indicates that drug use by teens is influenced by those closest to them (Wade-Mdivanian et al., 2012). LiFE SPORTS provides 4 weeks of summer camp and year-round sports clinics focused on increasing social competence. Sports and physical activities are used as avenues to reach youth and to teach critical life skills, including raising awareness about the dangers of drug abuse. Coaches and staff are trained in the life skills they are teaching.

YOUTH TO YOUTH INTERNATIONAL

Youth to Youth International is a "community-based drug prevention and youth leadership program that utilizes the voices and leadership of youth to reach other youth and deter risk-taking behavior" (Wade-Mdivanian et al., 2012, p. 18). This program is working to grow by recruiting youth teams from high schools throughout the country. High schools that are invited to participate select a team of five to ten teens and at least one adult advisor. These teams then participate in training provided by Youth to Youth International, which works closely with the schools to develop a strong team. Students learn about prescription drugs, and the groups are trained in delivering the "pHARMING effects" presentation. These teams then implement programs in their own communities.

Teen Parenting Programs

The majority of teens who give birth before age 18 are less likely to complete high school; therefore, they are at a disadvantage in the job market and are more likely to raise their children in poverty (Rowen, Shaw-Perry, & Rager, 2005). Mentorship is an evidence-based intervention that provides guidance, emotional support, and goal-setting assistance for pregnant and parenting teens. The National Committee for the Prevention of Child Abuse program has adapted a set of procedures for mentors when working with pregnant and parenting teens:

1. Meet with the students often.
2. Encourage them to stay in school.
3. Support them with personal issues.
4. Provide them with community resources.
5. Suggest they engage in extracurricular activities such as cultural events or family outings.
6. Support the youth in developing conflict-resolution and good decision-making skills by modeling these behaviors.

Coca-Cola Valued Youth Program

Components of Teen Parent and Pregnancy Programs

- **Experienced mentor**
- **Strong role model**
- **Consistency**
- **Parental guidance and support**
- **Communication workshops**
- **Parenting classes**
- **Peer support**
- **Counseling**

The Coca-Cola Valued Youth Program (VYP) incorporates interventions that affect the whole adolescent, including intensive tutoring that focuses on academic achievement, individualized social services in after-school and extended-day learning centers, and family involvement. The purpose of this program is to increase self-esteem and school success, thereby decreasing the likelihood of dropout. Participants in this program are trained to tutor at-risk elementary school students. They participate in special tutoring classes and field trips and are recognized as role models. The program has demonstrated effectiveness in increasing students' sense of pride and self-awareness, increasing school attendance, and decreasing discipline problems (Lehr, Johnson, Bremer, Cosio, & Thompson, 2004).

Clinical and Mental Health Support

Cognitive-behavioral therapy (CBT) is used to change behavior through the active engagement of clients in understanding and taking control of their thoughts, feelings, and behaviors (Mayer, Van Acker, Lochman, & Gresham, 2009). The research on depression, anxiety, and poor anger management with adolescents suggests that certain family and community background factors such as neighborhood problems, low socioeconomic status, and minimal social support at home have a direct effect on students' behavior and engagement in school (Mayer et al., 2009). CBT is an important evidence-based component of a multidimensional intervention package that helps keep students engaged in school and decreases the risk of dropping out. Behaviors associated with depression, anxiety, and poor anger management are some of the most common among at-risk middle school and high school students. Addressing these behaviors plays an important role in helping students achieve success in school. Table 9.2 provides a brief list of some of the evidence-based CBT programs for adolescents.

Intervention Integrity

A focus on evidence-based practices in school has become more prevalent over the past 10 years, and as schools are implementing MTSS, the importance of ensuring treatment integrity of selected instruction and interventions has gained attention. Treatment integrity is the degree to which an intervention is implemented as planned. Sanetti, Gritter, and Dobey (2011) reported in their research that treatment integrity data are necessary for evidence-based interventions because they allow (1) researchers to draw valid conclusions about intervention effectiveness, (2) consumers to know whether a selected intervention can

TABLE 9.2. Evidence-Based CBT Programs

Coping Power Program

This is a multicomponent intervention program that addresses emotional awareness, relaxation training, social skills enhancement, positive social and personal goals, and peer pressure. There are a youth component and a parent component to this program, which can be delivered at the same time.

Anger Coping Program

This is an 18-session group intervention for aggressive youth. The program is designed to teach and reinforce goal setting, anger management, perspective taking, awareness of physiological arousal and anger, and social problem solving.

Fast Track

Fast Track is a comprehensive approach for reducing chronic and severe conduct problems, focused on developing cognitive skills and changing patterns of interaction among members of the student's social fields to promote consistent expectations for behavior. Fast Track incorporates five components, including parent training, home visits, social skills training, academic tutoring, and classroom interventions, such as positive behavior plans.

The Coping Cat and Second Step interventions described in Table 6.8 also have versions that are appropriate for students at the secondary level.

Note. Based on Mayer et al. (2009).

be adapted to their setting, (3) practitioners to ensure the intervention is implemented as intended in an applied setting, and (4) teams to evaluate the effectiveness of the intervention (p. 72). Research has shown that higher levels of treatment integrity lead to better intervention outcomes. Unfortunately, despite the fact that treatment integrity data are key to assessing the effectiveness of an intervention, they are rarely assessed in school. Treatment integrity checklists, along with professional coaching support, are examples of methods used to enhance and monitor treatment integrity.

Professional Development

To provide teachers with evidence-based strategies they could use to improve instruction, changes to the way professional development is delivered in schools is crucial. Chapter 6 explains the importance of ongoing professional development to train teachers in how to select appropriate interventions and deliver them with fidelity. Aligning professional development and training to priority schoolwide academic goals and conducting teacher observations in a collaborative, professional coaching model are two ways in which effective teaching practices can be taught. Many teachers in our schools are experts in particular areas of education, behavior, and child development. Empowering teachers by providing them with opportunities to share their knowledge and lead trainings in their schools can also lead to greater consistency and follow-through with implementation of best practices. Professional development should be ongoing and long-term, which is more likely to promote lasting, positive changes in teacher knowledge and practice. Systematic and explicit instruction, with modeling and feedback, are recommended for professional development. These learning opportunities should be built into the regular school schedule, with an emphasis on new research and practices as well as opportunities to implement and reflect upon new ideas (Biancarosa & Snow, 2006).

SUMMARY

Because there are often multiple reasons that students drop out of school, the research on dropout prevention at the secondary level recommends multiple intervention strategies. It is essential that we identify students off track for graduation as soon as possible to provide them with resources, support, and interventions that are evidence-based and that focus on reengagement with school. Model programs and interventions that include academic support, social competency and life skills development, and family involvement are highly recommended for secondary-level interventions. Professional development and treatment integrity of interventions are critical aspects for sustained systems and student growth.

BIG IDEAS

- As at the elementary level, dropout prevention in secondary schools involves high-quality Tier 1 academic and behavioral instruction, early identification of dropout risk, and targeted interventions to reduce risk and reengage students in school.
- Student engagement for middle and high school students can be enhanced through a positive school climate and classroom instruction and activities that are relevant, interesting, rigorous, and motivating.
- In addition to reading and math support, Tier 2 and Tier 3 interventions that build executive functioning skills, such as planning, organization, self-regulation, and time management, are important for secondary students.
- Effective Tier 2 and 3 interventions are often needed to provide social and mental health support. Evidence-based approaches include mentoring, building positive relationships with adults and peers, family strengthening strategies, drug abuse prevention and teen parenting programs, and cognitive-behavioral therapy.
- Transition years are the most important times for identifying students at risk and providing needed supports.

CHAPTER 10

The Role of Technical Education, Alternative High Schools, and Postsecondary Options in Dropout Prevention

National dropout statistics and the individual stories of so many American youth demonstrate that the traditional public school does not meet the needs of all students. Fortunately there are more and more alternatives for students who are not successful in a traditional school setting. Matching student goals with relevant educational opportunities has been shown to enhance school engagement, graduation rates, and future success. There is great variety in the types of alternative schools available today, including whom they serve, what subject areas or type of training is provided, and how and where the curricula are delivered. Of course, there is also great variety in the outcome measures associated with alternative schools and programs. In terms of preventing dropout, the research findings are mixed. Not surprisingly, successful outcomes depend on the unique characteristics and quality of the programs. The models described in this chapter have successfully increased graduation rates and fall into three broad categories: career and technology education (CTE), alternative school programs for students at risk, and postsecondary options. The case example in Box 10.1 portrays a student who benefited from one of these programs.

CAREER AND TECHNOLOGY EDUCATION

With changes in the global economy and workplace, academic skills and vocational skills are no longer seen as distinct, or separate, areas. For many students, an integrated model that emphasizes work skills without compromising academic coursework is beneficial for a

---

BOX 10.1. Case Example: Jade

Jade was a 10th-grade student who had been identified as being off track for high school graduation. She had experienced a difficult transition to high school, and over the past year she had become increasingly disengaged from school. Her academic achievement had been in the low-average range since elementary school. Jade repeatedly told her mother and friends that she hated school and wanted to drop out. According to her mother, it took hours each night to try to keep Jade motivated and on task with homework assignments. She was also concerned about Jade's mood and lack of motivation. Although Jade had no history of behavior problems at school, teachers described her as a daydreamer who was often inattentive in class and needed direct support to follow directions and complete tasks. She had a few friends but no strong connections with teachers. At home, Jade liked to cook and watch cooking competition shows on television.

To make school more interesting and relevant for Jade, the problem-solving team recommended that she enroll in culinary courses offered through the career and technical education program at the high school, while keeping core academic courses in her schedule. Jade's advisor also helped set up a job-shadowing experience with a local caterer. This experience provided a positive mentoring relationship and important lessons about work-related behavior and specific culinary skills. Jade's orientation began to shift to future goals for college and career, and she was hopeful that the job shadowing experience would turn into a summer internship opportunity.

Practical Application to Dropout Prevention

In high school, dropout prevention efforts always aim to increase student engagement, among other protective factors, and may offer alternative options for meeting graduation requirements. Jade felt disconnected and unhappy at school and expressed a desire to drop out. Work-based learning and community mentorship helped to make school feel more meaningful and rewarding. At the same time, it helped Jade understand the relevance of academic achievement to her future aspirations.

---

successful school-to-career transition. To address the need to better prepare students for postsecondary schooling and careers, Congress passed the School to Work Opportunities Act (STWOA) in 1994. The program was meant to improve students' knowledge, skills, and abilities to be successful in postsecondary education and employment by making school experiences more relevant and meaningful to students' future careers. School-to-work systems create links between academic and vocational classes, secondary and postsecondary education, and school and work environments. With these educational reforms in the 1990s came a variety of CTE programs. Research has found that some CTE, or school-to-work, programs are associated with improved attendance (Kemple, 2001; Institute on Education and the Economy, 2001) and high school completion rates (Plank, DeLuca, & Estacion, 2005; Kemple, 2001; Institute on Education and the Economy, 2001), increased likelihood of college attendance and postsecondary employment (Public Policy Institute of California, 2004), and higher earnings (Kemple, 2008). The National Dropout Prevention Center cites CTE as one among 15 strategies for preventing dropout.

Work-Based Learning

Internships, job shadowing, and service learning opportunities provide students with relevant ways to learn about a particular industry or occupation while engaging in meaningful community service. Students are more likely to become actively involved in their educations when they are able to apply what they are learning in the classroom to real-world settings, making high school courses seem more pertinent to their personal interests and future aspirations. An important benefit of internships, job shadowing, and service learning is broader exposure to positive role models, with added opportunities for students to build relationships with adults and make connections to the community. Forming relationships with teachers, coaches, and mentors based on mutual job and career interests or through public service enhances engagement in the learning process (Christenson et al., 2008).

> **Relevant and personally meaningful curricula and educational activities enhance student engagement.**

Career Academies

One model for delivering CTE is a school-within-a-school program. Career academies typically follow this model, in which a relatively small group of students and teachers stay together for several years and the high school curriculum is organized around a specific subject area or career (e.g., health, finance, computer technology). Career academies emphasize work-related knowledge and skills through internships and mentorships, while preparing students for postsecondary education (Public Policy Institute of California, 2004).

Research has shown that enrollment in a career academy is associated with better attendance, increases in the number of credits earned, and sustained gains in earning (Kemple, 2001, 2008). Outcomes related to high school graduation are mixed; some studies have found a significant decrease in the dropout rate (Kemple, 2001), whereas other results did not indicate significant improvement in graduation rates for students attending career academies (Kemple, 2008). Together, the evidence suggests that career academies, like other high school programs that provide students with work-related experiences, can help students acquire needed knowledge and skills for the labor market and ease the transition from school to work, while maintaining academic and postsecondary education goals. More work is needed to fine-tune career academy programming and extend its benefits through high school graduation.

Benefits of CTE

Researchers have identified several positive outcomes associated with CTE, which are listed in Table 10.1. In a study published by the National Research Center for Career and Technology Education, researchers found that a balance between CTE and academic courses was associated with lower dropout rates (Plank et al., 2005). Specifically, for students under the age of 15 at the beginning of ninth grade, a ratio of 1:2 CTE to core academic courses

TABLE 10.1. Potential Benefits of Career and Technical Education

- Enhance students' motivation and academic achievement.
- Increase personal and social competence related to work in general.
- Gain a broad understanding of an occupation or industry.
- Explore and plan for future career options.
- Acquire knowledge and skills related to the workplace in general and specific occupations.

Note. Based on Schargel and Smink (2001).

was beneficial for high school completion. For students who enter high school at age 15 or older, the relationship between course ratio and high school completion was not as powerful, suggesting that other factors better predict high school graduation for this population of students.

CTE can enhance a student's understanding of a particular career or industry and can also contribute to individual career planning. These experiences can also build personal competence in the workplace, as well as professional knowledge and skills related to a specific job. Finally, research suggests that students who participate in CTE show an increase in motivation and academic achievement (Schargel & Smink, 2001).

ALTERNATIVE SCHOOLING

Alternative schooling can be an option for many students, but it commonly serves middle and secondary students who are at risk for school failure due to poor grades, insufficient credits, truancy, or disruptive behavior or who are unable to attend a traditional school due to parenting or other family responsibilities. Students who have been suspended, expelled, or in the juvenile justice system can also be supported by alternative schools. At the same time, not all alternative schools are designed for students who are at risk for dropping out. Quality alternative school settings have small class sizes, individual attention, and support services. Although the aim of these programs is to reconnect students with their educations and with adults who will help them be successful, they also run the risk of disconnecting students from their mainstream schools, organizations, teachers, and peers. Considering the central role that student engagement plays in promoting school completion, careful attention and planning are needed to avoid this pitfall.

> **The objective of alternative schooling programs is to reconnect students with their educations, not disconnect them from their schools, communities, or peers.**

Alternative schooling can take many different forms, depending on local needs and resources. Generally, alternative *schools* are housed in a separate facility from the regular school, and alternative *programs* are housed and operated within regular schools. Table

10.2 describes the broad categories into which alternative schools and programs typically fall. In 2008, results of the Survey of Alternative Schools and Programs revealed that 64% of public school districts nationwide reported offering at least one alternative school or program for at-risk students, representing over 10,000 district-administered programs and serving 645,500 students (National Center for Education Statistics [NCES], 2010). Approximately one-third of school districts, and an even higher percentage in urban areas, do not have the capacity to serve the number of students in need of alternative programs (National Center for Education Statistics, 2010). This suggests that despite growth in the number and types of alternative services available for high-risk students, these programs do not reach all who need them.

TABLE 10.2. Alternative Schooling Models

School within a school

In this model, a separate classroom or wing provides an alternative environment, curriculum, and staff within a traditional school.

School without Walls

These programs provide training in various settings within the community.

Residential school

This is typically designed for students in need of social–emotional support, counseling, and/or specialized educational programs.

Separate alternative learning center

Delivered from a location outside of the traditional school, these programs provide training in specialized job areas or parenting. These centers may be located in businesses, universities, or other community settings.

Summer school

Summer school can be an opportunity for students to get caught up on credits or to pursue special interests, such as math or science.

Schools of choice

Students who wish to focus on a specific area of the curriculum can choose to attend magnet or charter schools. They offer specialized and often intensive learning opportunities, usually with specialized staff.

Last-chance or continuation schools

These programs are designed to provide continued education for students who are no longer attending the traditional school. Also known as dropout recovery programs, these schools provide flexible learning opportunities, accommodating barriers such as transportation, parenting responsibilities, health problems, or economic hardship experienced by many students who are already disconnected from school.

A key element of alternative schooling seems to be collaboration with outside agencies or organizations. According to NCES data (2010), 80% of districts reported collaborating with the criminal justice system, and other common partners include mental health agencies, child protective services, police departments, substance abuse clinics, and community organizations such as mentoring, job placement, or crisis intervention centers. Most of these programs are removed from regular schools, offered in separate facilities such as juvenile detention centers, charter schools, and community centers, and use distance education to deliver instruction. For specific examples, Table 10.3 lists selected evidence-based programs that have been shown to have a positive effect on staying in school, progressing in school (i.e., credit accrual), or completing school. It is important to note that some programs yield higher rates of high school graduation with a diploma, whereas others demonstrate a greater likelihood that participants will complete school by earning a General Education Development (GED) credential but have a lower chance of completing school with a diploma. Still

TABLE 10.3. Examples of Evidence-Based Alternative Education Programs

Talent Development high schools

The Talent Development model is a comprehensive school reform initiative that incorporates several research-based dropout prevention strategies: small learning communities with interdisciplinary teacher teams, research-based core curricula, targeted academic support, specially designed professional development, and parent and community involvement. Evidence suggests that this model is associated with improvements in credit accrual, attendance, and grade promotion (Kemple & Herlihy, 2004; Kemple, Herlihy, & Smith, 2005).

Job Corps

Job Corps is an education and vocational training program that provides individualized academic instruction and vocational training, as well as residential and social services and job placement assistance. Participants in this program have been found to be more likely to complete school by earning a GED (Schochet, Burghardt, & Glazerman, 2001).

Talent Search

Talent Search is a federal program that offers services to middle and high school students from low-income and first-generation college families. The program provides academic advising and tutoring, study skills training, career development, mentoring, college campus visits, and assistance applying to college and securing financial aid. A study on the effects of Talent Search found that participants had significantly higher school completion rates than students in a comparison group (Constantine, Seftor, Martin, Silva, & Myers, 2006).

High School Redirection

High School Redirection is an alternative high school program for students who are at risk for dropout. The High School Redirection curriculum focuses on academic skill development, including intensive reading intervention, credit accrual, and teachers as mentors. Schools also offer extracurricular activities and onsite child care. Although there is no evidence of a significant impact on school completion, the High School Redirection model has been shown to have positive effects on staying in school and progressing in school (Dynarski & Wood, 1997).

BOX 10.2. What Does GED Stand For?

- The General Education Development program provides an alternative option for students to earn a high school credential other than a diploma; this credential has become known as the GED. Many students who are at high risk for dropping out or who have already dropped out of high school choose to earn a GED certificate through "last chance" schools or adult education (Association for Career and Technical Education, 2007). Approximately 12% of high school credentials awarded each year are GEDs (Heckman, Humphries, & Mader, 2010).

- *Myth*: GED stands for General Equivalency Degree and is equivalent to a high school diploma.

- *Fact*: The GED is named for the General Education Development battery of tests, first introduced in 1942 for World War II veterans, and is not equivalent to a traditional high school diploma. On average, a student with a GED earns lower wages, works fewer hours, and is less likely to continue with postsecondary education than a student with a diploma (Heckman et al., 2010).

---

other programs do not differentiate between the two credentials for the purpose of research studies. For more information about why these distinctions matter, see Box 10.2.

POSTSECONDARY OPTIONS

Currently, almost two-thirds of jobs require skills associated with some postsecondary education, and many students are motivated to continue their educations beyond high school in order to improve their career opportunities and earning potential, although the transition is often difficult (Valentine et al., 2009). Postsecondary institutions, particularly community and technical colleges, are reporting a large percentage of students who fail college placement tests and need to take remedial courses (Valentine et al., 2009). This lack of sufficient readiness for postsecondary education is a drain on family, state, and postsecondary system resources. A natural extension to an increase in high school graduation rates is an expansion of postsecondary options, such as 2-year degrees and specialized certificates and degree programs, as well as access to college courses in high school, that lead to viable future educational and career goals.

Partnerships between high schools and community colleges in a credit-based program have the potential to improve retention and completion by preparing high school students for more academically rigorous settings and helping them focus on a major field of study. Such arrangements also provide high school students with the opportunity to accelerate learning through access to college courses, as well as the possibility for early completion of high school course credits and acquisition of college credits. Global and state university online courses provide an excellent opportunity to craft an individualized educational program of relevant high school and college-level courses.

Several models of transition programs exist to help students who are entering postsecondary institutions, transferring from 2-year to 4-year colleges, or transitioning from college to career. As an intervention to improve postsecondary performance, retention, or completion, these programs have mixed research evidence. Studies suggest that comprehensive interventions aimed at providing transition support may have positive short-term effects on school performance; however, it is difficult to determine which components of these programs contribute to positive outcomes (Valentine et al., 2009).

CHARACTERISTICS OF SUCCESSFUL PROGRAMS

With all of the variety in alternative schooling, there are several elements that seem to be common to the most successful CTE and alternative programs. Notably, these are many of the same factors emphasized throughout this book as having a positive impact on school completion, such as student engagement, relationship building, flexibility and differentiation of instruction, and family involvement. The American Institutes for Research conducted

> **Many of the qualities of successful CTE and alternative schooling programs are the same factors that enhance student engagement and graduation in all school settings.**

a study on effective alternative education programs for students in kindergarten through the twelfth grade (Quinn & Poirier, 2006). Findings revealed some common features in the implementation and functioning of these programs, shown in Table 10.4.

Student Engagement

Disengagement from school—from peers, teachers, and the curriculum—is a commonly cited reason that students drop out of school. CTE provides learning experiences that are applicable to the real world and relevant to students' future careers. "For many students, applying academic and technical skills to real-world activities, using computers and other tools, and being able to see how their learning is related to the world of work make CTE classes more interesting and motivating, and more educationally powerful than standard academic classes" (Advisory Committee for the National Assessment of Vocational Education, 2003, p. 2). Students in CTE programs are often involved in career and technical student organizations (CTEOs), which provide co-curricular activities, such as regional competitions, and help build leadership and other work skills. The various approaches to

---

TABLE 10.4. Evidence-Based Characteristics of Effective Alternative Programs

• Small class size	• High expectations of students
• Personalized school environment in which students are part of the decision-making process	• Application process for acceptance to the program
• Flexibility	• Special teacher training
• Effective classroom management	• Parent and community involvement
• Administrative support	• Collaboration

Note. Based on Quinn and Poirier (2006).

alternative schooling described in this chapter are designed with previously established evidence-based features, such as personalized learning environments and positive relationships with teachers, which enhance student engagement.

Relationship Building

Students benefit from a sense of belonging and meaningful adult relationships at school. In a survey of students who had dropped out of school, participants expressed a strong desire for individual attention and praise from their teachers (Bridgeland et al., 2006). Resiliency research has indicated that caring and involved teachers play an important protective role for children who are at risk for a host of negative outcomes (Cove, Eiseman, & Popkin, 2005; Werner & Smith, 1989). These relationships, particularly when they occur within a larger school climate that is based on respect and caring, have the power to enhance motivation, self-confidence, and optimism.

Like smaller learning communities described in Chapter 2 of this text, alternative educational programs that offer a maximum teacher-to-student ratio of 1:10 and a total student population under 250 tend to be more successful (Schargel & Smink, 2001). Students at risk for dropping out of school benefit from relationships with caring and committed staff who maintain high expectations for student achievement and behavior. CTE programs often incorporate mentoring, job shadowing, internship, and service-learning opportunities, which connect students with adults within the community and provide additional opportunities for relationship building.

Flexibility

Other characteristics of successful programs include a flexible schedule and learning programs individualized to students' learning styles and expectations. One example is a combination of courses from the traditional high school curriculum and career and technical education courses. Differentiating instruction and utilizing evidence-based practices developed in MTSS academic research have been shown to be successful in improving middle and high school students' academic skills (Burns et al., 2012). A true understanding of students' current skill levels is important for scaffolding learning experiences so that students can access their course content to meet current academic and course performance expectations. For example, many students who are counseled into career and technical education courses have low reading or math skills. Providing specific courses and/or supplementary instruction on the reading, vocabulary, and math skills needed to access the CTE course content can facilitate conceptual understanding. These academic supports can be provided within prescheduled intervention blocks and strategic direct instruction study halls. Additionally, when students demonstrate failure of course material, requiring that they repeat entire courses may not be necessary. Rather, reteaching course unit content to passing levels as soon as possible would help students acquire the needed skills to master course content, achieve course credits, and continue their educational experience efficiently and productively.

SUMMARY

The need to maximize the rates of high school and postsecondary success is a topic of national interest with clear economic implications at the local, state, and national levels. Today there are many educational opportunities and programs that can serve as alternatives to the traditional public school setting to meet students' needs. CTE and alternative schooling are important ways of offering students a variety of learning opportunities that prepare them for future schooling and careers. For those students who are at risk for dropping out of school, these programs offer the promise of a more inspiring and relevant educational experience. The core components of MTSS, including collaborative problem solving and data-based decision making to design flexible, small-group instruction, remain important strategies in alternative high school settings. Adhering to the MTSS model with an emphasis on increasing student engagement will lead to more successful outcomes. Although they will not be appropriate for all students at risk, alternative programs that focus on future careers, real-life experiences, and meaningful relationships are important elements of a comprehensive dropout prevention strategy.

BIG IDEAS

- Traditional school settings do not meet the needs of all students; many students benefit from specialized programming, more individualized attention, and flexibility.
- Several alternative education programs offer a good platform to foster student engagement and continued enrollment in school.
- Work-based learning, such as CTE and internships, provides opportunities to develop relationships and make relevant connections between schoolwork and job-related activities and responsibilities.
- Academic skill proficiency is important in order to access both traditional and CTE course content and to foster student success.

CHAPTER 11

Conclusion
Time for a Change

> When I was very young, most of my childhood heroes wore capes,
> flew through the air, or picked up buildings with one arm.
> They were spectacular and got a lot of attention.
> But as I grew, my heroes changed, so that now
> I can honestly say that anyone who does anything
> to help a child is a hero to me.
> —FRED ROGERS (2003, p. 145)

There are many factors that contribute to the dropout crisis in America, many challenges faced by families and schools, and many reasons why solutions seem out of reach. In this book we have listed the risk factors and warnings, as well as research-based recommendations about how to prevent and/or to respond to them. We conclude with future directions and a call for change.

THE PROMISE OF CONVERGING RESEARCH

An exciting trend in educational, child development, and clinical research is a convergence of scholarship, empirical findings, and recommendations to inform best practice school reform efforts. School readiness, MTSS, RTI, PBIS, and dropout prevention research outcomes are aligning with consistent themes emphasizing the importance of prevention and early intervention as early as prekindergarten, with evidence-based practices, and with a sharp focus on school-based protective factors: school engagement, attendance, prosocial behaviors, and academic achievement in literacy and math.

Given that the dropout problem is complex, the solution must be comprehensive.

As highlighted throughout this book, investments in high-quality preschool education and authentic parental involvement yield lifelong individual, family, educational, and societal benefits. Children who enter kindergarten with school readiness skills are more likely to be engaged in school and to experience long-term academic, social, and emotional success. Once they set foot in the doors of the school, research evidence supports the implementation of universal, schoolwide academic and behavior support systems to reduce behavioral and academic problems.

Researchers have consistently reported that academic failure and behavior problems as early as first grade are correlated with antisocial behavior and other problems later in life. With well-designed and consistently implemented early efforts that focus on providing academic and behavior supports and maximizing student engagement, these problems can be largely prevented. We know that establishing reading and behavioral skills *early* is predictive of later success in school. Without needed supports, problems tend to persist in a downward spiral of academic failure and disengagement, which perpetuates itself and becomes increasingly resistant to change. Figure 7.2 in Chapter 7 presented an illustration of this spiral effect.

This negative cycle can be turned around. The big three key risk indicators that have been emphasized throughout this book—academic performance, attendance, and behavior—are the same factors that we in schools have the power to change. As an alternative to Figure 7.2, we offer a positive spiral of engagement, shown in Figure 11.1. In this scenario, a continuum of high-quality instruction and behavior supports, positive relationships with teachers and peers, and academic and personal achievements foster increased and lasting engagement and success in school.

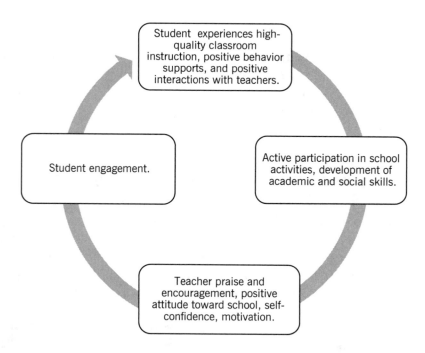

FIGURE 11.1. The positive spiral of engagement.

FACILITATING A PARADIGM SHIFT IN EDUCATION

Give me a place to stand, and with a lever I shall move the world.
—ARCHIMEDES

The principle of the lever, referred to by scientist and mathematician Archimedes, teaches us that finding the most effective leverage point results in the best opportunity for change. In terms of dropout prevention, early intervention in the elementary years represents a high leverage point; prevention and intervention efforts at this stage will have the greatest influence. Facilitating a paradigm shift in education also takes a high leverage point. To reverse the dropout trend and create positive momentum for higher levels of student engagement and high school completion requires systemic changes in our educational delivery system. A smarter use of school resources and expertise, a focus on school health and prevention, and high-quality teacher training are essential school reform efforts.

The purpose of this book is to guide educators toward strategies and supports that we know work: early identification of risk, prevention and early intervention, evidence-based instruction, MTSS, and data-based decision making. More specifically, we need dedicated teachers and mentors, parent and community partnerships, relevant and meaningful learn-

TABLE 11.1. Lessons Learned

- Dropping out of school is a process, not an event, and it can begin before a student even enters elementary school.
- Dropping out is a multifaceted process with wide-ranging individual and societal adverse effects that demands comprehensive and empirically based solutions.
- School engagement, academic skills, and prosocial behaviors are interrelated and equally essential for school success.
- Empirical evidence identifies early warning signs and prevention and intervention methods that are effective for reducing risk for dropout.
- The purpose of early risk identification is to resolve academic and behavior problems at a young age when intervention is most effective.
- The "big three" risk indicators are attendance, course performance, and behavior.
- Attendance and behavioral data are important for recognizing emerging internalizing and externalizing behavior problems.
- The key to effective dropout prevention is the link between early detection through EWS data and the implementation of MTSS in prekindergarten through 12th grade.
- The transition year is a school's best opportunity to intervene, so proactive planning and effective identification of students at risk as they enter middle school and high school are critical dropout prevention components.
- Traditional school settings do not meet the needs of all students; many students benefit from specialized programming, more individualized attention, and flexibility.
- Dropout prevention takes a village: schools, parents, families, and community partnerships.
- To resolve the current dropout crisis, dropout prevention must become a national priority with a mandate to provide every child with the opportunity to benefit from evidence-based practices.

ing activities, alternative pathways to meeting high school graduation requirements, and support for mental health needs. For a more detailed list of the lessons learned in dropout prevention, see Table 11.1.

We know what good reading and math instruction look like. We know the elements of a positive school climate and effective behavioral support. It is imperative that we provide high-quality evidence-based academic and behavior instruction for all children and regularly monitor the integrity of instruction, student response, and student engagement. Just as we want health care providers to use best practice treatments, we need to provide the best practice methods in schools for the development of academic, social, and emotional health. When we do this, we give our children the best chance for future success.

Many students and families face some sort of challenge, whether it is economic hardship, divorce, mental health issues, or learning difficulties. Rather than waiting for problems to escalate and compartmentalizing services for children, we need a systemwide, prekindergarten through 12th-grade continuum of supports, data sharing, and problem solving for *all* students. Along with the challenges, every student also comes through the doors with unique potential and future aspirations. We need to shepherd our children through the years and transitions with consistent attention, support, and advocacy so that these will be realized.

FUTURE DIRECTIONS

Our job as educators is to prepare students to complete school with the knowledge and skills to be successful in the future, while providing learning experiences that are relevant and engaging in the here and now. The pathway to accomplishing this task, although not without significant challenges, is clear. The primary research-to-practice void that remains is how to convince policy makers and educators to allocate the needed resources to proactively implement and sustain evidence-based prevention and intervention methods shown to increase school success and on-time high school completion.

Improving school experiences, achievements, and, ultimately, on-time graduation promises direct and substantial benefits at many levels: student, family, school, community, state, and national. The overarching aim of this book is to advocate for positive change in the education system. It stems from the fundamental belief that all children can learn when provided with needed supports. This is our vision for the future and hope for our nation's youth. It is time for a change, and it is possible.

REPRODUCIBLE MATERIALS

APPENDIX A. Checklist for Monitoring and Improving Family Engagement   147

APPENDIX B. Academic Intervention Record Form   149

APPENDIX C. Building an Early Warning System   151

APPENDIX D. Evidence-Based Interventions   152

APPENDIX E. Online Resources for Dropout Prevention and Intervention Methods   156

Checklist for Monitoring and Improving Family Engagement

	In Place	Needs Improvement	Not in Place	Priority	
				Low	High
Communication					
Conferences are held prior to the start of school, during the school year, and as needed, at convenient times.					
Teachers provide regular updates to families and encourage families to inform teachers about events, changes, etc., in their children's lives.					
The school clearly communicates information about school activities, schedules, policies, behavior expectations, and discipline procedures.					
Families are able to contact teachers directly.					
Teachers and administrators communicate with families regularly through a variety of means, including mail, e-mail, phone, and face-to-face interactions.					
Folders of student work, homework logs, and progress reports are sent between home and school regularly.					
Meetings and materials are translated for non-English-speaking families.					
Home visits are offered to families who are not able to visit the school regularly.					
Communication emphasizes positive observations and strengths.					
Informal activities, such as sporting events and coffee hours, promote interaction between school and home.					
Home–School Partnerships					
Parent workshops provide information on topics such as grade-level skills, strategies for supporting homework, preparing for transitions, and other ways to help children succeed at school.					

(continued)

Based on Michigan Department of Education (2004).

	In Place	Needs Improvement	Not in Place	Priority Low	High
Families are given information on how to assist children with new skills and learning at home.					
The school library loans books to families that they can read with their children.					
Teachers work with families and students in setting annual achievement goals.					
Volunteering					
The school encourages parent participation in the classroom, in the cafeteria, on field trips, or in school improvement projects.					
A volunteer orientation packet provides information on volunteer opportunities and instructions.					
School personnel welcome volunteers into the building and express appreciation for their involvement.					
Resources for Families					
The school provides access to community resources by offering meeting space and referrals for needed services.					
The school provides breakfast each morning.					
Representatives from parent organizations reach out to families and build connections among parents and with community groups.					
Family Involvement in Decision Making					
Families are provided with information about how the system works.					
Families are invited to be involved in school and districtwide committees.					
Families are asked to participate in discussions and decisions regarding school policies and curriculum.					

Academic Intervention Record Form

✓	Step	Notes
Identify and Define the Problem.		
	Collect baseline data.	
	Determine individual progress goal(s).	
Explore Alternative Interventions.		
	Ensure intervention is matched to student's skill level.	
	Determine trained personnel to deliver intervention.	
	Schedule a place and consistent time for intervention.	
	Determine a consistent progress monitoring schedule (e.g., weekly).	
	Determine appropriate intervention.	
Apply Selected Intervention.		
	Provide explicit and systematic instruction.	
	Provide multiple opportunities and adequate time for instruction (e.g., two to five times/week).	

(continued)

✓	Step	Notes
	Frequently review new material and skills.	
	Embed cuing and prompting strategies into the instruction.	
	Provide multiple opportunities for student(s) to respond and practice.	
	Give immediate corrective feedback to minimize errors.	
	Provide regular checks for understanding and generalization.	
	Intervention is implemented with fidelity by trained personnel.	
Look at Effects.		
	Complete progress monitoring on a regular basis.	
	Analyze progress monitoring data regularly (e.g., monthly) to assess rate of growth and response to intervention.	
	Tailor the intensity and level of instruction to the student's need based on results of regular progress monitoring.	
	Make data-based decision: Continue, modify, or discontinue intervention?	

Building an Early Warning System

1. Develop an EWS data collection system.

   a. The data system should track individual student attendance, course performance, promotion status, and behavior beginning in fourth grade.

   b. Provide training in the use of this system to members of the problem-solving team and other school personnel.

   c. Pay particular attention to transition years (usually grades 6 and 9).

   d. Include information on interventions and programs that individual students receive.

2. Establish a continuum of appropriate interventions.

3. Determine on-track and off-track criteria for high school graduation (recommended benchmarks given below).

   a. Attendance

      i. Students who miss more than 10% of instructional time (i.e., 2 days in the first 20 days of school, or approximately 10 days in a semester).

   b. Course performance

      i. One or more F in any course, particularly core academic courses.

      ii. GPA of 2.0 or less at end of ninth grade.

      iii. Ninth-grade students who do not earn enough credits to be promoted to tenth grade.

   c. Behavior

      i. Multiple ODRs or suspension.

4. Monitor attendance data monthly.

5. Monitor academic performance quarterly (course failures, GPA, credit accrual).

6. Monitor behavior data (ODRs, suspensions).

7. Identify and monitor students who have been retained.

8. Flag all students who meet criteria for being off track for graduation and provide targeted intervention.

9. Use the EWS data system to monitor progress.

Based on Kennelly and Monrad (2007); Heppen and Therriault (2008).

Evidence-Based Interventions

Behavior Interventions	Contact Information	Cost	Materials	Applicable Grade Levels
Check-In, Check-Out (CICO)	www.pbis.org/common/pbisresources/presentations/8APBS_Tier2_GettingStartedWorkbook.pdf	Free	Training is available. Produce your own materials.	Elementary and Secondary
Check and Connect	checkandconnect.umn.edu	Free	Training is available. No specific materials are required.	Secondary
PATHS	www.channing-bete.com/prevention-programs/paths/paths.html	Packages start at $350	Training is available. Materials are included with the purchased program.	Elementary
Skillstreaming the Elementary School Child	www.skillstreaming.com	Packages start at $79.95	Training is available. Materials are included with the purchased program.	Elementary
Skillstreaming the Adolescent	www.skillstreaming.com	Packages start at $79.95	Training is available. Materials are included with the purchased program.	Secondary
Coping Cat	www.workbookpublishing.com	Workbooks start at $24	Training is available. Materials are included with the purchased program.	Elementary and Secondary
Second Step	www.secondstep.org	Kits start at $189	Training is available. Materials are included with the purchased program.	PreK–9

(continued)

Evidence-Based Interventions *(page 2 of 4)*

Reading	Contact Information	Cost	Materials	Applicable Grade Levels
Reading Mastery	*www.mcgraw-hill.co.uk/sra/readingmastery.htm*	Quotes available based on materials	Training is available. Materials are included with the purchased program.	Elementary
Early Interventions in Reading 2012	*www.weareteachers.com/lessons-resources/details/sra-early-interventions-in-reading*	Quotes available based on materials	Training is available. Materials are included with the purchased program.	Grades K, 1, and 2
Corrective Reading Program	*www.mcgraw-hill.co.uk/sra/correctivereading.htm*	Quotes available based on materials	Training is available. Materials are included with the purchased program.	Grades 4–12
READ 180	*read180.scholastic.com/reading-intervention-program*	Quotes available based on materials	Training is available. Materials are included with the purchased program.	Grades 4–12
Scott Foresman Early Reading Intervention	*www.scottforesman.com/reading/eri/index.cfm?slide=7*	Quotes available based on materials	Training is available. Materials are included with the purchased program.	Elementary
PALS Reading (Peer-Assisted Learning Strategies)	*kc.vanderbilt.edu/pals/*	Packages start at $40	Training is available. Materials are included with the purchased program.	Elementary
Phonological Awareness and Word Analysis				
Lexia Reading	*www.lexialearning.co.nz/llreading.html*	Quotes available based on materials	Training is available. Materials are included with the purchased program.	Ages 4 to adult
Phoneme Segmentation	*www.bemidji.k12.mn.us/Curriculum/documents/PhonemeSegmentation InterventionStrategy.pdf*	Free	Materials are listed in the intervention.	Elementary
Phonological Awareness Training (PAT)	*www.ucl.ac.uk/educational-psychology/cpd/pat.htm*	Packets range from $25–$30	Materials are included with the purchased program.	Elementary

(continued)

Evidence-Based Interventions *(page 3 of 4)*

Fluency			
Partner Reading (PR)	www.readingrockets.org/strategies/partner_reading	Free	Reading Passage Partners	Elementary and Secondary
Quick Reads	www.rti4success.org	Free	Reading Passage	Elementary and Secondary
Repeated Reading	www.interventioncentral.com	Free	Reading Passage Timer	Elementary and Secondary
Listening Passage Preview (LPP)	www.interventioncentral.com	Free	Reading Passage Timer	Elementary and Secondary
Great Leaps	www.greatleaps.com	Packages range from $60 to $160	Materials are included with the purchased program.	Elementary and Secondary
Helping with Early Literacy with Practice Strategies (HELPS)	www.helpsprogram.org	Depends on materials used	Depends on strategies used	Elementary and Secondary
Read Naturally	www.readnaturally.com	Depends on materials purchased	Materials are included with the purchased program.	Elementary
Comprehension			
Collaborative Strategic Reading (CSR)	www.sedl.org/cgi-bin/mysql/buildingreading.cgi?showrecord=15	Free	Depends on strategies used	Elementary and Secondary
"Get the Gist"	www.interventioncentral.com	Free	Reading passage	Elementary and Secondary
Story Mapping	www.interventioncentral.com	Free	Reading materials	Elementary and Secondary

(continued)

Evidence-Based Interventions *(page 4 of 4)*

Math	Contact Information	Cost	Materials	Applicable Grade Levels
Time Practice, Practice, Practice	*RTI in the Classroom* (Brown-Chidsey, Bronaugh, & McGraw, 2009)	Free	Computation problems Timer Graph paper	Elementary and Secondary
Flashcards and Folding in New Items	*RTI in the Classroom* (Brown-Chidsey, Bronaugh, & McGraw, 2009)	Free	Blank 3 x 5 index cards Math computation problems Markers	Elementary and Secondary
Cover Copy Compare (CCC)	*www.interventioncentral.com*	Free	Computation problems Pencil	Elementary and Secondary
Peer-Assisted Learning Strategies (PALS)	*kc.vanderbilt.edu/pals*	Packages start at $40 for teacher manual and $30 for student materials	Training is available. Materials are included with the purchased program.	Elementary
Accelerated Math	*www.renlearn.com/am*	Quotes available for specific school needs	Training is available. Materials are included with the purchased program.	Elementary and Secondary
Reciprocal Peer Tutoring in Math	*Effective School Interventions* (Rathvon, 2008)	Free	Computation problems Pencil	Elementary and Secondary
Great Leaps Math	*www.greatleaps.com*	Packages range from $25 to $275	Materials are included with the purchased program.	Elementary and Secondary

155

Online Resources for Dropout Prevention and Intervention Methods

American Institutes for Research: Early Warning Systems in Education
www.earlywarningsystems.org

Blueprints for Healthy Youth Development
www.blueprintprogram.com

Center on Instruction
www.centeroninstruction.org

Florida Center for Reading Research
www.fcrr.org

Free Reading
www.freereading.net

International Reading Assocciation
www.reading.org

Intervention Central
www.interventioncentral.com

Khan Academy
www.khanacademy.org

Meadows Center for Preventing Educational Risk
www.meadowscenter.org

National Association of School Psychologists
www.nasponline.org

National Center on Intensive Intervention (NCII)
www.intensiveintervention

National Center for Response to Intervention (NCRTI)
www.rti4success

National High School Center
www.betterhighschools.org

National Mathematics Advisory Panel
www.ed.gov/MathPanel

National Reading Panel
www.nationalreadingpanel.org

RTI Action Network
www.rtinetwork.org

SEDL Advancing Research, Improving Education
www.sedl.org

Technical Assistance Center on Positive Behavior Intervention and Supports
www.pbis.org

Webmath
www.webmath.com

What Works Clearinghouse
www.ies.ed.gov/ncee/wwc

References

Advisory Committee for the National Assessment of Vocational Education. (2003). *Report of the Advisory Committee for the National Assessment of Vocational Education.* Washington, DC: U.S. Department of Education.

Akos, P., & Galassi, J. P. (2004). Middle and high school transitions as viewed by students, parents, and teachers. *Professional School Counseling, 7,* 212–221.

Alexander, K. L., Entwisle, D. R., & Horsey, C. S. (1997). From first grade forward: Early foundations of high school dropout. *Sociology of Education, 79,* 87–107.

Alexander, K. L., Entwisle, D. R., & Kabbani, N. (2001). The dropout process in life course perspective: Early risk factors at home and school. *Teachers College Record, 103,* 760–822.

Algozzine, B., Putnam, B., & Horner, R. (2010). *What comes first—the achievement or the behavior (problem)?* Charlotte: University of North Carolina Behavior and Reading Improvement Center.

Algozzine, B., Wang, C., & Violette, A. S. (2011). Rexamining the relationship between academic achievement and social behavior. *Journal of Positive Behavior Interventions, 13,* 3–16.

Allensworth, E., & Easton, J. Q. (2005). *The on-track indicator as a predictor of high school graduation.* Chicago: University of Chicago Consortium on Chicago School Research.

Allensworth, E., & Easton, J. Q. (2007). *What matters for staying on-track and graduating in Chicago public schools: A close look at course grades, failures and attendance in the freshman year.* Chicago: University of Chicago, Consortium on Chicago School Research. Retrieved from *http://ccsr.uchicago.edu/publications/07%20What%20Matters%20Final.pdf.*

Alliance for Excellent Education. (2007). *The high cost of high school dropouts: What the nation pays for inadequate high schools.* Washington, DC: Author. Retrieved from *www.all4ed.org/files/archive/publications/HighCost.pdf.*

Alliance for Excellent Education. (2011, November). *The high cost of high school dropouts: What the nation pays for inadequate high schools* (Issue Brief). Washington, DC: Author. Retrieved from *www.all4ed.org/ files/HighCost.pdf.*

Alvarez, M., & Anderson-Ketchmark, C. (2010). Review of an evidence-based school social work intervention: Check and Connect. *Children and Schools, 32,* 125–127.

Anderman, E. M., Maehr, M. L., & Midgley, C. (1999). Declining motivation after the transition to middle school: Schools can make a difference. *Journal of Research and Development in Education, 32,* 131–147.

Anderson, D., Munk, J., Young, K., Conley, L., & Caldarella, P. (2008). Teaching organizational skills to promote academic achievement in behaviorally challenged students. *Teaching Exceptional Children, 40,* 6–13.

Appleton, J. J., Christenson, S. L., & Furlong, M. J. (2008). Student engagement with school: Critical conceptual and methodological issues of the construct. *Psychology in the Schools, 45,* 369–386.

Association for Career and Technical Education. (2007, June). *Career and technical education's role in dropout prevention and recovery.* Alexandria, VA: Author.

August, D., & Shanahan, T. (2006). *Developing literacy in second-language learners: Report of the national literacy panel on language, minority children and youth.* Mahwah, NJ: Erlbaum.

Axtell, P. K., McCallum, R. S., Bell, S. M., & Poncy, B. (2009). Developing math automaticity using a classwide fluency building procedure for middle school students: A preliminary study. *Psychology in the Schools, 46,* 526–538.

Baker, S., Gersten, R., & Lee, D.-S. (2002). A synthesis of empirical research on teaching mathematics to low-achieving students. *Elementary School Journal, 103,* 51–73.

Balfanz, R. (2009). *Putting middle grade students on the graduation path: A policy and practice brief.* Retrieved from *http://web.jhu.edu/sebin/u/l/NMSA%20brief%20Balfanz.pdf.*

Balfanz, R., Bridgeland, J. M., Bruce, M., & Fox, J. H. (2012). *Building a grad nation: Progress and challenge in ending the high school dropout epidemic.* Retrieved from *www.americaspromise. org/Our-Work/Grad-Nation/Building-a-Grad-Nation.aspx.*

Balfanz, R., & Herzog, L. (2005, March). *Keeping middle grades students on track to graduation: Initial analysis and implications.* PowerPoint presentation at the second Regional Middle Grades Symposium, Philadelphia, PA.

Balfanz, R., Herzog, L., & Mac Iver, D. J. (2007). Preventing student disengagement and keeping students on the graduation path in urban middle grade schools: Early identification and effective interventions. *Educational Psychologist, 42,* 223–235.

Barrington, B. L., & Hendricks, B. (1989). Differentiating characteristics of high school graduates, dropouts, and nongraduates. *Journal of Educational Research, 82,* 309–319.

Belfield, C. R., & Levin, H. M. (2007). *The economic losses from high school dropouts in California.* Santa Barbara: California Dropout Research Project.

Benard, B. (1995, August). *Fostering resilience in children.* Chicago: University of Illinois Children's Research Center. Retrieved from *http://resilnet.uiuc.edu/library/benard95.html.*

Bender, W. N. (2012). *Project-based learning: Differentiating instruction for the 21st century.* Thousand Oaks, CA: Corwin.

Biancarosa, C., & Snow, C. E. (2006). *Reading Next: A vision for action and research in middle and high school literacy: A report to Carnegie Corporation of New York* (2nd ed.). Washington, DC: Alliance for Excellent Education.

Bridgeland, J., Dilulio, J. J., & Morison, K. B. (2006). *The silent epidemic: Perspectives of high school dropouts.* Washington, DC: Civic Enterprises. Retrieved from *www.ignitelearning.com/pdf/ TheSilentEpidemic3-06FINAL.pdf.*

Brown-Chidsey, R., & Andren, K. J. (2012). Introduction. In R. Brown-Chidsey & K. J. Andren (Eds.), *Assessment for intervention: A problem-solving approach* (2nd ed., pp. 3–9). New York: Guilford Press.

Brown-Chidsey, R., Bronaugh, L., & McGraw, K. (2009). *RTI in the classroom: Guidelines and recipes for success.* New York: Guilford Press.

Brown-Chidsey, R., & Steege, M. W. (2010). *Response to intervention: Principles and strategies for effective practice* (2nd ed.). New York: Guilford Press.

Bryant, D. P., Bryant, B. R., Gersten, R., Scamacca, N., & Chavez, M. M. (2008). Mathematics intervention for first- and second-grade students with mathematics difficulties: The effects of tier 2 intervention delivered as booster lessons. *Remedial and Special Education, 29*, 20–32.

Burns, M. K., Codding, R. S., Boice, C. H., & Lukito, G. (2010). Meta-analysis of acquisition and fluency math interventions with instructional and frustration level skills: Evidence for a skill-by-treatment interaction. *School Psychology Review, 39*, 69–83.

Burns, S. M., Griffin, P., & Snow, C. E. (1999). *Starting out right: A guide to promoting children's reading success.* Washington, DC: National Academy Press.

Burns, M. K., Riley-Tillman, T. C., & VanDerHeyden, A. (2012). *RTI applications: Vol. 1. Academic and behavioral interventions.* New York: Guilford Press.

Calderon, M., Slavin, R., & Sanchez, M. (2011). Effective instruction for English learners. *Immigrant Children, 21*, 103–128.

Campbell, S. B. (1995). Behavior problems in preschool children: A review of recent research. *Journal of Child Psychology and Psychiatry, 36*, 113–149.

Carnevale, A. P., Smith, N., & Strohl, J. (2010). *Projections of employment and education demand 2008–2018.* Washington, DC: Georgetown Center on Education and the Workforce.

Carnine, D. W., Silbert, J., Kame'enui, E. J., & Tarver, S. G. (2009). *Direct instruction reading* (5th ed.). Upper Saddle River, NJ: Pearson.

Casey, A., & Howe, K. (2002). Best practices in early literacy skills. In A. Thomas & J. Grimes (Eds.), *Best practices in school psychology IV* (pp. 721–735). Bethesda, MD: National Association of School Psychologists.

Centers for Disease Control and Prevention. (2012). *Parent engagement: Strategies for involving parents in school health.* Atlanta, GA: U.S. Department of Health and Human Services.

Chafouleas, S., Riley-Tillman, T. C., & Sugai, G. (2007). *School-based behavioral assessment: Informing intervention and instruction.* New York: Guilford Press.

Chapman, C., Laird, J., Ifill, N., & Kewal Ramani, A. (2011). *Trends in high school dropout and completion rates in the United States: 1972–2009* (NCES Publication No. 2012-006). Washington, DC: Institute of Education Sciences, National Center for Education Statistics, Retrieved from *http://nces.ed.gov/pubs2012/2012006.pdf.*

Christenson, S. L., Reschly, A. L., Appleton, J. J., Berman-Young, S., Spanjers, D. M., & Varro, P. (2008). Best practices in fostering student engagement. In A. Thomas & J. Grimes (Eds.), *Best practices in school psychology V* (pp. 1099–1119). Bethesda, MD: National Association of School Psychologists.

Christenson, S. L., Sinclair, M. F., Lehr, C. A., & Godber, Y. (2001). Promoting successful school completion: Critical conceptual and methodological guidelines. *School Psychology Quarterly, 16*, 468–484.

Christenson, S. L., Sinclair, M. F., Lehr, C. A., & Hurley, C. M. (2000). Promoting successful school completion. In K. M. Minke & G. C. Bear (Eds.), *Preventing school—Promoting school success* (pp. 211–257). Bethesda, MD: National Association of School Psychologists.

Christenson, S., & Thurlow, M. (2004). School dropouts: Prevention, considerations, interventions, and challenges. *Current Direction in Psychological Science, 13*, 36–39.

Constantine, J. M., Seftor, N. S., Martin, E. S., & Myers, D. (2006). *A study of the effect of the Talent Search program on secondary and postsecondary outcomes in Florida, Indiana, and Texas: Final report from phase II of the national evaluation.* Washington, DC: U.S. Department of Education.

Cooney, S., & Bottoms, G. (2002). *Middle grades to high school: Mending a weak link.* Atlanta, GA: Southern Regional Education Board. Retrieved from *www.sreb.org/cgi-bin/MySQLdb.*

Cove, E., Eiseman, M., & Popkin, S. J. (2005). *Resilient children: Literature review and evidence from the HOPE VI panel study.* Washington, DC: Urban Institute. Retrieved from *www.urban. org/uploadedPDF/411255_resilient_children.pdf.*

Covington-Smith, S. (2008). *Addressing dropout-related factors at the local level: Recommendations for teachers.* Clemson, SC: National Dropout Prevention Center for Students with Disabilities. Retrieved from *www.ndpcsd.org/documents/LEA_Recommendations_for_Teachers. pdf.*

Coyne, M. D., Carnine, D. W., & Kame'enui, E. J. (2010). *Effective teaching strategies that accommodate diverse learners* (4th ed.). Upper Saddle River, NJ: Pearson.

Crone, D. A., Hawken, L. S., & Horner, R. H. (2010). *Responding to problem behavior in schools: The behavior education program* (2nd ed.). New York: Guilford Press.

Dalton, T., Martella, R. C., & Marchand-Martella, N. E. (1999). The effects of a self-management program in reducing off-task behavior. *Journal of Behavioral Education, 9,* 157–176.

Daly, E. J., III, Chafouleas, S., & Skinner, C. H. (2005). *Interventions for reading problems: Designing and evaluating effective strategies.* New York: Guilford Press.

Dawson, P., & Guare, R. (2010). *Executive skills in children and adolescents: A practical guide to assessment and intervention* (2nd ed.). New York: Guilford Press.

Dawson, P., & Guare, R. (2012). *Coaching students with executive skills deficits.* New York: Guilford Press.

Deno, S. L. (1985). Curriculum-based measurement: The emerging alternative. *Exceptional Children, 52,* 219–232.

Deno, S. L. (1986). Formative evaluation of individual student programs: A new role for school psychologists. *School Psychology Review, 15,* 348–374.

Deno, S. L. (2012). Problem-solving assessment. In R. Brown-Chidsey & K. J. Andren (Eds.), *Assessment for intervention: A problem-solving approach* (2nd ed., pp. 10–36). New York: Guilford Press.

Deno, S. L., Reschly, A. L., Lembke, E. S., Magnusson, D., Callender, S. A., Windram, H., et al. (2009). Developing a school-wide progress-monitoring system. *Psychology in the Schools, 46,* 44–55.

Denti, L., & Guerin, G. (1999). Dropout prevention: A case for enhanced early literacy efforts. *Clearing House, 72,* 231–235.

Denton, C., Fletcher, J., Anthony, J., & Francis, D. (2006). An evaluation of intensive intervention for students with persistent reading difficulties. *Journal of Learning Disabilities, 39,* 447–466.

Dotterer, A. M., & Lowe, K. (2011). Classroom context, school engagement, and academic achievement in early adolescence. *Journal of Youth and Adolescence, 40,* 1649–1660.

Duncan, G. J., Dowsett, C. J., Claessens, A., Magnuson, K., Huston, A. C., Klebanov, P., et al. (2007). School readiness and later achievement. *Developmental Psychology, 43,* 1428–1446.

Duncan, G. J., Ziol-Guest, K. M., & Kalil, A. (2010). Early childhood poverty and adult attainment, behavior, and health. *Child Development, 81,* 306–325.

Durlak, J., Dymnicki, A., Taylor, R., Weissberg, R., & Schellinger, K. (2011). The impact of enhancing students' social and emotional learning: A meta-analysis of school-based universal interventions. *Child Development, 82,* 405–422.

Dynarski, M., Clarke, L., Cobb, B., Finn, J., Rumberger, R., & Smink, J. (2008). *Dropout prevention: A practice guide* (NCEE Publication No. 2008-4025). Washington, DC: U.S. Department of Education, Institute of Education Sciences, National Center for Education Evaluation and Regional Assistance. Retreived from *http://ies.ed.gove/ncee/wwc.*

Dynarski, M., & Wood, R. (1997). *Helping high-risk youth: Results from the Alternative School Demonstration Program.* Princeton, NJ: Mathematics Policy Research.

Echevarria, J., & Hasbrouck, J. (2009). *Response to intervention and English learners.* Retrieved from *www.cal.org/create/publications/briefs/response-to-intervention-and-english-learners. html.*

Elliot, J., & Morrison, D. (2008). *Response to intervention blueprints: District level edition.* Alexandria, VA: National Association of State Directors of Special Education. Retrieved from *www. nasdse.org/projects/responsetointerventionrtiproject/tabid/411/default.aspx.*

Finn, J. (1989). Withdrawing from school. *Review of Educational Research, 59,* 117–142.

Fleming, C. B., Harachi, T. W., Cortes, R. C., Abbott, R. D., & Catalano, R. F. (2004). Level and change in reading scores and attention problems during elementary school as predictors of problem behavior in middle school. *Journal of Emotional and Behavioral Disorders, 12,* 130–144.

Flora, S. R. (2000). Praise's magic reinforcement ratio: Five to one gets the job done. *Behavior Analyst Today, 1,* 64–69.

Foorman, B. R., Francis, D. J., Fletcher, J. M., Schatschneider, C., & Mehta, P. (1998). The role of instruction in learning to read: Preventing reading failure in at-risk children. *Journal of Educational Psychology, 90,* 37–55.

Fox, L., Dunlap, G., Hemmeter, M. L., Joseph, G. E., & Strain, P. S. (2003). The teaching pyramid: A model for supporting social competence and preventing challenging behavior in young children. *Young Children, 58*(4), 48–52.

Francis, D., Rivera, M., Lesaux, N. K., Kieffer, M., & Rivera, H. (2006). *Practical guidelines for the education of English language learners: Research-based recommendations for instruction and academic interventions.* Retrieved from *www.centeroninstruction.org/files/ELL1-Interventions.pdf.*

Fredricks, J., Blumenfeld, P., & Paris, A. (2004). School engagement: Potential of the concept, state of the evidence. *Review of Educational Research, 74,* 59–109.

Fuchs, L. S., Fuchs, D., & Compton, D. L. (2010). Rethinking response to intervention at middle and high school. *School Psychology Review, 39,* 22–28.

Fuchs, L. S., Fuchs, D., Prentice, K., Burch, M., Hamlett, C. L., Owen, T., et al. (2003). Explicitly teaching for transfer: Effects on third-grade students' mathematical problem solving. *Journal of Educational Psychology, 95,* 293–305.

Gentle-Genitty, C. (2009). Best practice programs for low-income African American students transitioning from middle to high school. *National Association of Social Workers, 31,* 109–117.

Gersten, R., Beckmann, S., Clarke, B., Foegen, A., Marsh, L., Star, J. R., et al. (2009). *Assisting students struggling with mathematics: Response to Intervention (RtI) for elementary and middle schools* (NCEE Publication No. 2009-4060). Washington, DC: U.S. Department of Education. Retrieved June 23, 2009, from *http://ies.ed.gov/ncee/wwc/pdf/practiceguides/rti_math_ pg_042109.pdf.*

Gettinger, M., & Stoiber, K. (2007). Applying a response to intervention model for early literacy development in low-income children. *Topics in Early Childhood Special Education, 27,* 198–213.

Ginsburg, H. P., Sun Lee, J., & Boyd, J. S. (2008). *Mathematics education for young children: What it is and how to promote it.* Retrieved June 23, 2009, from *www.srcd.org/documents/publications/spr/22-1_early_childhood_math.pdf.*

Glover, T., & Vaughn, S. (Eds.). (2010). *The promise of response to intervention: Evaluating current science and practice.* New York: Guilford Press.

Good, R. H., Simmons, D. C., & Kame'enui, E. J. (2001). The importance and decision making utility of a continuum of fluency-based indicators of foundational reading skills for third-grade high-stakes outcomes. *Scientific Studies of Reading, 5,* 257–288.

Guare, R., & Dawson, P. (2009). *Smart but scattered: The revolutionary "executive skills" approach to helping kids reach their potential.* New York: Guilford Press.

Guare, R., Dawson, P., & Guare, C. (2013). *Smart but scattered teens: The "executive skills" program for helping teens reach their potential.* New York: Guilford Press.

Hammond, C., Linton, D., Smink, J., & Drew, S. (2007). *Dropout risk factors and exemplary programs.* Clemson, SC: National Dropout Prevention Center. Retrieved from *www.cisdetroit. org/research/2007/2007-DropoutRiskFactors-Full.pdf.*

Hamre, B. K., & Pianta, R. C. (2001). Early teacher–child relationships and the trajectory of children's school outcomes through eighth grade. *Child Development, 72,* 625–638.

Harwell, S. (2003). *Teacher professional development: It's not an event, it's a process.* Waco, TX: Center for Occupational Research and Development. Retrieved from *www.cord.org/upload-edfiles/HarwellPaper.pdf.*

Hawkins, R., Hale, A., Sheeley, W., & Ling, S. (2011). Repeated reading and vocabulary-previewing interventions to improve fluency and comprehension for struggling high school readers. *Psychology in the Schools, 48,* 59–77.

Haydon, T., Conroy, M. A., Scott, T. M., Sindelar, P. T., Barber, B. R., & Orlando, A.-M. (2010). A comparison of three types of opportunities to respond on student academic and social behaviors. *Journal of Emotional and Behavioral Disorders, 18,* 27–40.

Heckman, J. J., Humphries, J. E., & Mader, N. S. (2010). *The GED.* Cambridge, MA: National Bureau of Economic Research.

Henderson, A. T., & Mapp, K. L. (2002). *A new wave of evidence: The impact on school, family, and community connections on student achievement.* Austin, TX: Southwest Educational Development Laboratory.

Heppen, J. B., & Therriault, S. B. (2008). *Developing early warning systems to identify potential high school dropouts.* Washington, DC: National High School Center.

Herlihy, C. (2007). *State and district-level supports for successful transition into high school.* Washington, DC: National High School Center.

Hernandez, D. J. (2012). *Double jeopardy: How third-grade reading skills and poverty influence high school graduation.* Baltimore: Annie E. Casey Foundation.

Hosp, J. L., Hosp, M. K., Howell, K. W., & Allison, R. (2014). *The ABCs of curriculum-based evaluation: A practical guide to effective decision making.* New York: Guilford Press.

Hosp, M. K., Hosp, J. L., & Howell, K. W. (2007). *The ABCs of CBM: A practical guide to curriculum-based measurement.* New York: Guilford Press.

Huffman, L. C., Mehlinger, S. L., & Kerivan, A. S. (2000). *Risk factors for academic and behavioral problems at the beginning of school.* Bethesda, MD: National Institute of Mental Health.

Institute on Education and the Economy. (2001). *School-to-work: Making a difference in education.* New York: Author.

Isaacs, J. B. (2012). *Starting school at a disadvantage: The school readiness of poor children.* Washington, DC: Brookings Institution.

Janosz, M., Archambault, I., Morizot, J., & Pagani, L. S. (2008). School engagement trajectories and their differential predictive relations to dropout. *Journal of Social Issues, 64,* 21–40.

Jimerson, S. (2001). Meta-analysis of grade retention research: Implications for practice in the 21st century. *School Psychology Review, 30,* 420–437.

Jimerson, S. R., Anderson, G. E., & Whipple, A. D. (2002). Winning the battle and losing the war: Examining the relation between grade retention and dropping out of high school. *Psychology in the Schools, 39,* 441–457.

Jimerson, S. R., Burns, M. K., & VanDerHeyden. A. (Eds.). (2007). *Handbook of response to intervention: The science and practice of assessment and intervention.* New York: Springer.

Jimerson, S. R., & Ferguson, P. (2007). A longitudinal study of grade retention: Academic and behavioral outcomes of retained students through adolescence. *School Psychology Quarterly, 22,* 314–339.

Jimerson, S. R., Reschly, A. L., & Hess, R. (2008). Best practices in increasing the likelihood of high school completion. In A. Thomas & J. Grimes (Eds.), *Best practices in school psychology V* (pp. 1085–1097). Bethesda, MD: National Association of School Psychologists.

Jimerson, S. R., Woehr, S. M., & Kaufman, A. M. (2007). *Grade retention and promotion: Information for parents.* Bethesda, MD: National Association of School Psychologists.

Johnson, W., McGue, M., & Iacono, W. G. (2006). Genetic and environmental influences on academic achievement trajectories during adolescence. *Developmental Psychology, 42,* 514–532.

Jones, R., Yssel, N., & Grant, C. (2012). Reading instruction in Tier 1: Bridging the gaps by nesting evidence-based interventions within differentiated instruction. *Psychology in Schools, 49,* 210–218.

Jordan, W. J., McPartland, J. M., & Lara, J. (1999). Rethinking the causes of high school dropout. *Prevention Researcher, 6,* 1–4.

Joseph, G. E., & Strain, P. S. (2003). Comprehensive evidence-based social–emotional curricula for young children: An analysis of efficacious adoption potential. *Topics in Early Childhood Special Education, 23,* 65–76.

Juel, C. (1998). What kind of one-on-one tutoring helps a poor reader? In C. Hulme & R. M. Joshi (Eds.), *Reading and spelling: Development and disorders* (pp. 449–471). Mahwah, NJ: Erlbaum.

Kaestle, C. F., Campbell, A., Finn, J. D., Johnson, S. T., & Mikulecky, L. J. (2001). Adult literacy and education in America. *Education Statistics Quarterly, 3,* 67–72.

Kam, C., Greenberg, M. T., & Kusche, C. A. (2004). Sustained effects of the PATHS curriculum on the social and psychological adjustment of children in special education. *Journal of Emotional and Behavioral Disorders, 12,* 66–78.

Kamil, M. L., Borman, G. D., Dole, J., Kral, C. C., Salinger, T., & Torgesen, J. (2008). *Improving adolescent literacy: Effective classroom and intervention practices: A practice guide* (NCEE Publication No. 2008-4027). Washington, DC: U.S. Department of Education. Retrieved from *http://ies.ed.gov/ncee/wwc.*

Kamps, D. M., Wills, H. P., Greenwood, C. R., Thorne, S., Lazo, J. F., Crockett, J. L., et al. (2003). Curriculum influences on growth in early reading fluency for students with academic and behavioral risks: A descriptive study. *Journal of Emotional and Behavioral Disorders, 11,* 211–224.

Kazdin, A. E. (1987). Treatment of antisocial behavior in children: Current status and future directions. *Psychological Bulletin, 102,* 187–203.

Kearney, C. A. (2008). School absenteeism and school refusal behavior in youth: A contemporary review. *Clinical Psychology Review, 28,* 451–471.

Kemple, J. J. (2001). *Career academies: Impacts on transitions to postsecondary education and employment.* New York: Manpower Demonstration Research Corporation.

Kemple, J. J. (2008). *Career academies: Long-term impacts on work, education, and transitions to adulthood.* New York: Manpower Demonstration Research Corporation.

Kemple, J. J., & Herlihy, C. M. (2004). *The Talent Development High School Model: Context, components, and initial impacts on students' performance and attendance.* New York: Manpower Demonstration Research Corporation.

Kemple, J. J., Herlihy, C. M., & Smith, T. J. (2005). *Making progress toward graduation: Evidence from the Talent Development High School Model.* New York: Manpower Demonstration Research Corporation.

Kennelly, L., & Monrad, M. (2007). *Approaches to dropout prevention: Heeding early warning signs with appropriate interventions.* Washington, DC: National High School Center. Retrieved from *www.betterhighschools.org.*

Kilpatrick, J., Swafford, J., & Findell, B. (2001). *Adding it up: Helping children learn mathematics.* Washington, DC: National Academies Press.

Kortering, L., Hess, R., & Braziel, P. (1997). School dropout. In G. Bear, K. Minke, & A. Thomas (Eds.), *Children's needs: II. Development, problems and alternatives* (pp. 511–521). Bethesda, MD: National Association of School Psychologists.

Kortering, L. J., & Braziel, P. M. (1999). School dropout from the perspective of former students. *Remedial and Special Education, 20,* 78–83.

Koughan, F. (Writer), & Robertson, M. (Director/Producer). (2012, July 17). *Middle school moment* [Television broadcast]. Boston, MA: WGBH Educational Foundation.

Kurns, S., & Tilly, D. (2008). *Response to intervention blueprints: School building level edition.* Alexandria, VA: National Association of State Directors of Special Education. Retrieved from *www.nasdse.org/projects/responsetointerventionrtiproject/tabid/411/default.aspx.*

Lam, S. F., Jimerson, S., Kikas, E., Cefai, C., Veiga, F. H., Nelson, B., et al. (2012). Do girls and boys perceive themselves as equally engaged in school?: The results of an international study from 12 countries. *Journal of School Psychology, 50,* 77–94.

Lane, K. L. (2007). Identifying and supporting students at risk for emotional and behavioral disorders within multi-level models: Data driven approaches to conducting secondary interventions with an academic emphasis. *Education and Treatment of Children, 30,* 135–164.

Lane, K. L., Barton-Arwood, S. M., Nelson, J. R., & Wehby, J. (2008). Academic performance of students with emotional and behavioral disorders served in a self-contained setting. *Journal of Behavioral Education, 17,* 43–62.

Lane, K. L., & Menzies, H. M. (2002). Promoting achievement and minimizing risk: Phase I. The impact of a school-based primary intervention program. *Preventing School Failure, 47,* 26–32.

Lane, K. L., Menzies, H. M., Bruhn, A. L., & Crnobori, M. (2011). *Managing challenging behaviors in schools: Research-based strategies that work.* New York: Guilford Press.

Lawrence, J. F., White, C., & Snow, C. E. (2010). The words students need. *Educational Leadership, 68,* 22–26.

Learning Point Associates. (2004). *A closer look at the five essential components of effective reading instruction: A review of scientifically based reading research for teachers.* Naperville, IL: Author. Retrieved from *www.learningpt.org/pdfs/literacy/components.pdf.*

Lee, Y. Y., Sugai, G., & Horner, R. (1999). Using an instructional intervention to reduce problem and off-task behaviors. *Journal of Postive Behavior Interventions, 1,* 195–204.

Lehr, C. A., Johnson, D. R., Bremer, C. D., Cosio, A., & Thompson, M. (2004). *Essential tools: Increasing rates of school completion: Moving from policy and research to practice.* Minneapolis:

University of Minnesota, Institute on Community Integration, National Center on Secondary Education and Transition.

Lewis, T. J., Hudson, S., Richter, M., & Johnson, N. (2004). Scientifically supported practices in emotional and behavioral disorders: A proposed approach and brief review of current practices. *Behavioral Disorders, 29,* 247–259.

Loeber, R., & Farrington, D. P. (2000). Young children who commit crime: Epidemiology, developmental origins, risk factors, early interventions, and policy implications. *Developmental Psychopathology, 12,* 737–762.

Maag, J. W. (2001). Rewarded by punishment: Reflections on the disuse of positive reinforcement in schools. *Exceptional Children, 67,* 173–186.

Marchand-Martella, N., Martella, R., Orlob, M., & Ebey, T. (2000). Conducting action research in a rural high school setting using peers as corrective reading instructors for students with disabilities. *Rural Special Education Quarterly, 19,* 5–13.

Massetti, G., & Bracken, S. (2010). Classroom academic and social context: Relationships among emergent literacy, behavioural functioning and teacher curriculum goals in kindergarten. *Early Child Development and Care, 180,* 359–375.

Mayer, M., Van Acker, R., Lochman, J., & Gresham, F. (2009). *Cognitive behavioral interventions for emotional and behavioral disorders.* New York: Guilford Press.

McConaughy, S. H., Kay, P., Welkowita, J. A., Hewitt, K., & Fitzgerald, M. D. (2010). *Collaborating with parents for early school success: The achieving–behaving–caring program.* New York: Guilford Press.

McIntosh, K., Flannery, K. B., Sugai, G., Braun, D., & Cochrane, K. L. (2008). Relationships between academics and problem behavior in the transition from middle to high school. *Journal of Positive Behavior Interventions, 10,* 243–255.

McIntosh, K., Horner, R. H., Chard, D. J., Boland, J. B., & Good, R. H. (2006). The use of reading and behavior screening measures to predict nonresponse to school-wide positive behavior support: A longitudinal analysis. *School Psychology Review, 35,* 275–291.

McIntosh, K., Horner, R. H., Chard, D. J., Dickey, C. R., & Braun, D. H. (2008). Reading skills and function of problem behavior in typical school settings. *Journal of Special Education, 42,* 131–147.

Michigan Department of Education. (2004). *Parent engagement information and tools: Moving beyond parent involvement to parent engagement.* Retrieved from *http://michigan.gov/documents/Parent_Involvement_Part_1_12-16-04_111426_7.pdf.*

Moats, L. C. (2001). When older students can't read. *Educational Leadership, 58,* 36–40.

Monrad, M. (2007). *High school dropout: A quick stats fact sheet.* Washington, DC: National High School Center.

Moroz, K. R., & Jones, K. J. (2002). The effects of positive peer reporting on children's social involvement. *School Psychology Review, 31,* 235–245.

National Center for Education Statistics. (2010). *Alternative schools and programs for public school students at risk of educational failure: 2007-08* (NCES 2010-026). Washington, DC: U.S. Government Printing Office.

National Center for Education Statistics. (2011). *High school graduates, by sex and control of school: Selected years, 1869–70 through 2020–21.* Retrieved from *http://nces.ed.gov/programs/digest/d11/tables/dt11_111.asp.*

National Institute of Child Health and Human Development. (2000). *Report of the National Reading Panel: Teaching children to read: An evidence-based assessment of the scientific research literature on reading and its implications for reading instruction* (NIH Publication No. 00-4769). Washington, DC: U.S. Government Printing Office.

National Mathematics Advisory Panel. (2008). *Foundations for success: The final report of the National Mathematics Advisory Panel.* Washington, DC: National Academies Press.

National Research Council. (2003). *Engaging schools: Fostering high school students' motivation to learn.* Washington, DC: National Academies Press.

Neild, R. C., & Balfanz, R. (2006). *Unfulfilled promises: The dimensions and characteristics of Philadelphia's dropout crisis, 2000–2005.* Baltimore: Center for Social Organization of Schools.

Neild, R. C., Balfanz, R., & Herzog, L. (2007). An early warning system. *Educational Leadership, 65,* 28–33.

Nelson, J. R., Benner, G. J., Lane, K., & Smith, B. W. (2004). Academic achievement of K–12 students with emotional and behavioral disorders. *Exceptional Children, 71,* 59–73.

Nelson, J. R., Stage, S. A., Epstein, M. H., & Pierce, C. D. (2005). Effects of a prereading intervention on the literacy and social skills of children. *Exceptional Children, 72,* 29–45.

Neuman, S. B., & Dickinson, D. K. (Eds.). (2011). *Handbook of early literacy research* (Vol. 3). New York: Guilford Press.

No Child Left Behind Act of 2001, Public Law No. 107-110, § 115, Stat. 1425 (2002).

Organization for Economic Cooperation and Development. (2013). Strong performers and successful reformers: Lessons from PISA 2012 for the United States. OECD Publishing. Retreived from *www.oecd.org/pisa/keyfindings/PISA2012_US%20report_ebook(eng).pdf.*

O'Shaughnessy, T., Lane, K. L., Gresham, F. M., & Beebe-Frankenberger, M. (2003). Children placed at risk for learning and behavioral difficulties: Implementing a school-wide system of early identification and intervention. *Remedial and Special Education, 24,* 27–35.

Osterling, K. L., & Hines, A. M. (2006). Mentoring adolescent foster youth: Promoting resilience during developmental transitions. *Child and Family Social Work, 11,* 242–253.

Partin, T. C., Robertson, R. E., Maggin, D. M., Oliver, R. M., & Wehby, J. H. (2010). Using teacher praise and opportunities to respond to promote appropriate student behavior. *Preventing School Failure, 54,* 172–178.

Peek, S. (2009). Integrating effective and beneficial interventions to increase student attendance in an elementary school setting. *Georgia School Counselors Association Journal, 16,* 9–20.

Phillips, D. C. K., Foote, C. J., & Harper, L. J. (2008, June 22). Strategies for effective vocabulary instruction. *Reading Improvement, 45,* 62–68.

Plank, S., Deluca, S., & Estacion, A. (2005). *Dropping out of high school and the place of career and technical education: A survival analysis of surviving high school.* St. Paul, MN: National Research Center for Career and Technical Education.

Pohl, A. J. (2013, February). *Check and connect: An introduction to implementation.* Paper presented at the meeting of the National Association of School Psychologists, Seattle, WA.

Public Policy Institute of California. (2004). *The effects of school-to-career programs on postsecondary enrollment and employment.* San Francisco: Author.

Quinn, M. M., & Poirier, J. M. (2006). *Study of effective alternative education programs: Final grant report.* Washington, DC: American Institutes for Research.

Rathvon, N. (2008). *Effective school interventions.* New York: Guilford Press.

Redding, S., Langdon, J., Meyer, J., & Sheley, P. (2004). *The effects of comprehensive parent engagement on student learning outcomes.* Cambridge, MA: Harvard Family Research Project. Available at *www.adi.org/solidfoundation/resources/Harvard.pdf.*

Reed, D. K., Wexler, J., & Vaughn, S. (2012). *RTI for reading at the secondary level: Recommended literacy practices and remaining questions*. New York: Guilford Press.

Reschly, A., & Christenson, S. L. (2006). Promoting school completion. In G. Bear & K. Minke (Eds.), *Children's needs: III. Understanding and addressing the developmental needs of children* (pp. 103–113). Bethesda, MD: National Association of School Psychologists.

Reschly, A. L. (2010). Reading and school completion: Critical connections and Matthew effects. *Reading and Writing Quarterly: Overcoming Learning Difficulties, 26*, 67–90.

Riley-Tillman, C. T., & Burns, M. K. (2009). *Evaluating educational interventions: Single-case design for measuring response to intervention*. New York: Guilford Press.

Roberts, G., Torgesen, J., Boardman, A., & Scammacca, N. (2008). Evidence-based strategies for reading instruction of older students with learning disabilities. *Learning Disabilities Research and Practice, 23*, 63–69.

Rogers, F. (2003). *The world according to Mr. Rogers: Important things to remember*. New York: Family Communications, Inc.

Rosenshine, B. (1986). Synthesis of research on explicit instruction. *Educational Leadership, 43*, 60–69.

Rowen, W., Shaw-Perry, M., & Rager, R. (2005). Essential components of a mentoring program for pregnant and parenting teens. *American Journal of Health Studies, 20*, 225–232.

Rumberger, R. W. (1987). High school dropouts: A review of issues and evidence. *Review of Educational Research, 57*, 101–121.

Rumberger, R. W. (2004). Why students drop out of school. In G. Orfield (Ed.), *Dropouts in America: Confronting the graduation rate crisis* (pp. 131–155). Cambridge, MA: Harvard Education Press.

Rumberger, R. W., & Lim, S. A. (2008). *Why students drop out: A review of 25 years of research*. Santa Barbara: California Dropout Research Project.

Sanetti, L., Gritter, K., & Dobey, L. (2011). Treatment integrity of interventions with children in the school psychology literature from 1995 to 2008. *School Psychology Review, 40*, 72–84.

Scarborough, H. (2001). Connecting early language and literacy to later reading (dis)abilities. In S. B. Neuman & D. K. Dickinson (Eds.), *Handbook of early literacy research* (pp. 97–110). New York: Guilford Press.

Schargel, F., & Smink, J. (2001). *Strategies to help solve our school dropout problem*. Larchmont, NY: Eye on Education.

Schochet, P. Z., Burghardt, J., & Glazerman, S. (2001). *National Job Corps study: The impacts of Job Corps on participants' employment and related outcomes*. Princeton, NJ: Mathematica Policy Research.

School-Wide Information System. (2012a). *ISIS–SWIS manual for facilitator, coordinators and users*. Retrieved from *www.swis.org/index.php?page=resources;rid=10167*.

School-Wide Information System. (2012b). *SWIS: Becoming swift at SWIS: User's manual (Version 4.4)*. Retrieved from *www.swis.org/index.php?page=resources;cid=4*.

Shannon, G. S., & Bylsma, P. (2003). *Helping students finish school: Why students drop out and how to help them graduate*. Olympia, WA: Office of the Superintendent of Public Instruction. Retrieved from *www.k12.wa.us/research/pubdocs/dropoutreport2006.pdf*.

Shapiro, E. (2011). *Academic skills problems: Direct assessment and intervention* (4th ed.). New York: Guilford Press.

Shinn, M. (2012). Identifying and validating academic problems in a multi-tiered system of services and supports model in a time of shifting paradigms. In R. Brown-Chidsey & K. J. Andren (Eds.), *Assessment for intervention: A problem-solving approach* (2nd ed., pp. 199–228). New York: Guilford Press.

Simonsen, B., Fairbanks, S., Briesch, A., Myers, D., & Sugai, G. (2008). Evidence-based practices in classroom management: Considerations for research to practice. *Education and Treatment of Children, 31*, 351–380.

Sinclair, M. F., Christenson, S. L., & Thurlow, M. L. (2005). Promoting school completion of urban secondary youth with emotional or behavioral disabilities. *Exceptional Children, 71*, 465–482.

Skinner, C. H., McLaughlin, T. F., & Logan, P. (1997). Cover, copy, and compare: A self-managed academic intervention effective across skills, students, and settings. *Journal of Behavioral Education, 7*, 295–306.

Slavin, R. E., & Cheung, A. (2004). How do English language learners learn to read? *Educational Leadership, 60*, 12–16.

Snow, C. E., Burns, S. M., & Griffin, P. (Eds.). (1998). *Preventing reading difficulties in young children*. Washington, DC: National Academy Press.

Spaulding, S., Irvin, L., Horner, R., May, S., Emeldi, M., Tobin, T., et al. (2010). Schoolwide social-behavior climate, student problem behavior, and related administrative decisions. *Journal of Positive Behavior Interventions, 12*, 60–85.

Stanovich, K. E. (1986). Matthew effects in reading: Some consequences of individual differences in the acquisition of literacy. *Reading Research Quarterly, 21*, 360–406.

Stecker, P. M., Fuchs, L. S., & Fuchs, D. (2005). Using curriculum-based measurement to improve student achievement: Review of research. *Psychology in the Schools, 42*, 795–819.

Stecker, P. M., Lembke, E. S., & Foegen, A. (2008). Using progress-monitoring data to improve instructional decision making. *Preventing School Failure, 52*, 48–58.

Steege, M. W., & Watson, S. (2009). *Conducting school-based functional behavioral assessments: A practitioner's guide* (2nd ed.). New York: Guilford Press.

Stillwell, R., & Sable, J. (2013). *Public school graduates and dropouts from the common core of data: School year 2009–10: First look (provisional data)* (NCES Publication No. 2013-309). Retrieved from *http://files.eric.ed.gov/fulltext/ED538847.pdf*.

Stormont, M., Reinke, W. M., Herman, K. C., & Lembke, E. S. (2012). *Academic and behavior supports for at-risk students: Tier 2 interventions*. New York: Guilford Press.

Stout, K. E., & Christenson, S. L. (2009). Staying on track for high school graduation: Promoting student engagement. *Prevention Researcher, 16*(3), 17–20.

Sugai, G., & Horner, R. H. (2002). The evolution of discipline practices: School-wide positive behavior supports. *Child and Family Behavior Therapy, 24*, 23–50.

Supovitz, J. (2008). *Building system capacity for improving high school graduation rates in California*. Santa Barbara: California Dropout Research Project. Retrieved from *www.hewlett.org/uploads/files/Building_System_Capacity_for_Improving_High_School_Graduation_Rates_in_California.pdf*.

Sutherland, K. S. (2000). Promoting positive interactions between teachers and students with emotional/behavioral disorders. *Preventing School Failure, 44*, 110–115.

Swanson, C. (2004). *Who graduates? Who doesn't? A statistical portrait of public high school graduation, class of 2001*. Washington, DC: Urban Institute, Education Policy Center.

Sylva, K., & Evans, E. (1999). Preventing failure at school. *Children and Society, 13*, 278–286.

Todd, A., Campbell, A., Meyer, G., & Horner, R. (2008). The effects of a targeted intervention to reduce problem behaviors. *Journal of Positive Behavioral Supports, 10*, 46–55.

Torgesen, J. K. (1998). Catch them before they fall: Identification and assessment to prevent reading failure in young children. *American Educator, 1,* 1–8.

Torgesen, J. K., & Burgess, S. R. (1998). Consistency of reading-related phonological processes throughout early childhood: Evidence from longitudinal-correlational and instructional studies. In J. Metsala & L. Ehri (Eds.), *Word recognition in beginning reading* (pp. 161–188). Hillsdale, NJ: Erlbaum.

Townsend, L., Flisher, A. J., & King, G. (2007). A systematic review of the relationship between high school dropout and substance use. *Clinical Child and Family Psychology Review, 10,* 295–317.

U.S. Bureau of Labor Statistics. (2011). *Labor force statistics from the current population survey.* Retrieved from *http://data.bls.gov/cgi-bin/surveymost.*

U.S. Department of Education. (2010). *ESEA blueprint for reform.* Washington, DC: U.S. Department of Education, Office of Planning, Evaluation, and Policy Development.

Valentine, J. C., Hirschy, A. S., Bremer, C. D., Novillo, W., Castellano, M., & Banister, A. (2009). *Systematic reviews of research: Postsecondary transitions—identifying effective models and practices.* Louisville, KY: National Research Center for Career and Technical Education.

VanDerHeyden, A. M., & Burns, M. K. (2009). Performance indicators in math: Implications for brief experimental analysis of academic performance. *Journal of Behavioral Education, 18,* 71–91.

VanDerHeyden, A. M., & Witt, J. C. (2008). Best practices in can't do/won't do assessment. In A. Thomas & J. Grimes (Eds.), *Best practices in school psychology V* (pp. 131–139). Bethesda, MD: National Association of School Psychologists.

VanderVen, K. (2004). Adults are still needed!: Intergenerational and mentoring activities. *Reclaiming Children and Youth, 13,* 94–102.

Vaughn, S. (2010, February). *Intensity of intervention to achieve student growth: Perspectives from the NICHD LDRC research projects.* Paper presented at the Pacific Coast Research Conference, Coronado, CA.

Vaughn, S., Chard, D., Bryant, D., Coleman, M., Tyler, B. J., Linan-Thompson, S., et al. (2000). Fluency and comprehension interventions for third grade students. *Remedial and Special Education, 21,* 325–335.

Vaughn, S., Cirino, P. T., Wanzek, J., Wexler, J., Fletcher, J. M., Denton, C. A., et al. (2010). Response to intervention for middle school students with reading difficulties: Effects of a primary and secondary intervention. *School Psychology Review, 39,* 3–21.

Vaughn, S., & Fletcher, J. M. (2010). Thoughts on rethinking RTI with secondary students. *School Psychology Review, 39,* 296–299.

Vaughn, S., & Fletcher, J. M. (2012). Response to intervention with secondary school students with reading difficulties. *Journal of Learning Disabilities, 45,* 244–256.

Vaughn, S., Fletcher, J. M., Francis, D. J., Denton, C. A., Wanzek, J., Wexler, J., et al. (2008). Response to intervention with older students with reading difficulties. *Learning and Individual Differences, 18,* 338–345.

Vaughn, S., Wexler, J., Roberts, G., Barth, A. E., Cirino, P. T., Romain, M., et al. (2011). The effects of individualized and standardized interventions on middle school students with reading disabilities. *Exceptional Children, 77,* 391–407.

Vellutino, F. R., Scanlon, D. M., Small, S., & Fanuele, D. P. (2006). Response to intervention as a vehicle for distinguishing between children with and without reading disabilities: Evidence for the role of kindergarten and first-grade interventions. *Journal of Learning Disabilities, 39,* 157–169.

Wade-Mdivanian, R., Anderson-Butcher, D., Hale, K., Kwiek, N., Smock, J., Radigan, D., et al. (2012). Utilizing business, university, and community resources to target adolescent prescription drug abuse. *Prevention Researcher, 19,* 17–20.

Walker, H. M., Forness, S. R., Kauffman, J. M., Epstein, M. H., Gresham, F. M., Nelson, C. M., et al. (1998). Macrosocial validation: Referencing outcomes in behavioral disorders to societal issues and problems. *Behavioral Disorders, 24,* 7–18.

Walker, H. M., Kavanagh, K., Stiller, B., Golly, A., Severson, H. H., & Feil, E. G. (1998). First step to success: An early intervention approach for preventing school anti-social behavior. *Journal of Emotional and Behavioral Disorders, 6,* 66–80.

Walker, H. M., & Severson, H. (1992). *Systematic Screening for Behavior Disorders: Technical manual.* Longmont, CO: Sopris West.

Walker, H. M., & Severson, H. (2002). Developmental prevention of at-risk outcomes for vulnerable antisocial children and youth. In K. L. Lane, F. M. Gresham, & T. E. O'Shaughnessy (Eds.), *Interventions for children with or at risk for emotional and behavioral disorders* (pp. 177–194). Boston: Allyn & Bacon.

Wanzek, J., & Vaughn, S. (2007). Research-based implications from extensive early reading interventions. *School Psychology Review, 36,* 541–561.

Werner, E., & Smith, R. (1989). *Vulnerable but invincible: A longitudinal study of resilient children and youth.* New York: Adams, Bannister, & Cox.

Whitehurst, G. J., & Lonigan, C. J. (1998). Child development and emergent literacy. *Child Development, 69,* 848–872.

Whitehurst, G. J., & Lonigan, C. J. (2001). Emergent literacy: Development from prereaders to readers. In S. B. Neuman & D. K. Dickinson (Eds.), *Handbook of early literacy research* (pp. 11–29). New York: Guilford Press.

Wimmer, M. B. (2003). *School refusal: Assessment and intervention within school settings.* Bethesda, MD: National Association of School Psychologists.

Wise, B. (2008). *Raising the grade: How high school reform can save our youth and our nation.* Hoboken, NJ: Jossey-Bass.

Young, E. L, Caldarella, P., Richardson, M. J., & Young, K. R. (2011). *Positive behavior support in secondary schools: A practical guide.* New York: Guilford Press.

Zins, J., Weissberg, R., Wang, M., & Walberg, H. J. (Eds.). (2004). *Building academic success on social and emotional learning: What does the research say?* New York: Teachers College Press.

Index

Absenteeism. *See* Attendance
Academic achievement. *See also* Academic
 performance
 multi-tiered systems of support and, 33–36, 34*f*, 35*f*
 school reform and, 10–11
 social behavior and, 28–33, 30*f*, 32*f*, 36
Academic performance. *See also* Academic
 achievement
 behavior links and, 28–36
 converging research and, 142
 early warning systems (EWS) and, 98–103, 100*f*, 102*f*
 paradigm shift in education and, 143*t*
 problem-solving model and, 107
 risk factors and, 42–44
 secondary level of education and, 94–95, 96–97, 96*f*,
 104, 107
Alternative schooling
 characteristics of successful programs, 138–139, 138*t*
 overview, 87, 134–137, 135*t*, 136*t*, 140
 paradigm shift in education and, 143*t*
Assessments. *See also* Screening; Universal screening
 academic achievement and, 97
 curriculum-based screening and, 42–43, 48*f*, 49
 data management systems, 57–61, 59*f*
 early identification and, 46–49, 47*t*, 48*f*
 Tier 1 reading instruction and, 71
At-risk indicators, 13, 93–98, 95*t*, 96*f*, 104, 143*t*.
  See also Academic performance; Attendance;
  Behavioral problems; Risk factors
Attendance
 early warning systems (EWS) and, 98–103, 100*f*,
 102*f*
 engagement and, 31–32, 32*f*
 family collaboration and, 19
 paradigm shift in education and, 143*t*
 problem-solving model and, 107, 109, 109*f*
 reasons for dropping out and, 6

 risk factors and, 44–45
 secondary level of education and, 94–95, 95*t*, 104,
 109, 109*f*
 targeted interventions (Tiers 2 and 3), 78, 78*t*

Behavioral problems
 converging research and, 142
 early warning systems (EWS) and, 98–103, 100*f*,
 102*f*
 engagement and, 31–32
 overview, 28–36, 45, 52
 paradigm shift in education and, 143*t*
 Positive Behavioral Interventions and Supports
  (PBIS) and, 74–76, 75*f*, 76*t*
 problem-solving model and, 107, 108*f*
 risk factors and, 42
 secondary level of education and, 94–95, 97–98, 104,
 113, 113*f*, 122–124, 123*t*, 124*f*

Career and technology education (CTE), 131–134, 134*t*,
 138–139, 138*t*, 140
Check and Connect intervention, 86, 122, 123*t*, 152
Check-In, Check-Out (CICO) intervention
 data management systems and, 59, 59*f*
 overview, 84, 86, 152
 secondary level of education and, 122–124, 124*f*
Classroom climate, 74–76, 75*f*, 76*t*
Classroom management, 10–11, 138*t*
Coaching, 71, 119, 129–130
Cognitive-behavioral therapy (CBT), 88*t*, 120, 128, 129*t*
Collaboration, 138*t*, 143*t*
Collaborative Strategic Reading (CSR) intervention,
 83*t*, 154
Communication, 21–22, 21*t*, 110–111, 147–148
Community collaboration
 alternative education programs, 138*t*
 family collaboration and, 21*t*

Community collaboration *(cont.)*
    overview, 24–26, 26*t*
    paradigm shift in education and, 143*t*
    secondary level of education and, 126–128
Completion, school. *See* High school completion
Comprehension
    list of interventions, 154
    secondary level of education and, 117–118, 121
    targeted interventions (Tiers 2 and 3), 83*t*–84*t*
    Tier 1 reading instruction and, 71, 72*t*
Curriculum-based measurement (CBM), 50–51, 58. *See also* Screening; Universal screening
Curriculum-based screening measures, 42–43, 48*f*, 49. *See also* Assessments; Screening

Data-based decision making, 61–63, 62*t*, 63*f*
Decision making, 21*t*, 22–23, 61–63, 62*t*, 63*f*, 148
Disengagement. *See also* School engagement
    attendance and, 44–45
    converging research and, 142, 142*f*
    dropping out as a process and, 6–9, 7*f*, 9*f*
    early identification of, 13
    multi-tiered systems of support and, 35
    overview, 31, 52
    reasons for dropping out and, 6
    risk factors and, 39
    secondary level of education and, 98, 99*f*
Dropout rates, 3–6, 13, 39. *See also* Graduation rates

Early education, 42–43, 67–68. *See also* Early intervention; Preschool programs
Early identification, 46–49, 47*t*, 48*f*, 77–78, 143*t*
Early intervention. *See also* Early education; Intervention
    converging research and, 142
    importance of, 66–67
    overview, 65–66, 88–89, 89*t*
    primary prevention (Tier 1) and, 68–77, 69*t*, 72*t*, 75*f*, 76*t*, 77*f*
    targeted interventions (Tiers 2 and 3), 77–88, 78*t*, 81*t*–84*t*, 85*t*, 88*t*
Early warning systems (EWS), 98–103, 100*f*, 102*f*, 143*t*, 151
Elementary education. *See* Early education
Engagement, school. *See* School engagement
Evidence-based intervention. *See also* Intervention
    alternative education programs, 136–137, 136*t*, 138–139, 138*t*
    converging research and, 141–142, 142*f*
    early intervention and, 67–68
    list of, 152–155
    paradigm shift in education and, 143*t*
    primary prevention (Tier 1) and, 115–119
    secondary level of education and, 115–130
    targeted interventions (Tiers 2 and 3), 77–88, 78*t*, 81*t*–84*t*, 85*t*, 88*t*
Executive function skills, 31–32, 80, 85*t*, 125–126

Family collaboration. *See also* Parental involvement
    forms for, 147–148
    overview, 18–23, 20*f*, 21*t*, 24*f*, 76–77, 77*f*
    paradigm shift in education and, 143*t*
Family factors, 7–8, 7*f*, 109*f*
Fluency
    list of interventions, 154
    risk factors and, 42–43
    secondary level of education and, 117–118, 121
    targeted interventions (Tiers 2 and 3), 82*t*–83*t*
    Tier 1 reading instruction and, 71, 72*t*
Forms and resources, 147–157

Grade retention. *See* Retention, grade
Graduation rates, 4, 5, 13, 100. *See also* Dropout rates; High school completion

High school. *See* Secondary level of education
High school completion. *See also* Dropout rates; Graduation rates
    benefits of, 4–5
    early warning systems (EWS) and, 100, 100*f*
    engagement and, 31–32, 32*f*
    international educational status and, 5
    school reform and, 10–11
Homework, 6, 32*f*, 120

Instruction. *See also* Intervention
    can't do/won't do and, 60
    core instruction, 70–71
    data-based decision making and, 61–63, 62*t*, 63*f*
    direct instruction, 43, 70–71
    multi-tiered systems of support and, 35, 71, 72*t*, 73, 74, 77–88, 78*t*, 81*t*–84*t*, 85*t*, 88*t*
    school reform and, 10–11
    secondary level of education and, 117
    summative and formative assessment and, 47–49, 47*t*, 48*f*
Integrated approach, 28–29, 33–36, 34*f*, 35*f*
Intervention. *See also* Early intervention; Evidence-based intervention; Instruction; Multi-tiered systems of support (MTSS); Prevention efforts; Primary prevention (Tier 1); Secondary prevention (Tier 2); Targeted interventions; Tertiary prevention (Tier 3)
    academic interventions, 24–25, 78–80, 121–122. See also Intervention
    behavioral interventions, 84–87, 85, 120, 122–124, 123*t*, 124*f*, 152
    data-based decision making and, 61–63, 62*t*, 63*f*
    early intervention, 39–46
    early warning systems (EWS) and, 98–103, 100*f*, 102*f*
    forms and resources for, 147–157
    list of, 152–155
    multi-tiered systems of support and, 11–13, 12*t*
    paradigm shift in education and, 143*t*
    problem-solving model, 53–57, 55*f*, 56*t*, 57*t*